2011

LLEWELLYN'S

MOON
SIGN
BOOK

MW00674653

Llewellyn's 2011 Moon Sign Book®

ISBN 978-0-7387-1133-1

© Llewellyn Publications, Woodbury, MN, USA. All rights reserved. No part of this book may be used or reproduced in any manner whatsoever, including Internet usage, without written permission from Llewellyn Worldwide Ltd. except for brief quotations embodied in critical articles or reviews.

Cover Design: Kevin R. Brown
Cover Illustrations: Sal Dell'Aquila/The July Group
Editor: Nicole Edman
Designer: Sharon Leah
Stock photography models used for illustrative purposes only and may not endorse or represent the book's subject.
Copyright 2010 Llewellyn Worldwide. All rights reserved.
Typography owned by Llewellyn Worldwide Ltd.

Any Internet references contained in this work are current at publication time, but the publisher cannot guarantee that a specific location will continue to be maintained.

Astrological data compiled and programmed by Rique Pottenger. Based on the earlier work of Neil F. Michelsen.

You can order Llewellyn annuals and books from *New Worlds*, Llewellyn's catalog. To request a free copy of the catalog, call toll-free 1-877-NEW-WRLD, or visit our Web site at www.llewellyn.com.

Llewellyn is a registered trademark of Llewellyn Worldwide Ltd.
2134 Wooddale Drive, Woodbury, MN 55125-2989 USA
Moon Sign Book® is registered in U.S. Patent and Trademark Office.
Moon Sign Book is a trademark of Llewellyn Worldwide Ltd. (Canada).
Printed in the USA

Llewellyn Worldwide Ltd.
2143 Wooddale Drive
Woodbury, MN 55125-3989
www.llewellyn.com

Table of Contents

2010 © Igor Korionov. Image from BigStockPhoto.com

What's Different About the Moon Sign Book?

Readers have asked why *Llewellyn's Moon Sign Book* says that the Moon is in Taurus when some almanacs indicate that the Moon is in the previous sign of Aries on the same date. It's because there are two different zodiac systems in use today: the tropical and the sidereal. *Llewellyn's Moon Sign Book* is based on the tropical zodiac.

The tropical zodiac takes 0 degrees of Aries to be the Spring Equinox in the Northern Hemisphere. This is the time and date when the Sun is directly overhead at noon along the equator, usually about March 20–21. The rest of the signs are positioned at 30-degree intervals from this point.

The sidereal zodiac, which is based on the location of fixed stars, uses the positions of the fixed stars to determine the starting point of

0 degrees of Aries. In the sidereal system, 0 degrees of Aries always begins at the same point. This does create a problem though, because the positions of the fixed stars, as seen from Earth, have changed since the constellations were named. The term "precession of the equinoxes" is used to describe the change.

Precession of the equinoxes describes an astronomical phenomenon brought about by the Earth's wobble as it rotates and orbits the Sun. The Earth's axis is inclined toward the Sun at an angle of about 23½ degrees, which creates our seasonal weather changes. Although the change is slight, because one complete circle of the Earth's axis takes 25,800 years to complete, we can actually see that the positions of the fixed stars seem to shift. The result is that each year, in the tropical system, the Spring Equinox occurs at a slightly different time.

Does Precession Matter?

There is an accumulative difference of about 23 degrees between the Spring Equinox (0 degrees Aries in the tropical zodiac and 0 degrees Aries in the sidereal zodiac) so that 0 degrees Aries at Spring Equinox in the tropical zodiac actually occurs at about 7 degrees Pisces in the sidereal zodiac system. You can readily see that those who use the other almanacs may be planting seeds (in the garden and in their individual lives) based on the belief that it is occurring in a fruitful sign, such as Taurus, when in fact it would be occurring in Gemini, one of the most barren signs of the zodiac. So, if you wish to plant and plan activities by the Moon, it is helpful to follow *Llewellyn's Moon Sign Book*. Before we go on, there are important things to understand about the Moon, her cycles, and their correlation with everyday living. For more information about gardening by the Moon, see page 65.

Weekly Almanac

Your Guide to Lunar Gardening & Good Timing for Activities

2010 © Zach Vanwanger. Image from BigStockPhoto.com

*To forget how to dig the earth and to tend the soil
is to forget ourselves.*
~Mohandas K. Gandhi

♑ January

January 1

Snowy, Flowy, Blowy, / Showery, Flowery, Bowery
Hoppy, Croppy, Droppy, / Breezy, Sneezy, Freezy.

~GEORGE ELLIS, "THE TWELVE MONTHS"

Date	Qtr.	Sign	Activity
Dec 31, 8:21 pm–Jan 3, 2:39 am	4th	Sagittarius	Cultivate. Destroy weeds and pests. Harvest fruits and root crops for food. Trim to retard growth.

January is a cold month. In zones 7 and 8, the temperature will dip below 40°F. In zone 3, along the U.S.-Canada border, the temperature can drop to 40° below zero. The cold can damage plants this month—and so can wind, ice, and snow. Prune weather-damaged branches as soon as possible to prevent future decay, using sharp tools to make clean cuts. Even uprooted trees can be saved if they are immediately righted and staked.

_____

_____

_____

JANUARY

S	M	T	W	T	F	S
						1
2	3	4	5	6	7	8
9	10	11	12	13	14	15
16	17	18	19	20	21	22
23	24	25	26	27	28	29
30	31					

2010 © Kent Abrahamson. Image from BigStockPhoto.com

January 2–8

And pluck till times and times are done
The silver apples of the moon / The golden apples of the sun.

~W. B. YEATS

Date	Qtr.	Sign	Activity
Dec 31, 8:21 pm– Jan 3, 2:39 am	4th	Sagittarius	Cultivate. Destroy weeds and pests. Harvest fruits and root crops for food. Trim to retard growth.
Jan 3, 2:39 am– Jan 4, 4:03 am	4th	Capricorn	Plant potatoes and tubers. Trim to retard growth.
Jan 4, 4:03 am– Jan 5, 11:08 am	1st	Capricorn	Graft or bud plants. Trim to increase growth.
Jan 7, 9:57 pm– Jan 10, 10:24 am	1st	Pisces	Plant grains, leafy annuals. Fertilize (chemical). Graft or bud plants. Irrigate. Trim to increase growth.

With the New Moon in Capricorn, it's the perfect time to plan landscapes and gardens. One of the best planning tools is the USDA Hardiness Zones Map, which was revised in the 1990s (see http://www.garden.org/zipzone/). It's tempting to introduce plants and trees that grow well in a neighboring zone; don't do it. Plants are adaptable over time, but it only takes one cold winter to destroy what took a decade or more to grow.

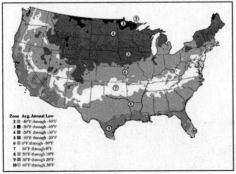

Zone Avg. Annual Low
2 ▦ -40°F through -50°F
3 ▦ -30°F through -40°F
4 ▦ -20°F through -30°F
5 ▦ -10°F through -20°F
6 ▦ 0°F through -10°F
7   10°F through 0°F
8 ▦ 20°F through 10°F
9 ▦ 30°F through 20°F
10 ▦ 40°F through 30°F

Image from WilsonBrosNursery.com

January 4
4:03 am EST

JANUARY

S	M	T	W	T	F	S
						1
2	3	4	5	6	7	8
9	10	11	12	13	14	15
16	17	18	19	20	21	22
23	24	25	26	27	28	29
30	31					

January 9–15

I love snow, and all the forms
Of the radiant frost.

~Percy Bysshe Shelley

Date	Qtr.	Sign	Activity
Jan 7, 9:57 pm– Jan 10, 10:24 am	1st	Pisces	Plant grains, leafy annuals. Fertilize (chemical). Graft or bud plants. Irrigate. Trim to increase growth.
Jan 12, 10:37 pm– Jan 15, 8:23 am	2nd	Taurus	Plant annuals for hardiness. Trim to increase growth.

Plant *Gaultheria*—commonly known as box berry, ground holly, creeping wintergreen, spice berry, teaberry, and *winisbugons* (Ojibwe, "dirty leaf")—for a hardy, colorful groundcover that grows well in Alaska, California, Minnesota, Michigan, and places between. *Gaultheria* produces bell-like white flowers in summer, which are followed by red berries in autumn that add a touch of color to winterscapes and provide food for hungry birds, deer, and small rodents.

_____

_____

_____

_____

January 12
6:31 am EST

<table>
<tr><th colspan="7">January</th></tr>
<tr><th>S</th><th>M</th><th>T</th><th>W</th><th>T</th><th>F</th><th>S</th></tr>
<tr><td></td><td></td><td></td><td></td><td></td><td></td><td>1</td></tr>
<tr><td>2</td><td>3</td><td>4</td><td>5</td><td>6</td><td>7</td><td>8</td></tr>
<tr><td>9</td><td>10</td><td>11</td><td>12</td><td>13</td><td>14</td><td>15</td></tr>
<tr><td>16</td><td>17</td><td>18</td><td>19</td><td>20</td><td>21</td><td>22</td></tr>
<tr><td>23</td><td>24</td><td>25</td><td>26</td><td>27</td><td>28</td><td>29</td></tr>
<tr><td>30</td><td>31</td><td></td><td></td><td></td><td></td><td></td></tr>
</table>

2010 © Emery Walters. Image from BigStockPhoto.com

January 16–22

Winning isn't everything, but wanting to win is.

~VINCE LOMBARDI

Date	Qtr.	Sign	Activity
Jan 17, 2:29 pm– Jan 19, 4:21 pm	2nd	Cancer	Plant grains, leafy annuals. Fertilize (chemical). Graft or bud plants. Irrigate. Trim to increase growth.
Jan 19, 4:21 pm– Jan 19, 5:16 pm	3rd	Cancer	Plant biennials, perennials, bulbs and roots. Prune. Irrigate. Fertilize (organic).
Jan 19, 5:16 pm– Jan 21, 6:10 pm	3rd	Leo	Cultivate. Destroy weeds and pests. Harvest fruits and root crops for food. Trim to retard growth.
Jan 21, 6:10 pm– Jan 23, 6:59 pm	3rd	Virgo	Cultivate, especially medicinal plants. Destroy weeds and pests. Trim to retard growth.

Tea made from the leaves of the *Gaultheria procumbens* plant is said to relieve symptoms of rheumatism, and oil of wintergreen has aspirin-like qualities. Native Americans used the tea to treat fevers, colds, and headaches. Wintergreen oil has long been used to flavor chewing gum and candy. Overdoses of wintergreen oil can be toxic, however, so use with caution.

2010 © Helena Eriksson. Image from BigStockPhoto.com

○
January 19
4:21 pm EST

JANUARY

S	M	T	W	T	F	S
						1
2	3	4	5	6	7	8
9	10	11	12	13	14	15
16	17	18	19	20	21	22
23	24	25	26	27	28	29
30	31					

~~ January 23–29

Excellence is not an exception, it is a prevailing attitude.

~COLIN POWELL

Date	Qtr.	Sign	Activity
Jan 21, 6:10 pm– Jan 23, 6:59 pm	3rd	Virgo	Cultivate, especially medicinal plants. Destroy weeds and pests. Trim to retard growth.
Jan 25, 9:15 pm– Jan 26, 7:57 am	3rd	Scorpio	Plant biennials, perennials, bulbs and roots. Prune. Irrigate. Fertilize (organic).
Jan 26, 7:57 am– Jan 28, 1:55 am	4th	Scorpio	Plant biennials, perennials, bulbs and roots. Prune. Irrigate. Fertilize (organic).
Jan 28, 1:55 am– Jan 30, 9:04 am	4th	Sagittarius	Cultivate. Destroy weeds and pests. Harvest fruits and root crops for food. Trim to retard growth.

On January 27–29 in 1922, the Knickerbocker Storm left more than 2 feet of heavy snow covering the southern and mid-Atlantic American coast. The storm—which got its name from the resulting collapse of the roof on the Knickerbocker Theater in Washington, D.C.—also produced 10-foot high drifts that stopped trains between Manassas and Clifton, Virginia.

_____

_____

_____

◑

January 26
7:57 am EST

JANUARY
S	M	T	W	T	F	S
						1
2	3	4	5	6	7	8
9	10	11	12	13	14	15
16	17	18	19	20	21	22
23	24	25	26	27	28	29
30	31					

2010 © Lane Erickson. Image from BigStockPhoto.com

February 〜〜

January 30–February 5

Nature admits no lie.

~THOMAS CARLYLE

Date	Qtr.	Sign	Activity
Jan 28, 1:55 am– Jan 30, 9:04 am	4th	Sagittarius	Cultivate. Destroy weeds and pests. Harvest fruits and root crops for food. Trim to retard growth.
Jan 30, 9:04 am– Feb 1, 6:21 pm	4th	Capricorn	Plant potatoes and tubers. Trim to retard growth.
Feb 1, 6:21 pm– Feb 2, 9:31 pm	4th	Aquarius	Cultivate. Destroy weeds and pests. Harvest fruits and root crops for food. Trim to retard growth.
Feb 4, 5:24 am– Feb 6, 5:45 pm	1st	Pisces	Plant grains, leafy annuals. Fertilize (chemical). Graft or bud plants. Irrigate. Trim to increase growth.

B arn owls (*Tyto alba*), egrets (*Ardea alba egretta*), and the flowers on *Spirea alba* and *Morus alba* have something in common. All of them are white. *Alba* means "white" in Latin and "daybreak" in Italian. The fairy tale *Snow White* originated in Germany, where winters are snowy, but, alas, while Albany, New York, is also snowy, the city was named after a Duke and has nothing to do with snow.

February 2
9:31 pm EST

2010 © Paul Gibbings. Image from BigStockPhoto.com

FEBRUARY

S	M	T	W	T	F	S
			1	2	3	4	5
6	7	8	9	10	11	12
13	14	15	16	17	18	19
20	21	22	23	24	25	26
27	28					

~~~ February 6–12

Don't be afraid of death so much as an inadequate life.

~BERTOLT BRECHT

Date	Qtr.	Sign	Activity
Feb 4, 5:24 am– Feb 6, 5:45 pm	1st	Pisces	Plant grains, leafy annuals. Fertilize (chemical). Graft or bud plants. Irrigate. Trim to increase growth.
Feb 9, 6:22 am– Feb 11, 2:18 am	1st	Taurus	Plant annuals for hardiness. Trim to increase growth.
Feb 11, 2:18 am– Feb 11, 5:20 pm	2nd	Taurus	Plant annuals for hardiness. Trim to increase growth.

The lime-colored coleus in the Versa collection (*Solenostemon scutellarioides*) will brighten any garden spot. Hardy to zone 4 and tolerant of sunlight or shade, this coleus' limey foliage provides a perfect background for soft white, pink, and purple flowers. For a more dramatic look and extended color, pair this coleus with red fountain grass ('Rubrum') and autumn mums. Fountain grass will not survive temperatures below 35°F, so plan to bring it inside during cold months.

February 11
2:18 am EST

FEBRUARY

S	M	T	W	T	F	S
		1	2	3	4	5
6	7	8	9	10	11	12
13	14	15	16	17	18	19
20	21	22	23	24	25	26
27	28					

2010 © Sheri Armstrong. Image from BigStockPhoto.com

February 13–19 〜〜〜

A heart that loves is always young.

~GREEK PROVERB

Date	Qtr.	Sign	Activity
Feb 14, 12:48 am– Feb 16, 4:14 am	2nd	Cancer	Plant grains, leafy annuals. Fertilize (chemical). Graft or bud plants. Irrigate. Trim to increase growth.
Feb 18, 3:36 am– Feb 18, 4:39 am	3rd	Leo	Cultivate. Destroy weeds and pests. Harvest fruits and root crops for food. Trim to retard growth.
Feb 18, 4:39 am– Feb 20, 4:01 am	3rd	Virgo	Cultivate, especially medicinal plants. Destroy weeds and pests. Trim to retard growth.

Give houseplants some extra love this week. While houseplants require less watering during winter because they are resting, they do like to have dust and grease removed from their leaves. Firm-leaved plants can be cleaned with a soft sponge or cloth and a very mild solution of dishsoap and tepid water. Large plants can be placed in the shower for an occasional "bath."

February 18
3:36 am EST

FEBRUARY

S	M	T	W	T	F	S
		1	2	3	4	5
6	7	8	9	10	11	12
13	14	15	16	17	18	19
20	21	22	23	24	25	26
27	28					

2010 © Judy Drietz. Image from BigStockPhoto.com

February 20–26

Holding on to anger is like grasping a hot coal with the intent of throwing it at someone else; you are the one who gets burned.

~GUATAMA BUDDHA

Date	Qtr.	Sign	Activity
Feb 18, 4:39 am– Feb 20, 4:01 am	3rd	Virgo	Cultivate, especially medicinal plants. Destroy weeds and pests. Trim to retard growth.
Feb 22, 4:29 am– Feb 24, 7:46 am	3rd	Scorpio	Plant biennials, perennials, bulbs and roots. Prune. Irrigate. Fertilize (organic).
Feb 24, 7:46 am– Feb 24, 6:26 pm	3rd	Sagittarius	Cultivate. Destroy weeds and pests. Harvest fruits and root crops for food. Trim to retard growth.
Feb 24, 6:26 pm– Feb 26, 2:32 pm	4th	Sagittarius	Cultivate. Destroy weeds and pests. Harvest fruits and root crops for food. Trim to retard growth.

Aloe vera, which is cultivated in tropic and subtropical regions, loves sunshine. It will flourish inside, too, if it is properly planted and cared for. Use moderately fertile, fast-draining soil and plant in a wide shallow pot to accommodate its shallow, wide-spreading root system. The pot should have a drainage hole, and a mixture of fertile, coarse sand and granite grit will keep aloe vera plants healthy.

February 24
6:26 pm EST

FEBRUARY

S	M	T	W	T	F	S
		1	2	3	4	5
6	7	8	9	10	11	12
13	14	15	16	17	18	19
20	21	22	23	24	25	26
27	28					

2010 © Hernan Anton. Image from BigStockPhoto.com

March ♓

February 27–March 5

It is better to die on your feet than to live on your knees.

~DOLORES IBÁRRURI

Date	Qtr.	Sign	Activity
Feb 26, 2:32 pm–Mar 1, 12:14 am	4th	Capricorn	Plant potatoes and tubers. Trim to retard growth.
Mar 1, 12:14 am–Mar 3, 11:47 am	4th	Aquarius	Cultivate. Destroy weeds and pests. Harvest fruits and root crops for food. Trim to retard growth.
Mar 3, 11:47 am–Mar 4, 3:46 pm	4th	Pisces	Plant biennials, perennials, bulbs and roots. Prune. Irrigate. Fertilize (organic).
Mar 4, 3:46 pm–Mar 6, 12:14 am	1st	Pisces	Plant grains, leafy annuals. Fertilize (chemical). Graft or bud plants. Irrigate. Trim to increase growth.

Get started early with your spring cleaning by removing last year's dead foliage from perennial gardens. Before new growth begins, feed plants with a good fertilizer. This is a good time to trim and thin plants so they don't take over where they are unwanted.

March 4
3:46 pm EST

MARCH

S	M	T	W	T	F	S
		1	2	3	4	5
6	7	8	9	10	11	12
13	14	15	16	17	18	19
20	21	22	23	24	25	26
27	28	29	30	31		

2010 © Anne Kitzman. Image from BigStockPhoto.com

March 6–12

"Hope" is the thing with feathers – That perches in the soul –
And sings the tune without the words – And never stops at all.

~Emily Dickinson

Date	Qtr.	Sign	Activity
Mar 4, 3:46 pm– Mar 6, 12:14 am	1st	Pisces	Plant grains, leafy annuals. Fertilize (chemical). Graft or bud plants. Irrigate. Trim to increase growth.
Mar 8, 12:52 pm– Mar 11, 12:31 am	1st	Taurus	Plant annuals for hardiness. Trim to increase growth.

Are you hungry for fresh vegetables? Do what the pros do: start seeds inside in containers. If you have at least eight hours of good sunlight from a south-facing window, you can enjoy fresh salad greens this month. You'll need seeds, fertile soil, and 8-inch-deep containers that have drainage holes and are not translucent or opaque (the roots will burn if exposed to sunlight). Plant, water, and watch. Make sure the soil doesn't dry out while your seeds sprout and grow, but don't overwater either.

_____

_____

_____

_____

March 12
6:45 pm EST

			March			
S	M	T	W	T	F	S
		1	2	3	4	5
6	7	8	9	10	11	12
13	14	15	16	17	18	19
20	21	22	23	24	25	26
27	28	29	30	31		

2010 © V. J. Matthew. Image from BigStockPhoto.com

March 13–19

Autumn arrives in the early morning, but spring at the close of a winter day.

~ELIZABETH BOWEN

Date	Qtr.	Sign	Activity
Mar 13, 10:29 am– Mar 15, 3:33 pm	2nd	Cancer	Plant grains, leafy annuals. Fertilize (chemical). Graft or bud plants. Irrigate. Trim to increase growth.
Mar 19, 2:10 pm– Mar 19, 4:03 pm	3rd	Virgo	Cultivate, especially medicinal plants. Destroy weeds and pests. Trim to retard growth.

There is more to lettuce than meets the eye, especially the dark-colored varieties. Most salad greens contain vitamin C and potassium, but the dark green, red, and purple varieties are also good sources of betacarotene and folic acid. In addition to color and nutrients, radicchio, arugula, endive, chicory, and escarole add taste and texture to salads.

O

March 19
2:10 pm EDT
Daylight Saving Time begins
March 13, 2:00 am

MARCH

S	M	T	W	T	F	S
		1	2	3	4	5
6	7	8	9	10	11	12
13	14	15	16	17	18	19
20	21	22	23	24	25	26
27	28	29	30	31		

2010 © Melinda Fawver. Image from BigStockPhoto.com

March 20–26

Buttercups and daisies / Oh, the pretty flowers;
Coming ere the Springtime, / To tell of sunny hours.

~MARY HOWITT

Date	Qtr.	Sign	Activity
Mar 21, 3:17 pm– Mar 23, 4:45 pm	3rd	Scorpio	Plant biennials, perennials, bulbs and roots. Prune. Irrigate. Fertilize (organic).
Mar 23, 4:45 pm– Mar 25, 9:57 pm	3rd	Sagittarius	Cultivate. Destroy weeds and pests. Harvest fruits and root crops for food. Trim to retard growth.
Mar 25, 9:57 pm– Mar 26, 8:07 am	3rd	Capricorn	Plant potatoes and tubers. Trim to retard growth.
Mar 26, 8:07 am– Mar 28, 7:00 am	4th	Capricorn	Plant potatoes and tubers. Trim to retard growth.

The potato industry held its first Potato Expo in 2009. They met again in Florida in 2010 to talk about everything: "hot" potato trends, consumer attitudes toward biotechnology, food safety on the farm, climate change, innovation, and how the size of a seed piece affects the yield. One focus, according to growers, was on varieties "targeted for fresh consumption," because French fry sales have been down.

◑

March 26
8:07 am EDT

MARCH

S	M	T	W	T	F	S
			1	2	3	4	5
6	7	8	9	10	11	12
13	14	15	16	17	18	19
20	21	22	23	24	25	26
27	28	29	30	31		

2010 © Bernd Lang. Image from BigStockPhoto.com

April

March 27–April 2

Green, I love you green. Green Wind. Green Branches.
~Federico García Lorca

Date	Qtr.	Sign	Activity
Mar 26, 8:07 am– Mar 28, 7:00 am	4th	Capricorn	Plant potatoes and tubers. Trim to retard growth.
Mar 28, 7:00 am– Mar 30, 6:38 pm	4th	Aquarius	Cultivate. Destroy weeds and pests. Harvest fruits and root crops for food. Trim to retard growth.
Mar 30, 6:38 pm– Apr 2, 7:16 am	4th	Pisces	Plant biennials, perennials, bulbs and roots. Prune. Irrigate. Fertilize (organic).
Apr 2, 7:16 am– Apr 3, 10:32 am	4th	Aries	Cultivate. Destroy weeds and pests. Harvest fruits and root crops for food. Trim to retard growth.

B aby" carrots that come in a bag are great when convenience is a priority, but they're not true baby carrots; they are carrots that have been peeled and shaped to look like baby carrots. "Real" baby carrots are not easy to find, but they can be grown in the garden. Look for 'Minicor' or 'Baby Sweet Hybrid' seeds for baby carrots that will be bright and the right size and shape.

APRIL

S	M	T	W	T	F	S
					1	2
3	4	5	6	7	8	9
10	11	12	13	14	15	16
17	18	19	20	21	22	23
24	25	26	27	28	29	30

2010 © Jun Yan Loke. Image from BigStockPhoto.com

April 3–9

For winter's rains and ruins are over . . .
Blossom by blossom the spring begins.

~ALGERNON CHARLES SWINBURNE

Date	Qtr.	Sign	Activity
Apr 2, 7:16 am– Apr 3, 10:32 am	4th	Aries	Cultivate. Destroy weeds and pests. Harvest fruits and root crops for food. Trim to retard growth.
Apr 4, 7:46 pm– Apr 7, 7:22 am	1st	Taurus	Plant annuals for hardiness. Trim to increase growth.
Apr 9, 5:02 pm– Apr 11, 8:05 am	1st	Cancer	Plant grains, leafy annuals. Fertilize (chemical). Graft or bud plants. Irrigate. Trim to increase growth.

Problems in the garden are often related to problems in the soil. Root crops, like carrots and parsnips, prefer deep, sandy, well-composted soil that is not too compacted. (Don't walk too closely to the plants.) Raised-bed gardens work well for root crops, as well. Overfeeding will cause extra "feeder" roots to grow, and overwatering will cause cracking.

●

April 3
10:32 am EDT

APRIL

S	M	T	W	T	F	S
					1	2
3	4	5	6	7	8	9
10	11	12	13	14	15	16
17	18	19	20	21	22	23
24	25	26	27	28	29	30

2010 © Kelly Shor-O'Dell. Image from BigStockPhoto.com

April 10–16

Fair daffodils, we weep to see / You haste away so soon.

~ROBERT HERRICK

Date	Qtr.	Sign	Activity
Apr 9, 5:02 pm– Apr 11, 8:05 am	1st	Cancer	Plant grains, leafy annuals. Fertilize (chemical). Graft or bud plants. Irrigate. Trim to increase growth.
Apr 11, 8:05 am– Apr 11, 11:37 pm	2nd	Cancer	Plant grains, leafy annuals. Fertilize (chemical). Graft or bud plants. Irrigate. Trim to increase growth.
Apr 16, 2:59 am– Apr 17, 10:44 pm	2nd	Libra	Plant annuals for fragrance and beauty. Trim to increase growth.

N ow is the time to think about daffodils for next spring. Order bulbs in April, May, or June (growers will ship them in September). When bulbs arrive, keep them in a cool, airy place until the ground has cooled. Choose a sunny, well-drained space to plant them next fall. Planting tips appear in the September section of this almanac.

2010 © Norman Chan. Image from BigStockPhoto.com

April 11
8:05 am EDT

APRIL

S	M	T	W	T	F	S
					1	2
3	4	5	6	7	8	9
10	11	12	13	14	15	16
17	18	19	20	21	22	23
24	25	26	27	28	29	30

April 17–23

When I orbited the Earth in a spaceship, I saw for the first time how beautiful our planet is. Mankind, let us preserve and increase this beauty, not destroy it!

~Yuri Gagarin

Date	Qtr.	Sign	Activity
Apr 16, 2:59 am– Apr 17, 10:44 pm	2nd	Libra	Plant annuals for fragrance and beauty. Trim to increase growth.
Apr 18, 2:19 am– Apr 20, 2:50 am	3rd	Scorpio	Plant biennials, perennials, bulbs and roots. Prune. Irrigate. Fertilize (organic).
Apr 20, 2:50 am– Apr 22, 6:24 am	3rd	Sagittarius	Cultivate. Destroy weeds and pests. Harvest fruits and root crops for food. Trim to retard growth.
Apr 22, 6:24 am– Apr 24, 1:59 pm	3rd	Capricorn	Plant potatoes and tubers. Trim to retard growth.

Leaf tips of spring-blooming bulbs may be showing up in northern gardens this month. Top-dressing with a 5-10-10 fertilizer as they emerge, and a 0-10-10 fertilizer as they flower, will encourage growth that produces beautiful blooms. Continue watering for three weeks after blooming time, and leave the growth until it is yellow.

○
April 17
10:44 pm EDT

April

S	M	T	W	T	F	S
					1	2
3	4	5	6	7	8	9
10	11	12	13	14	15	16
17	18	19	20	21	22	23
24	25	26	27	28	29	30

2009 © Timur Djafarov. Image from BigStockPhoto.com

April 24–30

Who has learned to garden who did not at the same time learn to be patient?

~H. L. V. FLETCHER

Date	Qtr.	Sign	Activity
Apr 22, 6:24 am–Apr 24, 1:59 pm	3rd	Capricorn	Plant potatoes and tubers. Trim to retard growth.
Apr 24, 1:59 pm–Apr 24, 10:47 pm	3rd	Aquarius	Cultivate. Destroy weeds and pests. Harvest fruits and root crops for food. Trim to retard growth.
Apr 24, 10:47 pm–Apr 27, 12:57 am	4th	Aquarius	Cultivate. Destroy weeds and pests. Harvest fruits and root crops for food. Trim to retard growth.
Apr 27, 12:57 am–Apr 29, 1:33 pm	4th	Pisces	Plant biennials, perennials, bulbs and roots. Prune. Irrigate. Fertilize (organic).
Apr 29, 1:33 pm–May 2, 1:58 am	4th	Aries	Cultivate. Destroy weeds and pests. Harvest fruits and root crops for food. Trim to retard growth.

Blooming forsythia signals that it's time to prune roses. Trim one-half to two-thirds of ever-blooming roses, hybrid teas, and Grandifloras, and remove old woody stems. Cut healthy canes to different lengths (18–24 inches) to encourage blooming. Remove one-third of old canes (and dead, dying, or diseased canes) to keep shrub roses and climbers looking their best.

2010 © Bonnie Watton. Image from BigStockPhoto.com

April 24
10:47 pm EDT

APRIL

S	M	T	W	T	F	S
					1	2
3	4	5	6	7	8	9
10	11	12	13	14	15	16
17	18	19	20	21	22	23
24	25	26	27	28	29	30

May

May 1–7

A garden is the best alternative therapy.

~GERMAINE GREER

Date	Qtr.	Sign	Activity
Apr 29, 1:33 pm– May 2, 1:58 am	4th	Aries	Cultivate. Destroy weeds and pests. Harvest fruits and root crops for food. Trim to retard growth.
May 2, 1:58 am– May 3, 2:51 am	4th	Taurus	Plant potatoes and tubers. Trim to retard growth.
May 3, 2:51 am– May 4, 1:09 pm	1st	Taurus	Plant annuals for hardiness. Trim to increase growth.
May 6, 10:32 pm– May 9, 5:35 am	1st	Cancer	Plant grains, leafy annuals. Fertilize (chemical). Graft or bud plants. Irrigate. Trim to increase growth.

Celebrate and welcome spring with a garden tea party. Send out real invitations, bring out the pretty dishes, prepare or purchase sandwiches or pastries, and gather some early blooms from the garden for a centerpiece. Tea parties don't have to be perfect (but try to avoid times when neighbors are known to mow their lawns). Plan for the unexpected, and enjoy the day.

May 3
2:51 am EDT

			MAY			
S	M	T	W	T	F	S
1	2	3	4	5	6	7
8	9	10	11	12	13	14
15	16	17	18	19	20	21
22	23	24	25	26	27	28
29	30	31				

2010 © Tatiana Emshanova. Image from BigStockPhoto.com

May 8–14

I have a garden of my own, / But so with roses overgrown,
And lilies, that you would it guess / To be a little wilderness.

~ANDREW MARVELL

Date	Qtr.	Sign	Activity
May 6, 10:32 pm– May 9, 5:35 am	1st	Cancer	Plant grains, leafy annuals. Fertilize (chemical). Graft or bud plants. Irrigate. Trim to increase growth.
May 13, 11:56 am– May 15, 12:31 pm	2nd	Libra	Plant annuals for fragrance and beauty. Trim to increase growth.

Party Hosting Tips:
- Make a "to-do" list.
- Clean only the rooms that your guests will occupy.
- Make easy centerpieces by clustering different size, same-color candles in the middle of the table, or use a pedestal cake stand to give them extra height.
- Send leftovers home with guests in purchased containers.

2010 © Graça Victoria. Image from BigStockPhoto.com

May 10
4:33 pm EDT

			MAY			
S	M	T	W	T	F	S
1	2	3	4	5	6	7
8	9	10	11	12	13	14
15	16	17	18	19	20	21
22	23	24	25	26	27	28
29	30	31				

May 15–21

A garden is never so good as it will be next year.

~THOMAS COOPER

Date	Qtr.	Sign	Activity
May 13, 11:56 am– May 15, 12:31 pm	2nd	Libra	Plant annuals for fragrance and beauty. Trim to increase growth.
May 15, 12:31 pm– May 17, 7:09 am	2nd	Scorpio	Plant grains, leafy annuals. Fertilize (chemical). Graft or bud plants. Irrigate. Trim to increase growth.
May 17, 7:09 am– May 17, 1:22 pm	3rd	Scorpio	Plant biennials, perennials, bulbs and roots. Prune. Irrigate. Fertilize (organic).
May 17, 1:22 pm– May 19, 4:16 pm	3rd	Sagittarius	Cultivate. Destroy weeds and pests. Harvest fruits and root crops for food. Trim to retard growth.
May 19, 4:16 pm– May 21, 10:32 pm	3rd	Capricorn	Plant potatoes and tubers. Trim to retard growth.
May 21, 10:32 pm– May 24, 8:24 am	3rd	Aquarius	Cultivate. Destroy weeds and pests. Harvest fruits and root crops for food. Trim to retard growth.

Plants started from seeds and grown indoors need to be "hardened off" (toughened up) before they are planted outdoors. To harden off plants indoors, withhold water, lower the temperature, and increase the ventilation. Of course, don't overdo this treatment or the plant won't make it to the great outdoors!

○
May 17
7:09 am EDT

MAY

S	M	T	W	T	F	S
1	2	3	4	5	6	7
8	9	10	11	12	13	14
15	16	17	18	19	20	21
22	23	24	25	26	27	28
29	30	31				

2010 © Maria Zubareva. Image from BigStockPhoto.com

May 22–28

The red rose whispers of passion, And the white rose breathes of love; O, the red rose is a falcon, And the white rose is a dove.

~JOHN BOYLE O'REILLY

Date	Qtr.	Sign	Activity
May 21, 10:32 pm– May 24, 8:24 am	3rd	Aquarius	Cultivate. Destroy weeds and pests. Harvest fruits and root crops for food. Trim to retard growth.
May 24, 8:24 am– May 24, 2:52 pm	3rd	Pisces	Plant biennials, perennials, bulbs and roots. Prune. Irrigate. Fertilize (organic).
May 24, 2:52 pm– May 26, 8:36 pm	4th	Pisces	Plant biennials, perennials, bulbs and roots. Prune. Irrigate. Fertilize (organic).
May 26, 8:36 pm– May 29, 9:02 am	4th	Aries	Cultivate. Destroy weeds and pests. Harvest fruits and root crops for food. Trim to retard growth.

Young plants can be hardened off outdoors by gradually increasing their exposure to sunlight and temperature variations. Plants can be placed in partial sunlight and breezy air for short time periods that are gradually increased over several days. The difference in the plants' durability will be noticeable.

2010 © Stefan Fierros. Image from BigStockPhoto.com

May 24
2:52 pm EDT

MAY

S	M	T	W	T	F	S
						1
2	3	4	5	6	7	8
9	10	11	12	13	14	15
16	17	18	19	20	21	22
23	24	25	26	27	28	29
30	31					

June

May 29–June 4

What is a weed? A plant whose virtues have not been discovered.

~RALPH WALDO EMERSON

Date	Qtr.	Sign	Activity
May 26, 8:36 pm– May 29, 9:02 am	4th	Aries	Cultivate. Destroy weeds and pests. Harvest fruits and root crops for food. Trim to retard growth.
May 29, 9:02 am– May 31, 7:56 pm	4th	Taurus	Plant potatoes and tubers. Trim to retard growth.
May 31, 7:56 pm– Jun 1, 5:03 pm	4th	Gemini	Cultivate. Destroy weeds and pests. Harvest fruits and root crops for food. Trim to retard growth.
Jun 3, 4:36 am– Jun 5, 11:03 am	1st	Cancer	Plant grains, leafy annuals. Fertilize (chemical). Graft or bud plants. Irrigate. Trim to increase growth.

Before buying expensive perennials for the yard, stop and evaluate. If the plants have a lot of foliage but small roots, they will not do as well as plants that have fewer leaves and larger roots. It's the roots that count.

●

June 1
5:03 pm EDT

JUNE

S	M	T	W	T	F	S
			1	2	3	4
5	6	7	8	9	10	11
12	13	14	15	16	17	18
19	20	21	22	23	24	25
26	27	28	29	30		

2010 © Natalia Lukiyanova. Image from BigStockPhoto.com

June 5–11

Earth laughs in flowers.

~Ralph Waldo Emerson

Date	Qtr.	Sign	Activity
Jun 3, 4:36 am– Jun 5, 11:03 am	1st	Cancer	Plant grains, leafy annuals. Fertilize (chemical). Graft or bud plants. Irrigate. Trim to increase growth.
Jun 9, 6:31 pm– Jun 11, 8:33 pm	2nd	Libra	Plant annuals for fragrance and beauty. Trim to increase growth.
Jun 11, 8:33 pm– Jun 13, 10:38 pm	2nd	Scorpio	Plant grains, leafy annuals. Fertilize (chemical). Graft or bud plants. Irrigate. Trim to increase growth.

Trees and flowers make great companions. Plant flowers around the trunks of trees. They add color to the yard, but the flowers also protect the tree trunks from lawn mower injury. The best flowers for this purpose are partial sunlight and shade-loving annuals such as impatiens, coleus, and hostas. Many white flowers enjoy shady spots, and they are often more fragrant than other colors.

June 8
10:11 pm EDT

2010 © Bill Zolis. Image from BigStockPhoto.com

June

S	M	T	W	T	F	S
				1	2	3	4
5	6	7	8	9	10	11
12	13	14	15	16	17	18
19	20	21	22	23	24	25
26	27	28	29	30		

June 12–18

Give me books, fruit, French wine, and fine weather and a
little music out of doors, played by somebody I do not know.

~John Keats

Date	Qtr.	Sign	Activity
Jun 11, 8:33 pm– Jun 13, 10:38 pm	2nd	Scorpio	Plant grains, leafy annuals. Fertilize (chemical). Graft or bud plants. Irrigate. Trim to increase growth.
Jun 15, 4:14 pm– Jun 16, 1:59 am	3rd	Sagittarius	Cultivate. Destroy weeds and pests. Harvest fruits and root crops for food. Trim to retard growth.
Jun 16, 1:59 am– Jun 18, 7:47 am	3rd	Capricorn	Plant potatoes and tubers. Trim to retard growth.
Jun 18, 7:47 am– Jun 20, 4:45 pm	3rd	Aquarius	Cultivate. Destroy weeds and pests. Harvest fruits and root crops for food. Trim to retard growth.

I f aphids and other pests won't stay away from the roses, try this: place one or two cloves of garlic among the roses. Replace the garlic when you notice the pests have returned.

_____

_____

_____

_____

○
June 15
4:14 pm EDT

	June					
S	M	T	W	T	F	S
			1	2	3	4
5	6	7	8	9	10	11
12	13	14	15	16	17	18
19	20	21	22	23	24	25
26	27	28	29	30		

2010 © Wanda Mascari. Image from BigStockPhoto.com

June 19–25

I value my garden more for being full of blackbirds than of
cherries, and very frankly give them fruit for their songs.

~JOSEPH ADDISON

Date	Qtr.	Sign	Activity
Jun 18, 7:47 am– Jun 20, 4:45 pm	3rd	Aquarius	Cultivate. Destroy weeds and pests. Harvest fruits and root crops for food. Trim to retard growth.
Jun 20, 4:45 pm– Jun 23, 4:24 am	3rd	Pisces	Plant biennials, perennials, bulbs and roots. Prune. Irrigate. Fertilize (organic).
Jun 23, 4:24 am– Jun 23, 7:48 am	3rd	Aries	Cultivate. Destroy weeds and pests. Harvest fruits and root crops for food. Trim to retard growth.
Jun 23, 7:48 am– Jun 25, 4:53 pm	4th	Aries	Cultivate. Destroy weeds and pests. Harvest fruits and root crops for food. Trim to retard growth.
Jun 25, 4:53 pm– Jun 28, 3:56 am	4th	Taurus	Plant potatoes and tubers. Trim to retard growth.

This is the time to dig up flower bulbs (daffodils, for example)
that need to be removed from the soil and replanted in late
fall. Wash the bulbs and let them dry completely (a week or
more). Store them in an onion sack (or another ventilated bag) so
air can circulate and minimize rot.

2010 © Cornelia Pithart. Image from BigStockPhoto.com

June 23
7:48 am EDT

JUNE

S	M	T	W	T	F	S
			1	2	3	4
5	6	7	8	9	10	11
12	13	14	15	16	17	18
19	20	21	22	23	24	25
26	27	28	29	30		

July

June 26–July 2

Bumblebees creep inside the foxgloves, and evening commences.

~ELIZABETH BISHOP

Date	Qtr.	Sign	Activity
Jun 25, 4:53 pm– Jun 28, 3:56 am	4th	Taurus	Plant potatoes and tubers. Trim to retard growth.
Jun 28, 3:56 am– Jun 30, 12:13 pm	4th	Gemini	Cultivate. Destroy weeds and pests. Harvest fruits and root crops for food. Trim to retard growth.
Jun 30, 12:13 pm– Jul 1, 4:54 am	4th	Cancer	Plant biennials, perennials, bulbs and roots. Prune. Irrigate. Fertilize (organic).
Jul 1, 4:54 am– Jul 2, 5:43 pm	1st	Cancer	Plant grains, leafy annuals. Fertilize (chemical). Graft or bud plants. Irrigate. Trim to increase growth.

Urban gardeners can encourage birds to visit and nest in their yards by planting shrubs and trees that provide year-round food and shelter. The following are excellent for attracting birds:

- Bayberry (*Myrica pensylvanica*), early spring and fall
- Serviceberry (*Amelanchier spp.*), early summer through fall
- Virginia creeper (*Parthenocissus quinquefolia*), late summer through winter

July 1
4:54 am EDT

		JULY				
S	M	T	W	T	F	S
					1	2
3	4	5	6	7	8	9
10	11	12	13	14	15	16
17	18	19	20	21	22	23
24	25	26	27	28	29	30
31						

2010 © Dmitry Maslov. Image from BigStockPhoto.com

July 3–9

*The first requisite of a good citizen in this Republic of ours is
that he shall be able and willing to pull his weight.*

~THEODORE ROOSEVELT

Date	Qtr.	Sign	Activity
Jul 1, 4:54 am– Jul 2, 5:43 pm	1st	Cancer	Plant grains, leafy annuals. Fertilize (chemical). Graft or bud plants. Irrigate. Trim to increase growth.
Jul 6, 11:54 pm– Jul 8, 2:29 am	1st	Libra	Plant annuals for fragrance and beauty. Trim to increase growth.
Jul 8, 2:29 am– Jul 9, 2:31 am	2nd	Libra	Plant annuals for fragrance and beauty. Trim to increase growth.
Jul 9, 2:31 am– Jul 11, 5:47 am	2nd	Scorpio	Plant grains, leafy annuals. Fertilize (chemical). Graft or bud plants. Irrigate. Trim to increase growth.

Mid- to late July is the height of the wild blueberry season
in places like northern Minnesota, the Upper Peninsula of
Michigan, and Maine. Scout out locations now, though. Some of
the best wild blueberries grow in "boggy" areas. They like rocky
areas, under ferns, and on the east or southeast side of rocky hills.
They are also commonly found near jack pine trees, but not red
pine, which they dislike. Happy hunting!

2010 © Alain Turgeon. Image from BigStockPhoto.com

◑

July 8
2:29 am EDT

JULY

S	M	T	W	T	F	S
					1	2
3	4	5	6	7	8	9
10	11	12	13	14	15	16
17	18	19	20	21	22	23
24	25	26	27	28	29	30
31						

July 10–16

I bought a cactus. A week later it died. And I got depressed, because I thought, "Damn. I am less nurturing than a desert."

~DEMETRI MARTIN

Date	Qtr.	Sign	Activity
Jul 9, 2:31 am– Jul 11, 5:47 am	2nd	Scorpio	Plant grains, leafy annuals. Fertilize (chemical). Graft or bud plants. Irrigate. Trim to increase growth.
Jul 13, 10:14 am– Jul 15, 2:40 am	2nd	Capricorn	Graft or bud plants. Trim to increase growth.
Jul 15, 2:40 am– Jul 15, 4:30 pm	3rd	Capricorn	Plant potatoes and tubers. Trim to retard growth.
Jul 15, 4:30 pm– Jul 18, 1:13 am	3rd	Aquarius	Cultivate. Destroy weeds and pests. Harvest fruits and root crops for food. Trim to retard growth.

If you have a great west-facing window, but houseplants don't do well there, it may be the perfect place for cactus. They love bright sunlight and dry air. Plant cactus in sandy loam, water well, and then ignore them. They need water only when the "meat" feels soft (poke the plant with a stick to avoid getting poked yourself). Feed with foliage plant food.

○
July 15
2:40 am EDT

JULY

S	M	T	W	T	F	S
					1	2
3	4	5	6	7	8	9
10	11	12	13	14	15	16
17	18	19	20	21	22	23
24	25	26	27	28	29	30
31						

2010 © Ragne Kabanova. Image from BigStockPhoto.com

July 17–23

In my garden I spend my days; in my library I spend my nights.

~ALEXANDER SMITH

Date	Qtr.	Sign	Activity
Jul 15, 4:30 pm– Jul 18, 1:13 am	3rd	Aquarius	Cultivate. Destroy weeds and pests. Harvest fruits and root crops for food. Trim to retard growth.
Jul 18, 1:13 am– Jul 20, 12:25 pm	3rd	Pisces	Plant biennials, perennials, bulbs and roots. Prune. Irrigate. Fertilize (organic).
Jul 20, 12:25 pm– Jul 23, 12:58 am	3rd	Aries	Cultivate. Destroy weeds and pests. Harvest fruits and root crops for food. Trim to retard growth.
Jul 23, 12:58 am– Jul 23, 1:02 am	3rd	Taurus	Plant potatoes and tubers. Trim to retard growth.
Jul 23, 1:02 am– Jul 25, 12:34 pm	4th	Taurus	Plant potatoes and tubers. Trim to retard growth.

As the summer heat settles in from coast to coast, garden plants need even more watering. Here is a way to use empty plastic jugs and save water too. Rinse the empty jug, punch holes in the lower portion, place the jug near thirsty plants, fill with water and replace the lid. Water will seep slowly into the ground. This method can also be used to fertilize plants.

2010 © Roman Milert. Image from BigStockPhoto.com

July 23
1:02 am EDT

		JULY				
S	M	T	W	T	F	S
					1	2
3	4	5	6	7	8	9
10	11	12	13	14	15	16
17	18	19	20	21	22	23
24	25	26	27	28	29	30
31						

July 24–30

Life is short, art long, opportunity fleeting, experience treacherous, judgment difficult.

~HIPPOCRATES

Date	Qtr.	Sign	Activity
Jul 23, 1:02 am– Jul 25, 12:34 pm	4th	Taurus	Plant potatoes and tubers. Trim to retard growth.
Jul 25, 12:34 pm– Jul 27, 9:11 pm	4th	Gemini	Cultivate. Destroy weeds and pests. Harvest fruits and root crops for food. Trim to retard growth.
Jul 27, 9:11 pm– Jul 30, 2:16 am	4th	Cancer	Plant biennials, perennials, bulbs and roots. Prune. Irrigate. Fertilize (organic).
Jul 30, 2:16 am– Jul 30, 2:40 pm	4th	Leo	Cultivate. Destroy weeds and pests. Harvest fruits and root crops for food. Trim to retard growth.

Many people recognize that seeds are living entities and that they need proper care even in their dormant state. Seeds should be cleaned of debris and stray seeds from other species. The cleaned seeds should be allowed to dry naturally (in sun or air), dried in silica gel, or vacuum dried, which helps keep pests away. Your dried seeds can be stored in earthen pots, baskets, or envelopes.

July 30
2:40 pm EDT

JULY

S	M	T	W	T	F	S
					1	2
3	4	5	6	7	8	9
10	11	12	13	14	15	16
17	18	19	20	21	22	23
24	25	26	27	28	29	30
31						

2010 © Marko Beric. Image from BigStockPhoto.com

August ♌

July 31–August 6

Imagination is the highest kite that one can fly.

~LAUREN BACALL

Date	Qtr.	Sign	Activity
Aug 3, 6:04 am– Aug 5, 7:57 am	1st	Libra	Plant annuals for fragrance and beauty. Trim to increase growth.
Aug 5, 7:57 am– Aug 6, 7:08 am	1st	Scorpio	Plant grains, leafy annuals. Fertilize (chemical). Graft or bud plants. Irrigate. Trim to increase growth.
Aug 6, 7:08 am– Aug 7, 11:21 am	2nd	Scorpio	Plant grains, leafy annuals. Fertilize (chemical). Graft or bud plants. Irrigate. Trim to increase growth.

New trees need to be watered every week for at least two years. Check the soil; if it feels like a damp sponge (damp, but not wet), it's OK. Never water if the soil is wet. How much is too much? If the soil is normal topsoil, about 10 gallons of water a week is sufficient for a tree with a trunk less than 2 inches wide.

_____

_____

_____

_____

2010 © Ints Tomsons. Image from BigStockPhoto.com

August 6
7:08 am EDT

		AUGUST				
S	M	T	W	T	F	S
		1	2	3	4	5	6
7	8	9	10	11	12	13
14	15	16	17	18	19	20
21	22	23	24	25	26	27
28	29	30	31			

♌ August 7–13

I stood upon that silent hill / And stared into the sky until
My eyes were blind with stars and still / I stared into the sky.

~RALPH HODGSON

Date	Qtr.	Sign	Activity
Aug 6, 7:08 am– Aug 7, 11:21 am	2nd	Scorpio	Plant grains, leafy annuals. Fertilize (chemical). Graft or bud plants. Irrigate. Trim to increase growth.
Aug 9, 4:38 pm– Aug 11, 11:47 pm	2nd	Capricorn	Graft or bud plants. Trim to increase growth.
Aug 13, 2:58 pm– Aug 14, 8:54 am	3rd	Aquarius	Cultivate. Destroy weeds and pests. Harvest fruits and root crops for food. Trim to retard growth.

Too much water on trees can be as bad as too little water. Excess water pushes oxygen from the soil, so without time to dry out, the roots will begin to die. Yellowing leaves can be a sign of overwatering. Too much mulch can also be a problem. If mulch is too deep, tree roots will form above the soil. Excess mulch around the trunk can cause trunk rot.

○
August 13
2:58 pm EDT

AUGUST

S	M	T	W	T	F	S
	1	2	3	4	5	6
7	8	9	10	11	12	13
14	15	16	17	18	19	20
21	22	23	24	25	26	27
28	29	30	31			

2010 © Rony Zmiri. Image from BigStockPhoto.com

August 14–20 ♌

Unholy battered old thing you were, my sunflower
O my soul, I loved you then!

~ALLEN GINSBERG, "SUNFLOWER SUTRA"

Date	Qtr.	Sign	Activity
Aug 13, 2:58 pm– Aug 14, 8:54 am	3rd	Aquarius	Cultivate. Destroy weeds and pests. Harvest fruits and root crops for food. Trim to retard growth.
Aug 14, 8:54 am– Aug 16, 8:01 pm	3rd	Pisces	Plant biennials, perennials, bulbs and roots. Prune. Irrigate. Fertilize (organic).
Aug 16, 8:01 pm– Aug 19, 8:36 am	3rd	Aries	Cultivate. Destroy weeds and pests. Harvest fruits and root crops for food. Trim to retard growth.
Aug 19, 8:36 am– Aug 21, 5:54 pm	3rd	Taurus	Plant potatoes and tubers. Trim to retard growth.

Chrysanthemum (*Chrysanthemum morifolium*) is a Chinese herb used to make cooling summer tea. It is also used to relieve gas, inflammation, and headaches. In the 1960s, a Russian taxonomist tried to differentiate the *morifolium*—pompon, Fufi, and spider mum—from hardy mums (*Dendranthema*) that make their appearance later in the fall. The International Botanical Congress failed to uphold that effort, and in 1995, *Dendranthema* was changed to *Chrysanthemum indicum*.

2009 © Darryl Brooks. Image from BigStockPhoto.com

AUGUST

S	M	T	W	T	F	S
	1	2	3	4	5	6
7	8	9	10	11	12	13
14	15	16	17	18	19	20
21	22	23	24	25	26	27
28	29	30	31			

♍ August 21–27

To put everything in balance is good, to put everything in harmony is better.

~VICTOR HUGO

Date	Qtr.	Sign	Activity
Aug 19, 8:36 am– Aug 21, 5:54 pm	3rd	Taurus	Plant potatoes and tubers. Trim to retard growth.
Aug 21, 5:54 pm– Aug 21, 8:53 pm	4th	Taurus	Plant potatoes and tubers. Trim to retard growth.
Aug 21, 8:53 pm– Aug 24, 6:31 am	4th	Gemini	Cultivate. Destroy weeds and pests. Harvest fruits and root crops for food. Trim to retard growth.
Aug 24, 6:31 am– Aug 26, 12:09 pm	4th	Cancer	Plant biennials, perennials, bulbs and roots. Prune. Irrigate. Fertilize (organic).
Aug 26, 12:09 pm– Aug 28, 2:13 pm	4th	Leo	Cultivate. Destroy weeds and pests. Harvest fruits and root crops for food. Trim to retard growth.

All trees will feel heat stress, even palm trees. Don't allow trees—especially young trees—to get dry. When trees appear "dull," a mixture of equal parts Epsom salts and manganese (two or three handfuls of each) dissolved in water will help trees produce chlorophyll and green up.

August 21
5:54 pm EDT

AUGUST

S	M	T	W	T	F	S
		1	2	3	4	5	6
7	8	9	10	11	12	13
14	15	16	17	18	19	20
21	22	23	24	25	26	27
28	29	30	31			

2010 © Nicole Edman

September ♍

August 28–September 3

There are two ways of spreading light: to be the candle or the mirror that reflects it.

~EDITH WHARTON

Date	Qtr.	Sign	Activity
Aug 26, 12:09 pm– Aug 28, 2:13 pm	4th	Leo	Cultivate. Destroy weeds and pests. Harvest fruits and root crops for food. Trim to retard growth.
Aug 28, 2:13 pm– Aug 28, 11:04 pm	4th	Virgo	Cultivate, especially medicinal plants. Destroy weeds and pests. Trim to retard growth.
Aug 30, 2:25 pm– Sep 1, 2:48 pm	1st	Libra	Plant annuals for fragrance and beauty. Trim to increase growth.
Sep 1, 2:48 pm– Sep 3, 5:03 pm	1st	Scorpio	Plant grains, leafy annuals. Fertilize (chemical). Graft or bud plants. Irrigate. Trim to increase growth.

The simplest way to preserve herbs is by quick-drying them. Wash sprigs and pat them dry with paper towels. Spread the sprigs in a very thin layer on an old window screen that has been set in a dry, airy place. Herb sprigs can also be tied in a bunch and then hung up to dry. When the herbs are completely dry, store them in glass jars with tight lids.

August 28
11:04 pm EDT

SEPTEMBER

S	M	T	W	T	F	S
				1	2	3
4	5	6	7	8	9	10
11	12	13	14	15	16	17
18	19	20	21	22	23	24
25	26	27	28	29	30	

2010 © Hazel Proudlove. Image from BigStockPhoto.com

♍ September 4–10

We are drowning in information, while starving for widsom.

~E. O. Wilson

Date	Qtr.	Sign	Activity
Sep 5, 10:03 pm– Sep 8, 5:42 am	2nd	Capricorn	Graft or bud plants. Trim to increase growth.
Sep 10, 3:26 pm– Sep 12, 5:27 am	2nd	Pisces	Plant grains, leafy annuals. Fertilize (chemical). Graft or bud plants. Irrigate. Trim to increase growth.

Prudent pruning:

• Remove all dead, diseased, and structurally unsound plant parts.

• Thin out weak or transplanted plants to balance the crown and root system.

• Prune trees and shrubs to maintain symmetry or eye-pleasing characteristics.

• Repair storm-damaged trees and shrubs and reshape what is left to a pleasing appearance.

_____

_____

_____

_____

◐
September 4
1:39 pm EDT

Sᴇᴘᴛᴇᴍʙᴇʀ

S	M	T	W	T	F	S
				1	2	3
4	5	6	7	8	9	10
11	12	13	14	15	16	17
18	19	20	21	22	23	24
25	26	27	28	29	30	

2009 © Bruce Shippee. Image from BigStockPhoto.com

September 11–17 ♍

I saw old Autumn in the misty morn
Stand shadowless like Silence, listening to silence.

~THOMAS HOOD

Date	Qtr.	Sign	Activity
Sep 10, 3:26 pm– Sep 12, 5:27 am	2nd	Pisces	Plant grains, leafy annuals. Fertilize (chemical). Graft or bud plants. Irrigate. Trim to increase growth.
Sep 12, 5:27 am– Sep 13, 2:49 am	3rd	Pisces	Plant biennials, perennials, bulbs and roots. Prune. Irrigate. Fertilize (organic).
Sep 13, 2:49 am– Sep 15, 3:25 pm	3rd	Aries	Cultivate. Destroy weeds and pests. Harvest fruits and root crops for food. Trim to retard growth.
Sep 15, 3:25 pm– Sep 18, 4:06 am	3rd	Taurus	Plant potatoes and tubers. Trim to retard growth.

Many perennials grow in ever-widening clumps that have holes in their center. To restore a plant's "clumped" look, divide it. In warm climates, the best time to divide and transplant perennials is in the fall. Use a sharp spade to cut through the middle of the clump, and then trim away loose roots with a sharp knife. Before transplanting, add compost to replenish the soil in the planting site.

2010 © Michael Klenetsky. Image from BigStockPhoto.com

September 12
5:27 am EDT

SEPTEMBER

S	M	T	W	T	F	S
				1	2	3
4	5	6	7	8	9	10
11	12	13	14	15	16	17
18	19	20	21	22	23	24
25	26	27	28	29	30	

♍ September 18–24

*A leaf, I would love the leaves, delighting in the redolent
disorder of the mortal life.*

~Theodore Roethke, "The Longing"

Date	Qtr.	Sign	Activity
Sep 15, 3:25 pm– Sep 18, 4:06 am	3rd	Taurus	Plant potatoes and tubers. Trim to retard growth.
Sep 18, 4:06 am– Sep 20, 9:39 am	3rd	Gemini	Cultivate. Destroy weeds and pests. Harvest fruits and root crops for food. Trim to retard growth.
Sep 20, 9:39 am– Sep 20, 2:53 pm	4th	Gemini	Cultivate. Destroy weeds and pests. Harvest fruits and root crops for food. Trim to retard growth.
Sep 20, 2:53 pm– Sep 22, 9:55 pm	4th	Cancer	Plant biennials, perennials, bulbs and roots. Prune. Irrigate. Fertilize (organic).
Sep 22, 9:55 pm– Sep 25, 12:49 am	4th	Leo	Cultivate. Destroy weeds and pests. Harvest fruits and root crops for food. Trim to retard growth.

If the ground has cooled sufficiently, it's time to plant daffodil bulbs. (If it's still too warm in your area, plant the week of October 23.) Choose a sunny location with good drainage. Amend soil as needed (slightly acidic is best), and plant 2-inch bulbs 4 inches deep. Daffodils need lots of water and good drainage.

*September 20
9:39 am EDT*

SEPTEMBER

S	M	T	W	T	F	S
				1	2	3
4	5	6	7	8	9	10
11	12	13	14	15	16	17
18	19	20	21	22	23	24
25	26	27	28	29	30	

2010 © Cornelia Pithart. Image from BigStockPhoto.com

October

September 25–October 1

In three words I can sum up everything I've learned about life—It goes on.

~ROBERT FROST

Date	Qtr.	Sign	Activity
Sep 22, 9:55 pm– Sep 25, 12:49 am	4th	Leo	Cultivate. Destroy weeds and pests. Harvest fruits and root crops for food. Trim to retard growth.
Sep 25, 12:49 am– Sep 27, 12:51 am	4th	Virgo	Cultivate, especially medicinal plants. Destroy weeds and pests. Trim to retard growth.
Sep 27, 7:09 am– Sep 29, 12:05 am	1st	Libra	Plant annuals for fragrance and beauty. Trim to increase growth.
Sep 29, 12:05 am– Oct 1, 12:42 am	1st	Scorpio	Plant grains, leafy annuals. Fertilize (chemical). Graft or bud plants. Irrigate. Trim to increase growth.

Trim suckers off of your 'Tiny Tim' or 'Patio' tomato (use suckers that are about 6 inches long). Dip the cut end in rooting compound and stick it in potting soil. Cover with plastic and place in indirect sunlight. After two weeks, if the plant has rooted, treat it as a seedling. These can be potted and grown inside near a south-facing window for fruit during the winter.

2010 © Richard Hill. Image from BigStockPhoto.com

September 27
7:09 am EDT

OCTOBER

S	M	T	W	T	F	S
						1
2	3	4	5	6	7	8
9	10	11	12	13	14	15
16	17	18	19	20	21	22
23	24	25	26	27	28	29
30	31					

♎ October 2–8

Do what you can, with what you have, where you are.

~Theodore Roosevelt

Date	Qtr.	Sign	Activity
Sep 29, 12:05 am– Oct 1, 12:42 am	1st	Scorpio	Plant grains, leafy annuals. Fertilize (chemical). Graft or bud plants. Irrigate. Trim to increase growth.
Oct 3, 4:16 am– Oct 3, 11:15 pm	1st	Capricorn	Graft or bud plants. Trim to increase growth.
Oct 3, 11:15 pm– Oct 5, 11:18 am	2nd	Capricorn	Graft or bud plants. Trim to increase growth.
Oct 7, 9:13 pm– Oct 10, 8:57 am	2nd	Pisces	Plant grains, leafy annuals. Fertilize (chemical). Graft or bud plants. Irrigate. Trim to increase growth.

Plant evergreens (*Rhododendrons*, *Kalmia*, and mountain laurel) and conifers (pines, hemlocks, spruce, cedars, fir, and so on) now to get a head start on spring. Keep in mind that conifers planted to the south of a house will provide shade as they grow, so make sure you want the shade before you plant.

◑
October 3
11:15 pm EDT

		O	CTOB	ER		
S	M	T	W	T	F	S
						1
2	3	4	5	6	7	8
9	10	11	12	13	14	15
16	17	18	19	20	21	22
23	24	25	26	27	28	29
30	31					

2010 © Timo Nurminen. Image from BigStockPhoto.com

October 9–15 ♎

I think that I shall never see / A billboard lovely as a tree.
Indeed, unless the billboards fall / I'll never see a tree at all.

~OGDEN NASH

Date	Qtr.	Sign	Activity
Oct 7, 9:13 pm– Oct 10, 8:57 am	2nd	Pisces	Plant grains, leafy annuals. Fertilize (chemical). Graft or bud plants. Irrigate. Trim to increase growth.
Oct 11, 10:06 pm– Oct 12, 9:35 pm	3rd	Aries	Cultivate. Destroy weeds and pests. Harvest fruits and root crops for food. Trim to retard growth.
Oct 12, 9:35 pm– Oct 15, 10:15 am	3rd	Taurus	Plant potatoes and tubers. Trim to retard growth.
Oct 15, 10:15 am– Oct 17, 9:38 pm	3rd	Gemini	Cultivate. Destroy weeds and pests. Harvest fruits and root crops for food. Trim to retard growth.

Do *not* prune flowering shrubs yet, even if they look a little shaggy. Wait until frost has definitely ended all growing activity for the season before pruning anything. When you do prune, cut off the largest shoots at ground level. Simply cutting off the ends of branches will stimulate growth in many side branches, which may not be desirable.

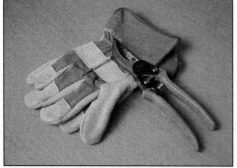

2010 © Dave Baxter. Image from BigStockPhoto.com

○
October 11
10:06 pm EDT

OCTOBER

S	M	T	W	T	F	S
						1
2	3	4	5	6	7	8
9	10	11	12	13	14	15
16	17	18	19	20	21	22
23	24	25	26	27	28	29
30	31					

October 16–22

*If I have a thousand ideas and only one turns out to be good,
I am satisfied.*

~ALFRED NOBEL

Date	Qtr.	Sign	Activity
Oct 15, 10:15 am– Oct 17, 9:38 pm	3rd	Gemini	Cultivate. Destroy weeds and pests. Harvest fruits and root crops for food. Trim to retard growth.
Oct 17, 9:38 pm– Oct 19, 11:30 pm	3rd	Cancer	Plant biennials, perennials, bulbs and roots. Prune. Irrigate. Fertilize (organic).
Oct 19, 11:30 pm– Oct 20, 6:06 am	4th	Cancer	Plant biennials, perennials, bulbs and roots. Prune. Irrigate. Fertilize (organic).
Oct 20, 6:06 am– Oct 22, 10:40 am	4th	Leo	Cultivate. Destroy weeds and pests. Harvest fruits and root crops for food. Trim to retard growth.
Oct 22, 10:40 am– Oct 24, 11:49 am	4th	Virgo	Cultivate, especially medicinal plants. Destroy weeds and pests. Trim to retard growth.

Fall is the best time to dethatch lawns because grass is still growing, making it possible to repair damaged or bare spots before weeds take over. Thatch should be removed if it is more than ¾-inch thick.

◑
October 19
11:30 pm EDT

OCTOBER						
S	M	T	W	T	F	S
						1
2	3	4	5	6	7	8
9	10	11	12	13	14	15
16	17	18	19	20	21	22
23	24	25	26	27	28	29
30	31					

2010 © Steve McSweeny. Image from BigStockPhoto.com

October 23–29 ♏

A good deed is never lost: he who sows courtesy reaps friendship; and he who plants kindness gathers love.

~St. Basil

Date	Qtr.	Sign	Activity
Oct 22, 10:40 am– Oct 24, 11:49 am	4th	Virgo	Cultivate, especially medicinal plants. Destroy weeds and pests. Trim to retard growth.
Oct 26, 11:08 am– Oct 26, 3:56 pm	4th	Scorpio	Plant biennials, perennials, bulbs and roots. Prune. Irrigate. Fertilize (organic).
Oct 26, 3:56 pm– Oct 28, 10:45 am	1st	Scorpio	Plant grains, leafy annuals. Fertilize (chemical). Graft or bud plants. Irrigate. Trim to increase growth.

Houseplants will indicate when they need to be fed. Here are some signs that they are hungry:

• large older leaves turn yellow (feed it)

• baby leaves are yellow (plant needs iron)

• the veins on older foliage are dark, while foliage itself is yellowish (plant needs iron)

2010 © Yevgen Kotyukh. Image from BigStockPhoto.com

October 26
3:56 pm EDT

OCTOBER

S	M	T	W	T	F	S
						1
2	3	4	5	6	7	8
9	10	11	12	13	14	15
16	17	18	19	20	21	22
23	24	25	26	27	28	29
30	31					

November

October 30–November 5

I am the daughter of Earth and Water,
And the nursling of the sky.

~PERCY BYSSHE SHELLEY

Date	Qtr.	Sign	Activity
Oct 30, 12:39 pm–Nov 1, 6:08 pm	1st	Capricorn	Graft or bud plants. Trim to increase growth.
Nov 4, 3:18 am–Nov 6, 2:02 pm	2nd	Pisces	Plant grains, leafy annuals. Fertilize (chemical). Graft or bud plants. Irrigate. Trim to increase growth.

B uy liquid fertilizers now, when they are on sale. You can keep the fertilizer sealed and protected from freezing for use next growing season.

November 2
12:38 pm EDT

NOVEMBER

S	M	T	W	T	F	S
		1	2	3	4	5
6	7	8	9	10	11	12
13	14	15	16	17	18	19
20	21	22	23	24	25	26
27	28	29	30			

2009 © Kimberly Soliz. Image from BigStockPhoto.com

November 6–12 ♏

When the power of love overcomes the love of power the
world will know peace.

~JIMI HENDRIX

Date	Qtr.	Sign	Activity
Nov 4, 3:18 am– Nov 6, 2:02 pm	2nd	Pisces	Plant grains, leafy annuals. Fertilize (chemical). Graft or bud plants. Irrigate. Trim to increase growth.
Nov 9, 2:45 am– Nov 10, 3:16 pm	2nd	Taurus	Plant annuals for hardiness. Trim to increase growth.
Nov 10, 3:16 pm– Nov 11, 3:10 pm	3rd	Taurus	Plant potatoes and tubers. Trim to retard growth.
Nov 11, 3:10 pm– Nov 14, 2:19 am	3rd	Gemini	Cultivate. Destroy weeds and pests. Harvest fruits and root crops for food. Trim to retard growth.

Now is the last best time to plant grass seed for new spring growth. The grass seed will remain dormant over winter and germinate when the soil warms in spring. Applying straw to protect seeds and maintain constant moisture is helpful, but it should be removed before snowfall (the exception to this rule is if erosion is a problem).

2010 © Le Do. Image from BigStockPhoto.com

○
November 10
3:16 pm EST
Daylight Saving Time ends
November 6, 2:00 am

NOVEMBER

S	M	T	W	T	F	S
		1	2	3	4	5
6	7	8	9	10	11	12
13	14	15	16	17	18	19
20	21	22	23	24	25	26
27	28	29	30			

♏ November 13–19

In all things of nature there is something of the marvelous.

~Aristotle

Date	Qtr.	Sign	Activity
Nov 11, 3:10 pm– Nov 14, 2:19 am	3rd	Gemini	Cultivate. Destroy weeds and pests. Harvest fruits and root crops for food. Trim to retard growth.
Nov 14, 2:19 am– Nov 16, 11:17 am	3rd	Cancer	Plant biennials, perennials, bulbs and roots. Prune. Irrigate. Fertilize (organic).
Nov 16, 11:17 am– Nov 18, 10:09 am	3rd	Leo	Cultivate. Destroy weeds and pests. Harvest fruits and root crops for food. Trim to retard growth.
Nov 18, 10:09 am– Nov 18, 5:19 pm	4th	Leo	Cultivate. Destroy weeds and pests. Harvest fruits and root crops for food. Trim to retard growth.
Nov 18, 5:19 pm– Nov 20, 8:16 pm	4th	Virgo	Cultivate, especially medicinal plants. Destroy weeds and pests. Trim to retard growth.

Prolong the beauty of cut flowers by keeping them in a mixture of 50 percent water and 50 percent lemon-lime soda. The sugar in the soda acts like an energy supply, and the citric acid slows down the growth of bacteria in the water.

_____

_____

_____

_____

◗

November 18
10:09 am EST

NOVEMBER

S	M	T	W	T	F	S
		1	2	3	4	5
6	7	8	9	10	11	12
13	14	15	16	17	18	19
20	21	22	23	24	25	26
27	28	29	30			

2009 © Lisa Turay. Image from BigStockPhoto.com

November 20–26

Youth is happy because it has the ability to see beauty.
Anyone who keeps the ability to see beauty never grows old.

~Franz Kafka

Date	Qtr.	Sign	Activity
Nov 18, 5:19 pm– Nov 20, 8:16 pm	4th	Virgo	Cultivate, especially medicinal plants. Destroy weeds and pests. Trim to retard growth.
Nov 22, 8:58 pm– Nov 24, 8:57 pm	4th	Scorpio	Plant biennials, perennials, bulbs and roots. Prune. Irrigate. Fertilize (organic).
Nov 24, 8:57 pm– Nov 25, 1:10 am	4th	Sagittarius	Cultivate. Destroy weeds and pests. Harvest fruits and root crops for food. Trim to retard growth.
Nov 26, 10:05 pm– Nov 29, 2:02 am	1st	Capricorn	Graft or bud plants. Trim to increase growth.

Exposure to extreme cold can kill fruit buds on peach trees and sweet cherries. Heating the air near the trees provides the best protection, but that may not be a practical solution. Covering trees with a floating row cover is also helpful.

_____

_____

_____

2010 © Sue Ashe. Image from BigStockPhoto.com

November 25
1:10 am EST

Nᴏᴠᴇᴍʙᴇʀ

S	M	T	W	T	F	S
		1	2	3	4	5
6	7	8	9	10	11	12
13	14	15	16	17	18	19
20	21	22	23	24	25	26
27	28	29	30			

December

November 27–December 3

I never think about the future—it comes soon enough.

~ALBERT EINSTEIN

Date	Qtr.	Sign	Activity
Nov 26, 10:05 pm– Nov 29, 2:02 am	1st	Capricorn	Graft or bud plants. Trim to increase growth.
Dec 1, 9:45 am– Dec 2, 4:52 am	1st	Pisces	Plant grains, leafy annuals. Fertilize (chemical). Graft or bud plants. Irrigate. Trim to increase growth.
Dec 2, 4:52 am– Dec 3, 8:51 pm	2nd	Pisces	Plant grains, leafy annuals. Fertilize (chemical). Graft or bud plants. Irrigate. Trim to increase growth.

Exposure to sun, snow, cold, and wind can cause serious damage to broadleaf evergreens, like rhododendrons. Protect susceptible plants by planting in sheltered locations and then protect them with burlap, plastic mesh, or snow fence. Anti-desiccant sprays will help to slow the rate of transpiration. These should be applied two or three times during early and late winter.

December 2
4:52 am EST

DECEMBER

S	M	T	W	T	F	S
				1	2	3
4	5	6	7	8	9	10
11	12	13	14	15	16	17
18	19	20	21	22	23	24
25	26	27	28	29	30	31

2010 © Phil Evaul. Image from BigStockPhoto.com

December 4–10

There really is no such thing as bad weather, only different kinds of good weather.

~JOHN RUSKIN

Date	Qtr.	Sign	Activity
Dec 2, 4:52 am– Dec 3, 8:51 pm	2nd	Pisces	Plant grains, leafy annuals. Fertilize (chemical). Graft or bud plants. Irrigate. Trim to increase growth.
Dec 6, 9:34 am– Dec 8, 9:52 pm	2nd	Taurus	Plant annuals for hardiness. Trim to increase growth.
Dec 10, 9:36 am– Dec 11, 8:26 am	3rd	Gemini	Cultivate. Destroy weeds and pests. Harvest fruits and root crops for food. Trim to retard growth.

Tree-topping is a common practice in urban areas. Utility companies send out crews to chop off trees under utility lines. Disagreements with the utility company are seldom settled in the landowner's favor. The best solution is prevention, which can be accomplished by careful planting.

2010 © Charles Vazquez. Image from BigStockPhoto.com

○
December 10
9:36 am EST

DECEMBER

S	M	T	W	T	F	S
				1	2	3
4	5	6	7	8	9	10
11	12	13	14	15	16	17
18	19	20	21	22	23	24
25	26	27	28	29	30	31

December 11–17

The frolic architecture of the snow.

~Ralph Waldo Emerson

Date	Qtr.	Sign	Activity
Dec 10, 9:36 am– Dec 11, 8:26 am	3rd	Gemini	Cultivate. Destroy weeds and pests. Harvest fruits and root crops for food. Trim to retard growth.
Dec 11, 8:26 am– Dec 13, 4:48 pm	3rd	Cancer	Plant biennials, perennials, bulbs and roots. Prune. Irrigate. Fertilize (organic).
Dec 13, 4:48 pm– Dec 15, 10:58 pm	3rd	Leo	Cultivate. Destroy weeds and pests. Harvest fruits and root crops for food. Trim to retard growth.
Dec 15, 10:58 pm– Dec 17, 7:48 pm	3rd	Virgo	Cultivate, especially medicinal plants. Destroy weeds and pests. Trim to retard growth.
Dec 17, 7:48 pm– Dec 18, 3:06 am	4th	Virgo	Cultivate, especially medicinal plants. Destroy weeds and pests. Trim to retard growth.

Kumquats are a delicate Asian citrus fruit that offers a pleasant alternative to other winter fruits. The tiny, oval-shaped kumquat will keep at room temperature for about three days and up to two weeks in the refrigerator. Choose firm kumquats to eat. Wash and then halve or quarter the fruit and eat with the skin on (seeds are edible, but you may choose to pass on them).

◑
December 17
7:48 pm EST

	December					
S	M	T	W	T	F	S
				1	2	3
4	5	6	7	8	9	10
11	12	13	14	15	16	17
18	19	20	21	22	23	24
25	26	27	28	29	30	31

2010 © Massimiliano Pieraccini. Image from BigStockPhoto.com

December 18–26

The greatest glory in living lies not in never falling, but in rising every time we fall.

~NELSON MANDELA

Date	Qtr.	Sign	Activity
Dec 17, 7:48 pm– Dec 18, 3:06 am	4th	Virgo	Cultivate, especially medicinal plants. Destroy weeds and pests. Trim to retard growth.
Dec 20, 5:33 am– Dec 22, 7:03 am	4th	Scorpio	Plant biennials, perennials, bulbs and roots. Prune. Irrigate. Fertilize (organic).
Dec 22, 7:03 am– Dec 24, 8:47 am	4th	Sagittarius	Cultivate. Destroy weeds and pests. Harvest fruits and root crops for food. Trim to retard growth.
Dec 24, 8:47 am– Dec 24, 1:06 pm	4th	Capricorn	Plant potatoes and tubers. Trim to retard growth.
Dec 24, 1:06 pm– Dec 26, 12:14 pm	1st	Capricorn	Graft or bud plants. Trim to increase growth.

Place holiday poinsettias near a sunny window to extend their flowering period. Check the soil every day and when it's dry to the touch, water it—but don't soak the soil.

2010 © David Davis. Image from BigStockPhoto.com

December 24
1:06 pm EST

DECEMBER

S	M	T	W	T	F	S
				1	2	3
4	5	6	7	8	9	10
11	12	13	14	15	16	17
18	19	20	21	22	23	24
25	26	27	28	29	30	31

December 25–31

*The place to be happy is here. The time to be happy is now.
The way to be happy is to make others so.*

~ROBERT G. INGERSOLL

Date	Qtr.	Sign	Activity
Dec 24, 1:06 pm– Dec 26, 12:14 pm	1st	Capricorn	Graft or bud plants. Trim to increase growth.
Dec 28, 6:45 pm– Dec 31, 4:48 am	1st	Pisces	Plant grains, leafy annuals. Fertilize (chemical). Graft or bud plants. Irrigate. Trim to increase growth.

Poinsettias can be held over for another year by allowing them to go dormant (store in a cool, dry place when leaves fall off). In spring, cut the stems back to 6 inches and start watering. From early October until they start to bloom, give plants 12 hours of sunlight and 12 hours of dark (in a closet or other dark area).

DECEMBER

S	M	T	W	T	F	S
					1	2	3
4	5	6	7	8	9	10
11	12	13	14	15	16	17
18	19	20	21	22	23	24
25	26	27	28	29	30	31

2010 © Jeremy Swinborne. Image from BigStockPhoto.com

2010 © Richard Lewis. Image from BigStockPhoto.com

Gardening by the Moon

Today, people often reject the notion of gardening according to the Moon's phase and sign. The usual nonbeliever is not a scientist but the city dweller who has never had any real contact with nature and little experience of natural rhythms.

Camille Flammarion, the French astronomer, testifies to the success of Moon planting, though:

"Cucumbers increase at Full Moon, as well as radishes, turnips, leeks, lilies, horseradish, and saffron; onions, on the contrary, are much larger and better nourished during the decline and old age of the Moon than at its increase, during its youth and fullness, which is the reason the Egyptians abstained from onions, on account of their antipathy to the Moon. Herbs gathered while the Moon increases are of great efficiency. If the vines are trimmed at night when the Moon is in the sign of the Lion, Sagittarius, the Scorpion, or the Bull, it will save them from field rats, moles, snails, flies, and other animals."

Dr. Clark Timmins is one of the few modern scientists to have conducted tests in Moon planting. Following is a summary of his experiments:

Beets: When sown with the Moon in Scorpio, the germination rate was 71 percent; when sown in Sagittarius, the germination rate was 58 percent.

Scotch marigold: When sown with the Moon in Cancer, the germination rate was 90 percent; when sown in Leo, the rate was 32 percent.

Carrots: When sown with the Moon in Scorpio, the germination rate was 64 percent; when sown in Sagittarius, the germination rate was 47 percent.

Tomatoes: When sown with the Moon in Cancer, the germination rate was 90 percent; but when sown with the Moon in Leo, the germination rate was 58 percent.

Two things should be emphasized. First, remember that this is only a summary of the results of the experiments; the experiments themselves were conducted in a scientific manner to eliminate any variation in soil, temperature, moisture, and so on, so that only the Moon sign is varied. Second, note that these astonishing results were obtained without regard to the phase of the Moon—the other factor we use in Moon planting, and which presumably would have increased the differential in germination rates.

Dr. Timmins also tried transplanting Cancer- and Leo-planted tomato seedlings while the Cancer Moon was waxing. The result was 100 percent survival. When transplanting was done with the waning Sagittarius Moon, there was 0 percent survival. Dr. Timmins' tests show that the Cancer-planted tomatoes had blossoms twelve days earlier than those planted under Leo; the Cancer-planted tomatoes had an average height of twenty inches at that time compared to fifteen inches for the Leo-planted; the first ripe tomatoes were gathered from the Cancer plantings eleven days ahead of the Leo plantings; and a count of the hanging fruit and its size and weight shows an advantage to the Cancer plants over the Leo plants of 45 percent.

Dr. Timmins also observed that there have been similar tests that did not indicate results favorable to the Moon planting theory. As a scientist, he asked why one set of experiments indicated a positive verification of Moon planting, and others did not. He checked these other tests and found that the experimenters had not followed the geocentric system for determining the Moon sign positions, but the heliocentric. When the times used in these other tests were converted to the geocentric system, the dates chosen often were found to be in barren, rather than fertile, signs. Without going into a technical explanation, it is sufficient to point out that geocentric and heliocentric positions often vary by as much as four days. This is a large enough differential to place the Moon in Cancer, for example, in the heliocentric system, and at the same time in Leo by the geocentric system.

Most almanacs and calendars show the Moon's signs heliocentrically—and thus incorrectly for Moon planting—while the *Moon Sign Book* is calculated correctly for planting purposes, using the geocentric system. Some readers are confused because the *Moon Sign Book* talks about first, second, third, and fourth quarters, while other almanacs refer to these same divisions as New Moon, first quarter, Full Moon, and fourth quarter. Thus the almanacs say first quarter when the *Moon Sign Book* says second quarter.

There is nothing complicated about using astrology in agriculture and horticulture in order to increase both pleasure and profit, but there is one very important rule that is often neglected—use common sense! Of course this is one rule that should be remembered in every activity we undertake, but in the case of gardening and farming by the Moon, if it is not possible to use the best dates for planting or harvesting, we must select the next best and just try to do the best we can.

This brings up the matter of the other factors to consider in your gardening work. The dates we give as best for a certain activity apply to the entire country (with slight time correction), but in your section of the country you may be buried under three feet of snow on a date we say is good to plant your flowers. So we have factors of weather, season, temperature, and moisture variations, soil conditions, your own available time and opportunity, and so forth. Some astrologers like to think it is all a matter of science, but gardening is also an art. In art, you develop an instinctive identification with your work and influence it with your feelings and wishes.

The *Moon Sign Book* gives you the place of the Moon for every day of the year so that you can select the best times once you have become familiar with the rules and practices of lunar agriculture. We give you specific, easy-to-follow directions so that you can get right down to work.

We give you the best dates for planting, and also for various related activities, including cultivation, fertilizing, harvesting, irrigation, and getting rid of weeds and pests. But we cannot tell you exactly when it's good to plant. Many of these rules were learned by observation and experience; as the body of experience grew, we could see various patterns emerging that allowed us to make judgments about new things. That's what you should do, too. After you have worked with lunar agriculture for a while and have gained a working knowledge, you will probably begin to try new things—and we hope you will share your experiments and findings with us. That's how the science grows.

Here's an example of what we mean. Years ago Llewellyn George suggested that we try to combine our bits of knowledge about what to expect in planting under each of the Moon signs in order to benefit from several lunar factors in one plant. From this came our rule for developing "thoroughbred seed." To develop thoroughbred seed, save the seed for three successive years from plants grown by the correct Moon sign and phase. You can plant in the first quarter phase and in the sign of Cancer for fruitfulness; the second year, plant seeds from the first year plants in Libra for beauty; and in the third year, plant the seeds from the second year plants in Taurus to produce hardiness. In a similar manner you can combine the fruitfulness of Cancer, the good root growth of Pisces, and the sturdiness and good vine growth of Scorpio. And don't forget the characteristics of Capricorn: hardy like Taurus, but drier and perhaps more resistant to drought and disease.

Unlike common almanacs, we consider both the Moon's phase and the Moon's sign in making our calculations for the proper timing of our work. It is perhaps a little easier to understand this if we remind you that we are all living in the center of a vast electromagnetic field that is the Earth and its environment in space. Everything that occurs within this electromagnetic field has an effect on everything else within the field. The Moon and the Sun are the most important of the factors affecting the life of the Earth, and it is their relative positions to the Earth that we project for each day of the year.

Many people claim that not only do they achieve larger crops gardening by the Moon, but that their fruits and vegetables are much tastier. A number of organic gardeners have also become lunar gardeners using the natural rhythm of life forces that we experience through the relative movements of the Sun and Moon. We provide a few basic rules and then give you day-by-day guidance for your gardening work. You will be able to choose the best dates to meet your own needs and opportunities.

Planting by the Moon's Phases
During the increasing or waxing light—from New Moon to Full Moon—plant annuals that produce their yield above the ground. An annual is a plant that completes its entire life cycle within

one growing season and has to be seeded each year. During the decreasing or waning light—from Full Moon to New Moon—plant biennials, perennials, and bulb and root plants. Biennials include crops that are planted one season to winter over and produce crops the next, such as winter wheat. Perennials and bulb and root plants include all plants that grow from the same root each year.

A simpler, less-accurate rule is to plant crops that produce above the ground during the waxing Moon, and to plant crops that produce below the ground during the waning Moon. Thus the old adage, "Plant potatoes during the dark of the Moon." Llewellyn George's system divided the lunar month into quarters. The first two from New Moon to Full Moon are the first and second quarters, and the last two from Full Moon to New Moon the third and fourth quarters. Using these divisions, we can increase our accuracy in timing our efforts to coincide with natural forces.

First Quarter

Plant annuals producing their yield above the ground, which are generally of the leafy kind that produce their seed outside the fruit. Some examples are asparagus, broccoli, brussels sprouts, cabbage, cauliflower, celery, cress, endive, kohlrabi, lettuce, parsley, and spinach. Cucumbers are an exception, as they do best in the first quarter rather than the second, even though the seeds are inside

the fruit. Also plant cereals and grains.

Second Quarter

Plant annuals producing their yield above the ground, which are generally of the viney kind that produce their seed

2009 © Doris Lambracht-Washington. Image from BigStockPhoto.com

inside the fruit. Some examples include beans, eggplant, melons, peas, peppers, pumpkins, squash, tomatoes, etc. These are not hard-and-fast divisions. If you can't plant during the first quarter, plant during the second, and vice versa. There are many plants that seem to do equally well planted in either quarter, such as watermelon, hay, and cereals and grains.

Third Quarter

Plant biennials, perennials, bulbs, root plants, trees, shrubs, berries, grapes, strawberries, beets, carrots, onions, parsnips, rutabagas, potatoes, radishes, peanuts, rhubarb, turnips, winter wheat, etc.

Fourth Quarter

This is the best time to cultivate, turn sod, pull weeds, and destroy pests of all kinds, especially when the Moon is in Aries, Leo, Virgo, Gemini, Aquarius, and Sagittarius.

The Moon in the Signs

Moon in Aries

Barren, dry, fiery, and masculine. Use for destroying noxious weeds.

Moon in Taurus

Productive, moist, earthy, and feminine. Use for planting many crops when hardiness is important, particularly root crops. Also used for lettuce, cabbage, and similar leafy vegetables.

Moon in Gemini

Barren and dry, airy and masculine. Use for destroying noxious growths, weeds, and pests, and for cultivation.

Moon in Cancer

Fruitful, moist, feminine. Use for planting and irrigation.

Moon in Leo
Barren, dry, fiery, masculine. Use for killing weeds or cultivation.

Moon in Virgo
Barren, moist, earthy, and feminine. Use for cultivation and destroying weeds and pests.

Moon in Libra
Semi-fruitful, moist, and airy. Use for planting crops that need good pulp growth. A very good sign for flowers and vines. Also used for seeding hay, corn fodder, and the like.

Moon in Scorpio
Very fruitful and moist, watery and feminine. Nearly as productive as Cancer; use for the same purposes. Especially good for vine growth and sturdiness.

Moon in Sagittarius
Barren and dry, fiery and masculine. Use for planting onions, seeding hay, and for cultivation.

Moon in Capricorn
Productive and dry, earthy and feminine. Use for planting potatoes and other tubers.

Moon in Aquarius
Barren, dry, airy, and masculine. Use for cultivation and destroying noxious growths and pests.

Moon in Pisces
Very fruitful, moist, watery, and feminine. Especially good for root growth.

A Guide to Planting

Plant	Quarter	
Coreopsis	2nd or 3rd	Libra
Corn	1st	Ca...
Corn for fodder	1st or 2nd	
Cosmo	2nd or 3...	
Cress	1st	
Crocus		
Cucumber		
Daffodil		
Dahl...		

Plant	Quarter	Signs
Annuals		
Apple tree		
Artichoke		
Asparagus		
Aster		
Barley		
Beans (bush & ...		
Beans (kidney, w...		
Beech tree		
Beets		
Biennials		
Broccoli		, Libra
Brussels sprouts		..., Scorpio, Pisces, Libra
Buckwheat	...t or 2nd	Capricorn
Bulbs	3rd	Cancer, Scorpio, Pisces
Bulbs for seed	2nd or 3rd	
Cabbage	1st	Cancer, Scorpio, Pisces, Taurus, Libra
Canes (raspberry, blackberry, & gooseberry)	2nd	Cancer, Scorpio, Pisces
Cantaloupe	1st or 2nd	Cancer, Scorpio, Pisces, Taurus, Libra
Carrots	3rd	Cancer, Scorpio, Pisces, Taurus, Libra
Cauliflower	1st	Cancer, Scorpio, Pisces, Libra
Celeriac	3rd	Cancer, Scorpio, Pisces
Celery	1st	Cancer, Scorpio, Pisces
Cereals	1st or 2nd	Cancer, Scorpio, Pisces, Libra
Chard	1st or 2nd	Cancer, Scorpio, Pisces
Chicory	2nd or 3rd	Cancer, Scorpio, Pisces
Chrysanthemum	1st or 2nd	Virgo
Clover	1st or 2nd	Cancer, Scorpio, Pisces

		Sign
		...ncer, Scorpio, Pisces
		Libra
		Libra
		Cancer, Scorpio, Pisces
	1st or 2nd	Virgo
	1st	Cancer, Scorpio, Pisces
	1st or 2nd	Libra, Virgo
	1st or 2nd	Libra, Virgo
Deciduous trees	2nd or 3rd	Cancer, Scorpio, Pisces, Virgo, Libra
Eggplant	2nd	Cancer, Scorpio, Pisces, Libra
Endive	1st	Cancer, Scorpio, Pisces, Libra
Flowers	1st	Cancer, Scorpio, Pisces, Libra, Taurus, Virgo
Garlic	3rd	Libra, Taurus, Pisces
Gladiola	1st or 2nd	Libra, Virgo
Gourds	1st or 2nd	Cancer, Scorpio, Pisces, Libra
Grapes	2nd or 3rd	Cancer, Scorpio, Pisces, Virgo
Hay	1st or 2nd	Cancer, Scorpio, Pisces, Libra, Taurus
Herbs	1st or 2nd	Cancer, Scorpio, Pisces
Honeysuckle	1st or 2nd	Scorpio, Virgo
Hops	1st or 2nd	Scorpio, Libra
Horseradish	1st or 2nd	Cancer, Scorpio, Pisces
Houseplants	1st	Cancer, Scorpio, Pisces, Libra
Hyacinth	3rd	Cancer, Scorpio, Pisces
Iris	1st or 2nd	Cancer, Virgo
Kohlrabi	1st or 2nd	Cancer, Scorpio, Pisces, Libra
Leek	2nd or 3rd	Sagittarius
Lettuce	1st	Cancer, Scorpio, Pisces, Libra, Taurus
Lily	1st or 2nd	Cancer, Scorpio, Pisces
Maple tree	2nd or 3rd	Taurus, Virgo, Cancer, Pisces
Melon	2nd	Cancer, Scorpio, Pisces
Moon vine	1st or 2nd	Virgo

Plant	Quarter	Sign
Morning glory	1st or 2nd	Cancer, Scorpio, Pisces, Virgo
Oak tree	2nd or 3rd	Taurus, Virgo, Cancer, Pisces
Oats	1st or 2nd	Cancer, Scorpio, Pisces, Libra
Okra	1st or 2nd	Cancer, Scorpio, Pisces, Libra
Onion seed	2nd	Cancer, Scorpio, Sagittarius
Onion set	3rd or 4th	Cancer, Pisces, Taurus, Libra
Pansies	1st or 2nd	Cancer, Scorpio, Pisces
Parsley	1st	Cancer, Scorpio, Pisces, Libra
Parsnip	3rd	Cancer, Scorpio, Taurus, Capricorn
Peach tree	2nd or 3rd	Cancer, Taurus, Virgo, Libra
Peanuts	3rd	Cancer, Scorpio, Pisces
Pear tree	2nd or 3rd	Cancer, Scorpio, Pisces, Libra
Peas	2nd	Cancer, Scorpio, Pisces, Libra
Peony	1st or 2nd	Virgo
Peppers	2nd	Cancer, Scorpio, Pisces
Perennials	3rd	
Petunia	1st or 2nd	Libra, Virgo
Plum tree	2nd or 3rd	Cancer, Pisces, Taurus, Virgo
Poppies	1st or 2nd	Virgo
Portulaca	1st or 2nd	Virgo
Potatoes	3rd	Cancer, Scorpio, Libra, Taurus, Capricorn
Privet	1st or 2nd	Taurus, Libra
Pumpkin	2nd	Cancer, Scorpio, Pisces, Libra
Quince	1st or 2nd	Capricorn
Radishes	3rd	Cancer, Scorpio, Pisces, Libra, Capricorn
Rhubarb	3rd	Cancer, Pisces
Rice	1st or 2nd	Scorpio
Roses	1st or 2nd	Cancer, Virgo
Rutabaga	3rd	Cancer, Scorpio, Pisces, Taurus
Saffron	1st or 2nd	Cancer, Scorpio, Pisces
Sage	3rd	Cancer, Scorpio, Pisces

Plant	Quarter	Sign
Salsify	1st	Cancer, Scorpio, Pisces
Shallot	2nd	Scorpio
Spinach	1st	Cancer, Scorpio, Pisces
Squash	2nd	Cancer, Scorpio, Pisces, Libra
Strawberries	3rd	Cancer, Scorpio, Pisces
String beans	1st or 2nd	Taurus
Sunflowers	1st or 2nd	Libra, Cancer
Sweet peas	1st or 2nd	
Tomatoes	2nd	Cancer, Scorpio, Pisces, Capricorn
Trees, shade	3rd	Taurus, Capricorn
Trees, ornamental	2nd	Libra, Taurus
Trumpet vine	1st or 2nd	Cancer, Scorpio, Pisces
Tubers for seed	3rd	Cancer, Scorpio, Pisces, Libra
Tulips	1st or 2nd	Libra, Virgo
Turnips	3rd	Cancer, Scorpio, Pisces, Taurus, Capricorn, Libra
Valerian	1st or 2nd	Virgo, Gemini
Watermelon	1st or 2nd	Cancer, Scorpio, Pisces, Libra
Wheat	1st or 2nd	Cancer, Scorpio, Pisces, Libra

Companion Planting Guide

Plant	Companions	Hindered by
Asparagus	Tomatoes, parsley, basil	None known
Beans	Tomatoes, carrots, cucumbers, garlic, cabbage, beets, corn	Onions, gladiolas
Beets	Onions, cabbage, lettuce, mint, catnip	Pole beans
Broccoli	Beans, celery, potatoes, onions	Tomatoes
Cabbage	Peppermint, sage, thyme, tomatoes	Strawberries, grapes
Carrots	Peas, lettuce, chives, radishes, leeks, onions, sage	Dill, anise
Citrus trees	Guava, live oak, rubber trees, peppers	None known
Corn	Potatoes, beans, peas, melon, squash, pumpkin, sunflowers, soybeans	Quack grass, wheat, straw, mulch
Cucumbers	Beans, cabbage, radishes, sunflowers, lettuce, broccoli, squash	Aromatic herbs
Eggplant	Green beans, lettuce, kale	None known
Grapes	Peas, beans, blackberries	Cabbage, radishes
Melons	Corn, peas	Potatoes, gourds
Onions, leeks	Beets, chamomile, carrots, lettuce	Peas, beans, sage
Parsnip	Peas	None known
Peas	Radishes, carrots, corn, cucumbers, beans, tomatoes, spinach, turnips	Onion, garlic
Potatoes	Beans, corn, peas, cabbage, hemp, cucumbers, eggplant, catnip	Raspberries, pumpkins, tomatoes, sunflowers
Radishes	Peas, lettuce, nasturtiums, cucumbers	Hyssop
Spinach	Strawberries	None known
Squash/Pumpkin	Nasturtiums, corn, mint, catnip	Potatoes
Tomatoes	Asparagus, parsley, chives, onions, carrots, marigolds, nasturtiums, dill	Black walnut roots, fennel, potatoes
Turnips	Peas, beans, brussels sprouts	Potatoes

Plant	Companions	Uses
Anise	Coriander	Flavor candy, pastry, cheeses, cookies
Basil	Tomatoes	Dislikes rue; repels flies and mosquitoes
Borage	Tomatoes, squash	Use in teas
Buttercup	Clover	Hinders delphinium, peonies, monkshood, columbine

Plant	Companions	Uses
Catnip		Repels flea beetles
Chamomile	Peppermint, wheat, onions, cabbage	Roman chamomile may control damping-off disease; use in herbal sprays
Chervil	Radishes	Good in soups and other dishes
Chives	Carrots	Use in spray to deter black spot on roses
Coriander	Plant anywhere	Hinders seed formation in fennel
Cosmos		Repels corn earworms
Dill	Cabbage	Hinders carrots and tomatoes
Fennel	Plant in borders away from garden	Disliked by all garden plants
Horseradish		Repels potato bugs
Horsetail		Makes fungicide spray
Hyssop		Attracts cabbage fly away from cabbage; harmful to radishes
Lavender	Plant anywhere	Use in spray to control insects on cotton, repels clothes moths
Lovage		Lures horn worms away from tomatoes
Marigolds		Pest repellent; use against Mexican bean beetles and nematodes
Mint	Cabbage, tomatoes	Repels ants, flea beetles, and cabbage worm butterflies
Morning glory	Corn	Helps melon germination
Nasturtiums	Cabbage, cucumbers	Deters aphids, squash bugs, and pumpkin beetles
Okra	Eggplant	Will attract leafhopper (use to trap insects away from other plants)
Parsley	Tomatoes, asparagus	Freeze chopped up leaves to flavor foods
Purslane		Good ground cover
Rosemary		Repels cabbage moths, bean beetles, and carrot flies
Savory		Plant with onions to give them added sweetness
Tansy		Deters Japanese beetles, striped cucumber beetles, and squash bugs
Thyme		Repels cabbage worms
Yarrow		Increases essential oils of neighbors

Moon Void-of-Course

By Kim Rogers-Gallagher

The Moon circles the Earth in about twenty-eight days, moving through each zodiac sign in two-and-a-half days. As she passes through the thirty degrees of each sign, she "visits" with the planets in numerical order, forming aspects with them. Because she moves one degree in just two to two-and-a-half hours, her influence on each planet lasts only a few hours. She eventually reaches the planet that's in the highest degree of any sign and forms what will be her final aspect before leaving the sign. From this point until she enters the next sign, she is referred to as void-of-course.

Think of it this way: the Moon is the emotional "tone" of the day, carrying feelings with her particular to the sign she's "wearing" at the moment. After she has contacted each of the planets, she symbolically "rests" before changing her costume, so her instinct is temporarily on hold. It's during this time that many people feel "fuzzy" or "vague." Plans or decisions made now often do not pan out. Without the instinctual "knowing" the Moon provides as she touches each planet, we tend to be unrealistic or exercise poor judgment. The traditional definition of the void Moon is that "nothing will come of this." Actions initiated under a void Moon are often wasted, irrelevant, or incorrect—usually because information is hidden, missing, or has been overlooked.

Although it's not a good time to initiate plans, routine tasks seem to go along just fine. This period is ideal for reflection. On the lighter side, remember there are good uses for the void Moon. It is the period when the universe seems to be most open to loopholes. It's a great time to make plans you don't want to fulfill or schedule things you don't want to do. See the table on pages 76–81 for a schedule of the Moon's void-of-course times.

Last Aspect		Moon Enters New Sign		
		January		
2	9:08 pm	3	Capricorn	2:39 am
5	7:15 am	5	Aquarius	11:08 am
7	3:51 pm	7	Pisces	9:57 pm
10	6:12 am	10	Aries	10:24 am
12	9:47 pm	12	Taurus	10:37 pm
15	7:47 am	15	Gemini	8:23 am
17	12:57 pm	17	Cancer	2:29 pm
19	4:26 pm	19	Leo	5:16 pm
21	1:57 pm	21	Virgo	6:10 pm
23	3:08 pm	23	Libra	6:59 pm
25	5:04 pm	25	Scorpio	9:15 pm
27	10:01 pm	28	Sagittarius	1:55 am
30	5:10 am	30	Capricorn	9:04 am
		February		
1	2:32 pm	1	Aquarius	6:21 pm
4	1:11 am	4	Pisces	5:24 am
6	2:13 pm	6	Aries	5:45 pm
9	2:31 am	9	Taurus	6:22 am
11	2:27 pm	11	Gemini	5:20 pm
13	10:19 pm	14	Cancer	12:48 am
16	2:06 am	16	Leo	4:14 am
18	3:36 am	18	Virgo	4:39 am
20	2:18 am	20	Libra	4:01 am
22	3:35 am	22	Scorpio	4:29 am
24	6:14 am	24	Sagittarius	7:46 am
26	1:08 pm	26	Capricorn	2:32 pm
28	11:03 pm	3/1	Aquarius	12:14 am

Last Aspect   Moon Enters New Sign

		March		
3	9:36 am	3	Pisces	11:47 am
5	11:34 pm	6	Aries	12:14 am
8	11:04 am	8	Taurus	12:52 pm
11	12:26 am	11	Gemini	12:31 am
13	9:10 am	13	Cancer	10:29 am
15	6:05 am	15	Leo	3:33 pm
17	3:58 pm	17	Virgo	4:53 pm
19	2:10 pm	19	Libra	4:03 pm
21	2:35 pm	21	Scorpio	3:17 pm
23	4:08 pm	23	Sagittarius	4:45 pm
25	9:25 pm	25	Capricorn	9:57 pm
27	11:17 pm	28	Aquarius	7:00 am
30	6:21 pm	30	Pisces	6:38 pm
		April		
3/31	9:44 am	2	Aries	7:16 am
4	6:04 am	4	Taurus	7:46 pm
5	7:02 pm	7	Gemini	7:22 am
8	10:24 pm	9	Cancer	5:02 pm
11	8:05 am	11	Leo	11:37 pm
13	3:58 pm	14	Virgo	2:40 am
15	4:49 pm	16	Libra	2:59 am
17	10:44 pm	18	Scorpio	2:19 am
20	12:53 am	20	Sagittarius	2:50 am
21	12:57 pm	22	Capricorn	6:24 am
23	8:13 pm	24	Aquarius	1:59 pm
26	7:28 am	27	Pisces	12:57 am
27	3:53 pm	29	Aries	1:33 pm

Last Aspect   Moon Enters New Sign

		May		
1	11:20 am	2	Taurus	1:58 am
3	2:51 am	4	Gemini	1:09 pm
6	4:12 pm	6	Cancer	10:32 pm
9	2:52 am	9	Leo	5:35 am
11	12:52 am	11	Virgo	9:59 am
12	10:52 pm	13	Libra	11:56 am
15	12:01 pm	15	Scorpio	12:31 pm
17	7:09 am	17	Sagittarius	1:22 pm
19	10:17 am	19	Capricorn	4:16 pm
21	5:04 pm	21	Aquarius	10:32 pm
24	3:40 am	24	Pisces	8:24 am
25	2:15 pm	26	Aries	8:36 pm
29	6:28 am	29	Taurus	9:02 am
31	11:37 am	31	Gemini	7:56 pm
		June		
3	4:08 am	3	Cancer	4:36 am
5	1:33 am	5	Leo	11:03 am
7	11:27 am	7	Virgo	3:33 pm
9	4:13 am	9	Libra	6:31 pm
11	4:04 am	11	Scorpio	8:33 pm
13	1:43 pm	13	Sagittarius	10:38 pm
15	11:31 pm	16	Capricorn	1:59 am
18	4:07 am	18	Aquarius	7:47 am
20	4:23 pm	20	Pisces	4:45 pm
21	10:51 pm	23	Aries	4:24 am
24	6:07 pm	25	Taurus	4:53 pm
27	12:24 pm	28	Gemini	3:56 am
30	3:33 am	30	Cancer	12:13 pm

Last Aspect   Moon Enters New Sign

			July		
1	7:37 am	2		Leo	5:43 pm
3	12:25 pm	4		Virgo	9:15 pm
5	8:19 pm	6		Libra	11:54 pm
8	2:29 am	9		Scorpio	2:31 am
10	9:05 am	11		Sagittarius	5:47 am
12	8:21 am	13		Capricorn	10:14 am
15	2:40 am	15		Aquarius	4:30 pm
17	8:23 am	18		Pisces	1:13 am
20	7:15 am	20		Aries	12:25 pm
22	5:34 pm	23		Taurus	12:58 am
25	9:12 am	25		Gemini	12:34 pm
27	8:35 pm	27		Cancer	9:11 pm
28	7:03 pm	30		Leo	2:16 am
			August		
1	2:20 am	1		Virgo	4:41 am
1	7:38 pm	3		Libra	6:04 am
5	7:56 am	5		Scorpio	7:57 am
7	11:14 am	7		Sagittarius	11:21 am
9	4:24 pm	9		Capricorn	4:38 pm
10	4:34 pm	11		Aquarius	11:47 pm
14	8:25 am	14		Pisces	8:54 am
15	4:21 am	16		Aries	8:01 pm
19	7:50 am	19		Taurus	8:36 am
21	7:59 pm	21		Gemini	8:53 pm
24	5:33 am	24		Cancer	6:31 am
25	9:04 am	26		Leo	12:09 pm
28	1:11 pm	28		Virgo	2:13 pm
29	6:15 pm	30		Libra	2:25 pm

Last Aspect   Moon Enters New Sign

		September		
1	1:35 pm	1	Scorpio	2:48 pm
3	3:41 pm	3	Sagittarius	5:03 pm
5	8:30 pm	5	Capricorn	10:03 pm
7	4:35 pm	8	Aquarius	5:42 am
10	1:32 pm	10	Pisces	3:26 pm
12	9:45 pm	13	Aries	2:49 am
15	1:10 pm	15	Taurus	3:25 pm
18	3:09 am	18	Gemini	4:06 am
20	12:33 pm	20	Cancer	2:53 pm
22	9:22 pm	22	Leo	9:55 pm
24	10:39 pm	25	Virgo	12:49 am
25	3:47 pm	27	Libra	12:51 am
28	9:51 pm	29	Scorpio	12:05 am
30	10:17 pm	10/1	Sagittarius	12:42 am
		October		
3	1:37 am	3	Capricorn	4:16 am
5	1:58 am	5	Aquarius	11:18 am
7	6:08 pm	7	Pisces	9:13 pm
8	12:51 pm	10	Aries	8:57 am
12	8:08 pm	12	Taurus	9:35 pm
15	6:51 am	15	Gemini	10:15 am
17	6:18 pm	17	Cancer	9:38 pm
19	11:30 pm	20	Leo	6:06 am
22	8:34 am	22	Virgo	10:40 am
23	4:47 pm	24	Libra	11:49 am
26	8:18 am	26	Scorpio	11:08 am
28	7:49 am	28	Sagittarius	10:45 am
30	9:30 am	30	Capricorn	12:39 pm

Last Aspect   **Moon Enters New Sign**

		November		
1	5:00 pm	1	Aquarius	6:08 pm
3	11:40 pm	4	Pisces	3:18 am
5	4:05 am	6	Aries	2:02 pm
9	12:46 am	9	Taurus	2:45 am
11	11:27 am	11	Gemini	3:10 pm
13	10:42 pm	14	Cancer	2:19 am
16	12:22 am	16	Leo	11:17 am
18	2:05 pm	18	Virgo	5:19 pm
20	5:21 pm	20	Libra	8:16 pm
22	6:04 pm	22	Scorpio	8:58 pm
24	6:04 pm	24	Sagittarius	8:57 pm
26	7:06 pm	26	Capricorn	10:05 pm
28	6:01 pm	29	Aquarius	2:02 am
		December		
1	6:27 am	1	Pisces	9:45 am
2	1:06 pm	3	Aries	8:51 pm
6	6:13 am	6	Taurus	9:34 am
8	6:39 pm	8	Gemini	9:52 pm
11	5:24 am	11	Cancer	8:26 am
13	11:05 am	13	Leo	4:48 pm
15	8:20 pm	15	Virgo	10:58 pm
17	9:29 pm	18	Libra	3:06 am
20	4:49 am	20	Scorpio	5:33 am
22	4:49 am	22	Sagittarius	7:03 am
24	6:36 am	24	Capricorn	8:47 am
26	8:36 am	26	Aquarius	12:14 pm
28	4:31 pm	28	Pisces	6:45 pm
30	8:37 am	31	Aries	4:48 am

2010 © Nicole Kuehl. Image from BigStockPhoto.com

The Moon's Rhythm

The Moon journeys around Earth in an elliptical orbit that takes about 27.33 days, which is known as a sidereal month (period of revolution of one body about another). She can move up to 15 degrees or as few as 11 degrees in a day, with the fastest motion occurring when the Moon is at perigee (closest approach to Earth). The Moon is never retrograde, but when her motion is slow, the effect is similar to a retrograde period.

Astrologers have observed that people born on a day when the Moon is fast will process information differently from those who are born when the Moon is slow in motion. People born when the Moon is fast process information quickly and tend to react quickly, while those born during a slow Moon will be more deliberate.

The time from New Moon to New Moon is called the synodic month (involving a conjunction), and the average time span between this Sun-Moon alignment is 29.53 days. Since 29.53 won't divide into 365 evenly, we can have a month with two Full Moons or two New Moons.

Moon Aspects

The aspects the Moon will make during the times you are considering are also important. A trine or sextile, and sometimes a conjunction, are considered favorable aspects. A trine or sextile between the Sun and Moon is an excellent foundation for success. Whether or not a conjunction is considered favorable depends upon the planet the Moon is making a conjunction to. If it's joining the Sun, Venus, Mercury, Jupiter, or even Saturn, the aspect is favorable. If the Moon joins Pluto or Mars, however, that would not be considered favorable. There may be exceptions, but it would depend on what you are electing to do. For example, a trine to Pluto might hasten the end of a relationship you want to be free of.

It is important to avoid times when the Moon makes an aspect to or is conjoining any retrograde planet, unless, of course, you want the thing started to end in failure.

After the Moon has completed an aspect to a planet, that planetary energy has passed. For example, if the Moon squares Saturn at 10:00 am, you can disregard Saturn's influence on your activity if it will occur after that time. You should always look ahead at aspects the Moon will make on the day in question, though, because if the Moon opposes Mars at 11:30 pm on that day, you can expect events that stretch into the evening to be affected by the Moon-Mars aspect. A testy conversation might lead to an argument, or more.

Moon Signs

Much agricultural work is ruled by earth signs—Virgo, Capricorn, and Taurus; and the air signs—Gemini, Aquarius, and Libra—rule flying and intellectual pursuits.

Each planet has one or two signs in which its characteristics are enhanced or "dignified," and the planet is said to "rule" that sign. The Sun rules Leo and the Moon rules Cancer, for example. The ruling planet for each sign is listed below. These should not be considered complete lists. We recommend that you purchase a book of planetary rulerships for more complete information.

Aries Moon

The energy of an Aries Moon is masculine, dry, barren, and fiery. Aries provides great start-up energy, but things started at this time may be the result of impulsive action that lacks research or necessary support. Aries lacks staying power.

Use this assertive, outgoing Moon sign to initiate change, but have a plan in place for someone to pick up the reins when you're impatient to move on to the next thing. Work that requires skillful, but not necessarily patient, use of tools—hammering, cutting down trees, etc.—is appropriate in Aries. Expect things to occur rapidly but to also quickly pass. If you are prone to injury or accidents, exercise caution and good judgment in Aries-related activities.

RULER: Mars

IMPULSE: Action

RULES: Head and face

Taurus Moon

A Taurus Moon's energy is feminine, semi-fruitful, and earthy. The Moon is exalted—very strong—in Taurus. Taurus is known as the farmer's sign because of its associations with farmland and precipitation that is the typical day-long "soaker" variety. Taurus energy is good to incorporate into your plans when patience, practicality, and perseverance are needed. Be aware, though, that you may also experience stubbornness in this sign.

Things started in Taurus tend to be long lasting and to increase in value. This can be very supportive energy in a marriage election. On the downside, the fixed energy of this sign resists change or the letting go of even the most difficult situations. A divorce following a marriage that occurred during a Taurus Moon may be difficult and costly to end. Things begun now tend to become habitual and hard to alter. If you want to make changes in something you started, it would be better to wait for Gemini. This is a good time to get a loan, but expect the people in charge of money to be cautious and slow to make decisions.

RULER: Venus

IMPULSE: Stability

RULES: Neck, throat, and voice

Gemini Moon

A Gemini Moon's energy is masculine, dry, barren, and airy. People are more changeable than usual and may prefer to follow intellectual pursuits and play mental games rather than apply themselves to practical concerns.

This sign is not favored for agricultural matters, but it is an excellent time to prepare for activities, to run errands, and write letters. Plan to use a Gemini Moon to exchange ideas, meet people, go on vacations that include walking or biking, or be in situations that require versatility and quick thinking on your feet.

RULER: Mercury

IMPULSE: Versatility

RULES: Shoulders, hands, arms, lungs, and nervous system

Cancer Moon

A Cancer Moon's energy is feminine, fruitful, moist, and very strong. Use this sign when you want to grow things—flowers, fruits, vegetables, commodities, stocks, or collections—for example. This sensitive sign stimulates rapport between people. Considered the most fertile of the signs, it is often associated with mothering. You can use this moontime to build personal friendships that support mutual growth.

Cancer is associated with emotions and feelings. Prominent Cancer energy promotes growth, but it can also turn people pouty and prone to withdrawing into their shells.

RULER: The Moon

IMPULSE: Tenacity

RULES: Chest area, breasts, and stomach

Leo Moon

A Leo Moon's energy is masculine, hot, dry, fiery, and barren. Use it whenever you need to put on a show, make a presentation, or entertain colleagues or guests. This is a proud yet playful energy that exudes self-confidence and is often associated with romance.

This is an excellent time for fund-raisers and ceremonies or to be straightforward, frank, and honest about something. It is advisable not to put yourself in a position of needing public approval or where you might have to cope with underhandedness, as trouble in these areas can bring out the worst Leo traits. There is a tendency in this sign to become arrogant or self-centered.

RULER: The Sun

IMPULSE: I am

RULES: Heart and upper back

Virgo Moon

A Virgo Moon is feminine, dry, barren, earthy energy. It is favorable for anything that needs painstaking attention—especially those things where exactness rather than innovation is preferred.

Use this sign for activities when you must analyze information or when you must determine the value of something. Virgo is the sign of bargain hunting. It's friendly toward agricultural matters with an emphasis on animals and harvesting vegetables. It is an excellent time to care for animals, especially training them and veterinary work.

This sign is most beneficial when decisions have already been made and now need to be carried out. The inclination here is to see details rather than the bigger picture.

There is a tendency in this sign to overdo. Precautions should be taken to avoid becoming too dull from all work and no play. Build a little relaxation and pleasure into your routine from the beginning.

RULER: Mercury

IMPULSE: Discriminating

RULES: Abdomen and intestines

Libra Moon

A Libra Moon's energy is masculine, semi-fruitful, and airy. This energy will benefit any attempt to bring beauty to a place or thing. Libra is considered good energy for starting things of an intellectual nature. Libra is the sign of partnership and unions, which make it an excellent time to form partnerships of any kind, to make agreements, and to negotiate. Even though this sign is good for initiating things, it is crucial to work with a partner who will provide incentive and encouragement, however. A Libra Moon accentuates teamwork (particularly teams of two) and artistic work (especially work that involves color). Make use of this sign when you are decorating your home or shopping for better quality clothing.

RULER: Venus

IMPULSE: Balance

RULES: Lower back, kidneys, and buttocks

Scorpio Moon

The Scorpio Moon is feminine, fruitful, cold, and moist. It is useful when intensity (that sometimes borders on obsession) is needed. Scorpio is considered a very psychic sign. Use this Moon sign when you must back up something you strongly believe in, such as union or employer relations. There is strong group loyalty here, but a Scorpio Moon is also a good time to end connections thoroughly. This is also a good time to conduct research.

The desire nature is so strong here that there is a tendency to manipulate situations to get what one wants or to not see one's responsibility in an act.

RULER: Pluto, Mars (traditional)

IMPULSE: Transformation

RULES: Reproductive organs, genitals, groin, and pelvis

Sagittarius Moon

The Moon's energy is masculine, dry, barren, and fiery in Sagittarius, encouraging flights of imagination and confidence in the flow of life. Sagittarius is the most philosophical sign. Candor and honesty are enhanced when the Moon is here. This is an excellent time to "get things off your chest" and to deal with institutions of higher learning, publishing companies, and the law. It's also a good time for sport and adventure.

Sagittarians are the crusaders of this world. This is a good time to tackle things that need improvement, but don't try to be the diplomat while influenced by this energy. Opinions can run strong, and the tendency to proselytize is increased.

RULER: Jupiter

IMPULSE: Expansion

RULES: Thighs and hips

Capricorn Moon

In Capricorn the Moon's energy is feminine, semi-fruitful, and earthy. Because Cancer and Capricorn are polar opposites, the Moon's energy is thought to be weakened here. This energy encourages the need for structure, discipline, and organization. This is a good time to set goals and plan for the future, tend to family business, and to take care of details requiring patience or a businesslike manner. Institutional activities are favored. This sign should be avoided if you're seeking favors, as those in authority can be insensitive under this influence.

RULER: Saturn

IMPULSE: Ambitious

RULES: Bones, skin, and knees

Aquarius Moon

An Aquarius Moon's energy is masculine, barren, dry, and airy. Activities that are unique, individualistic, concerned with humanitarian issues, society as a whole, and making improvements are favored under this Moon. It is this quality of making improvements that has caused this sign to be associated with inventors and new inventions.

An Aquarius Moon promotes the gathering of social groups for friendly exchanges. People tend to react and speak from an intellectual rather than emotional viewpoint when the Moon is in this sign.

RULER: Uranus and Saturn

IMPULSE: Reformer

RULES: Calves and ankles

Pisces Moon

A Pisces Moon is feminine, fruitful, cool, and moist. This is an excellent time to retreat, meditate, sleep, pray, or make that dreamed-of escape into a fantasy vacation. However, things are not always what they seem to be with the Moon in Pisces. Personal boundaries tend to be fuzzy, and you may not be seeing things clearly. People tend to be idealistic under this sign, which can prevent them from seeing reality.

There is a live and let live philosophy attached to this sign, which in the idealistic world may work well enough, but chaos is frequently the result. That's why this sign is also associated with alcohol and drug abuse, drug trafficking, and counterfeiting. On the lighter side, many musicians and artists are ruled by Pisces. It's only when they move too far away from reality that the dark side of substance abuse, suicide, or crime takes away life.

RULER: Jupiter and Neptune

IMPULSE: Empathetic

RULES: Feet

More About Zodiac Signs

Element (Triplicity)

Each of the zodiac signs is classified as belonging to an element; these are the four basic elements:

Fire Signs

Aries, Sagittarius, and Leo are action-oriented, outgoing, energetic, and spontaneous.

Earth Signs

Taurus, Capricorn, and Virgo are stable, conservative, practical, and oriented to the physical and material realm.

Air Signs

Gemini, Aquarius, and Libra are sociable and critical, and they tend to represent intellectual responses rather than feelings.

Water Signs

Cancer, Scorpio, and Pisces are emotional, receptive, intuitive, and can be very sensitive.

Quality (Quadruplicity)

Each zodiac sign is further classified as being cardinal, mutable, or fixed. There are four signs in each quadruplicity, one sign from each element.

Cardinal Signs

Aries, Cancer, Libra, and Capricorn represent beginnings and newly initiated action. They initiate each new season in the cycle of the year.

Fixed Signs

Taurus, Leo, Scorpio,
quo through stubborn
"between" time. For exam
really feels like summer.

Mutable Signs

Pisces, Gemini, Virgo, and Sagittar
ate situations. They represent the last
things are changing in preparation for th

Nature and Fertility

In addition to a sign's element and quality, e
classified as either fruitful, semi-fruitful, or bar
fication is the most important for readers who us
ing information in the *Moon Sign Book* because the
most events depends on the fertility of the sign occupie
Moon. The water signs of Cancer, Scorpio, and Pisces a
most fruitful. The semi-fruitful signs are the earth signs Tau
and Capricorn, and the air sign Libra. The barren signs correspond to fire-signs Aries, Leo, and Sagittarius; air-signs Gemini
and Aquarius; and earth-sign Virgo.

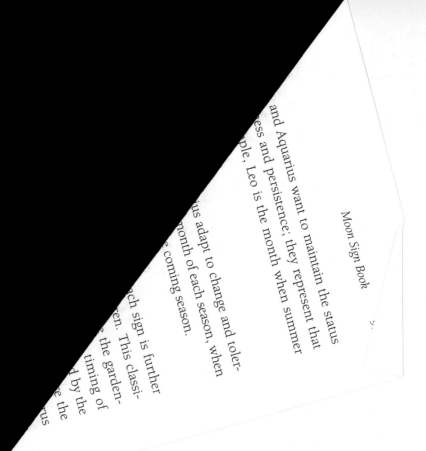

and Aquarius want to maintain the status
...ess and persistence; they represent that
...ple, Leo is the month when summer

...us adapt to change and toler-
...month of each season, when
...coming season.

...ach sign is further
...een. This classi-
... the garden-
... timing of
...d by the
...e the
...us

E lectional astrology is the art of electing times to begin any undertaking. Say, for example, you want to start a business. That business will experience ups and downs, as well as reach its potential, according to the promise held in the universe at the time the business was started—its birth time. The horoscope (birth chart) set for the date, time, and place that a business starts would indicate the outcome—its potential to succeed.

So, you might ask yourself the question: If the horoscope for a business start can show success or failure, why not begin at a time that is more favorable to the venture? Well, you can.

While no time is perfect, there are better times and better days to undertake specific activities. There are thousands of examples that prove electional astrology is not only practical, but that it can make a difference in our lives. There are rules for electing times to begin various activities—even shopping. You'll find detailed instructions about how to make elections beginning on page 107.

Personalizing Elections

The election rules in this almanac are based upon the planetary positions at the time for which the election is made. They do not depend on any type of birth chart. However, a birth chart based upon the time, date, and birthplace of an event has advantages. No election is effective for every person. For example, you may leave home to begin a trip at the same time as a friend, but each of you will have a different experience according to whether or not your birth chart favors the trip.

Not all elections require a birth chart, but the timing of very important events—business starts, marriages, etc.—would benefit from the additional accuracy a birth chart provides. To order a birth chart for yourself or a planned event, visit our Web site at www.llewellyn.com.

Some Things to Consider

You've probably experienced good timing in your life. Maybe you were at the right place at the right time to meet a friend whom you hadn't seen in years. Frequently, when something like that happens, it is the result of following an intuitive impulse—that "gut instinct." Consider for a moment that you were actually responding to planetary energies. Electional astrology is a tool that can help you to align with energies, present and future, that are available to us through planetary placements.

Significators

Decide upon the important significators (planet, sign, and house ruling the matter) for which the election is being made. The Moon is the most important significator in any election, so the

Moon should always be fortified (strong by sign and making favorable aspects to other planets). The Moon's aspects to other planets are more important than the sign the Moon is in.

Other important considerations are the significators of the Ascendant and Midheaven—the house ruling the election matter and the ruler of the sign on that house cusp. Finally, any planet or sign that has a general rulership over the matter in question should be taken into consideration.

Nature and Fertility

Determine the general nature of the sign that is appropriate for your election. For example, much agricultural work is ruled by the earth signs of Virgo, Capricorn, and Taurus; while the air signs—Gemini, Aquarius, and Libra—rule intellectual pursuits.

One Final Comment

Use common sense. If you must do something, like plant your garden or take an airplane trip on a day that doesn't have the best aspects, proceed anyway, but try to minimize problems. For example, leave early for the airport to avoid being left behind due to delays in the security lanes. When you have no other choice, do the best that you can under the circumstances at the time.

If you want to personalize your elections, please turn to page 107 for more information. If you want a quick and easy answer, you can refer to Llewellyn's Astro Almanac.

Llewellyn's Astro Almanac

The Astro Almanac tables, beginning on the next page, can help you find the dates best suited to particular activities. The dates provided are determined from the Moon's sign, phase, and aspects to other planets. Please note that the Astro Almanac does not take personal factors, such as your Sun and Moon sign, into account. The dates are general, and they will apply for everyone. Some activities will not have suitable dates during a particular month, so no dates will be shown.

Activity	January
Animals (Neuter or spay)	1, 2, 3, 4, 28, 29, 30, 31
Animals (Sell or buy)	5, 10, 15
Automobile (Buy)	5, 16, 22
Brewing	26
Build (foundation)	6
Business (Conducting for Self and Others)	9, 14, 24, 28
Business (Start new)	5, 15
Can Fruits and Vegetables	26
Can Preserves	26
Concrete (Pour)	20, 21
Construction (Begin new)	5, 14, 15, 19, 24, 28
Consultants (Begin work with)	2, 5, 7, 10, 12, 15, 19, 22, 27, 28
Contracts (Bid on)	5, 7, 10, 12, 15, 19
Cultivate	
Decorating	5, 6, 7, 15, 16, 17
Demolition	2, 19, 20, 28, 29
Electronics (Buy)	7
Entertain Guests	13, 14, 15, 20, 25
Floor Covering (Laying new)	20, 21, 22, 23, 24, 25
Habits (Break)	3, 30, 31
Hair (Cut to increase growth)	2, 3, 4, 7, 8, 9, 12, 13, 14, 15, 16, 19
Hair (Cut to decrease growth)	28, 29, 30, 31
Harvest (Grain for storage)	20, 21
Harvest (Root crops)	2, 20, 21, 28, 29
Investments (New)	14, 24
Loan (Ask for)	13, 14
Massage (Relaxing)	20, 25
Mow Lawn (Decrease growth)	3, 20, 21, 22, 23, 24, 28, 29, 30, 31
Mow Lawn (Increase growth)	5, 6, 10, 11, 12, 13, 14, 15, 16
Mushrooms (Pick)	18, 19, 20
Negotiate (Business for the Elderly)	6, 16, 20, 29
Prune for Better Fruit	2, 25, 26, 27, 28, 29
Prune to Promote Healing	3, 30, 31
Wean Children	2, 3, 4, 5, 6, 7, 28, 29, 30, 31
Wood Floors (Installing)	3, 30, 31
Write Letters or Contracts	5, 15, 19, 27

Activity	February
Animals (Neuter or spay)	1, 24, 25, 26, 27, 28
Animals (Sell or buy)	4, 9, 12, 16
Automobile (Buy)	1, 12, 13, 27, 28
Brewing	23
Build (foundation)	3
Business (Conducting for Self and Others)	8, 13, 22, 27
Business (Start new)	
Can Fruits and Vegetables	23
Can Preserves	23
Concrete (Pour)	
Construction (Begin new)	1, 8, 12, 13, 16, 24, 27
Consultants (Begin work with)	1, 6, 7, 12, 16, 22, 24, 27
Contracts (Bid on)	5, 6, 7, 12, 16
Cultivate	1, 2, 24
Decorating	2, 3, 4, 11, 12, 13
Demolition	24, 25
Electronics (Buy)	12
Entertain Guests	12, 13, 15
Floor Covering (Laying new)	1, 2, 19, 20, 21, 22
Habits (Break)	1, 25, 26, 27, 28
Hair (Cut to increase growth)	4, 5, 9, 10, 11, 12, 13, 16
Hair (Cut to decrease growth)	24, 25, 26, 27, 28
Harvest (Grain for storage)	24
Harvest (Root crops)	1, 24, 25, 26
Investments (New)	13, 22
Loan (Ask for)	9, 10, 11, 16, 17
Massage (Relaxing)	9
Mow Lawn (Decrease growth)	1, 19, 20, 21, 24, 25, 26, 27
Mow Lawn (Increase growth)	3, 6, 7, 8, 9, 10, 11,12, 16, 17
Mushrooms (Pick)	17, 18, 19
Negotiate (Business for the Elderly)	25
Prune for Better Fruit	22, 23, 24, 25, 26
Prune to Promote Healing	1, 27, 28
Wean Children	1, 2, 3, 4, 24, 25, 26, 27, 28
Wood Floors (Installing)	1, 26, 27, 28
Write Letters or Contracts	1, 11, 16, 28

Activity	March
Animals (Neuter or spay)	3, 26, 27, 31
Animals (Sell or buy)	6, 16
Automobile (Buy)	11, 12
Brewing	22, 23, 31
Build (foundation)	
Business (Conducting for Self and Others)	10, 15, 23, 28
Business (Start new)	
Can Fruits and Vegetables	4, 22, 23, 31
Can Preserves	22, 23
Concrete (Pour)	1, 2, 29, 30
Construction (Begin new)	1, 10, 11, 15, 16, 23, 24, 28, 29
Consultants (Begin work with)	1, 5, 6, 11, 16, 24, 25, 29, 30
Contracts (Bid on)	6, 11, 15, 16
Cultivate	1, 2, 3, 24, 25, 28, 29, 30
Decorating	11, 12, 13
Demolition	23, 24
Electronics (Buy)	11, 28, 30
Entertain Guests	8, 9, 11, 21
Floor Covering (Laying new)	1, 2, 20, 21, 28, 29, 30
Habits (Break)	1, 2, 27, 28, 29, 30
Hair (Cut to increase growth)	5, 8, 9, 10, 11, 12, 15
Hair (Cut to decrease growth)	3, 4, 23, 24, 25, 26, 27, 31
Harvest (Grain for storage)	15, 24, 25
Harvest (Root crops)	1, 2, 23, 24, 25, 28, 29, 30
Investments (New)	15, 23
Loan (Ask for)	9, 10, 16, 17
Massage (Relaxing)	21
Mow Lawn (Decrease growth)	1, 2, 20, 23, 24, 25, 26, 27, 28, 29, 30
Mow Lawn (Increase growth)	6, 7, 8, 9, 11, 12, 15, 16, 17, 18
Mushrooms (Pick)	18, 19, 20
Negotiate (Business for the Elderly)	2, 16, 24, 29
Prune for Better Fruit	21, 22, 23, 24, 25
Prune to Promote Healing	26, 27
Wean Children	1, 2, 3, 24, 25, 26, 27, 28, 29, 30
Wood Floors (Installing)	25, 26, 27
Write Letters or Contracts	5, 11, 15, 23, 28

Activity	April
Animals (Neuter or spay)	27, 28
Animals (Sell or buy)	5, 8, 13
Automobile (Buy)	7, 8
Brewing	18, 27, 28
Build (foundation)	
Business (Conducting for Self and Others)	8, 13, 22, 27
Business (Start new)	
Can Fruits and Vegetables	18, 27, 28
Can Preserves	18
Concrete (Pour)	25
Construction (Begin new)	8, 13, 21, 22, 26
Consultants (Begin work with)	3, 4, 8, 13, 21, 25, 26, 30
Contracts (Bid on)	4, 8, 11, 13
Cultivate	2, 20, 21, 25, 26, 30
Decorating	7, 8, 16, 17
Demolition	2, 20, 21, 29, 30
Electronics (Buy)	7, 8, 24, 25
Entertain Guests	5, 6, 7, 8, 9
Floor Covering (Laying new)	2, 24, 25, 26
Habits (Break)	2, 25, 26, 29, 30
Hair (Cut to increase growth)	4, 5, 6, 7, 8, 11
Hair (Cut to decrease growth)	20, 21, 22, 23, 27, 28
Harvest (Grain for storage)	20, 21
Harvest (Root crops)	2, 20, 21, 24, 25, 26, 29, 30
Investments (New)	13, 22
Loan (Ask for)	5, 6, 12, 13
Massage (Relaxing)	5, 11, 24
Mow Lawn (Decrease growth)	2, 20, 21, 22, 23, 24, 25, 29, 30
Mow Lawn (Increase growth)	4, 5, 6, 7, 8, 11, 12, 14, 16
Mushrooms (Pick)	16, 17, 18
Negotiate (Business for the Elderly)	8, 12, 25
Prune for Better Fruit	18, 19, 20
Prune to Promote Healing	22, 23
Wean Children	20, 21, 22, 23, 24, 25, 26
Wood Floors (Installing)	22, 23
Write Letters or Contracts	4, 7, 12, 20, 24, 30

Activity	May
Animals (Neuter or spay)	18, 19, 20, 24, 25, 26
Animals (Sell or buy)	6, 11
Automobile (Buy)	4, 5, 6, 20
Brewing	25, 26
Build (foundation)	10
Business (Conducting for Self and Others)	8, 12, 21, 27
Business (Start new)	
Can Fruits and Vegetables	25, 26
Can Preserves	2, 3, 30, 31
Concrete (Pour)	22, 30, 31
Construction (Begin new)	6, 8, 11, 12, 19, 21, 24, 27
Consultants (Begin work with)	1, 6, 10, 11, 19, 20, 24, 25, 29, 31
Contracts (Bid on)	6, 10, 11
Cultivate	1, 18, 19, 27, 28, 29
Decorating	4, 5, 6, 13, 14, 15
Demolition	1, 17, 18, 27
Electronics (Buy)	4, 6, 22
Entertain Guests	2, 3, 4, 5, 6, 11, 29
Floor Covering (Laying new)	2, 3, 21, 22, 29, 30, 31
Habits (Break)	1, 27, 29, 31
Hair (Cut to increase growth)	3, 4, 5, 9
Hair (Cut to decrease growth)	2, 18, 19, 20, 24, 25, 29, 30, 31
Harvest (Grain for storage)	18, 19, 22
Harvest (Root crops)	1, 17, 118, 19, 21, 22, 27, 31
Investments (New)	12, 21
Loan (Ask for)	3, 4, 9, 10
Massage (Relaxing)	11, 30
Mow Lawn (Decrease growth)	18, 19, 20, 21, 22, 27, 29, 30, 31
Mow Lawn (Increase growth)	4, 5, 9, 10, 11, 12, 13, 14
Mushrooms (Pick)	16, 17, 18
Negotiate (Business for the Elderly)	5, 22
Prune for Better Fruit	17, 18, 19
Prune to Promote Healing	20, 21
Wean Children	18, 19, 20, 21, 22, 24
Wood Floors (Installing)	19, 20, 21
Write Letters or Contracts	4, 9, 17, 31

Activity	June
Animals (Neuter or spay)	16, 17, 18
Animals (Sell or buy)	3, 5, 7, 9
Automobile (Buy)	1, 28, 29
Brewing	21, 22
Build (foundation)	6
Business (Conducting for Self and Others)	6, 11, 20, 26
Business (Start new)	7
Can Fruits and Vegetables	21, 22
Can Preserves	26, 27
Concrete (Pour)	19, 20, 26, 27
Construction (Begin new)	3, 6, 7, 11, 16, 20, 26, 30
Consultants (Begin work with)	3, 5, 7, 11, 16, 20, 21, 26, 27, 30
Contracts (Bid on)	3, 5, 7, 11, 16
Cultivate	1, 23, 24, 28, 29, 30
Decorating	1, 2, 3, 9, 10, 11
Demolition	15, 23, 24
Electronics (Buy)	1, 11, 18, 28
Entertain Guests	1, 2, 4, 5, 9, 26, 27
Floor Covering (Laying new)	1, 18, 19, 25, 26, 27, 28, 29
Habits (Break)	24, 28, 29, 30
Hair (Cut to increase growth)	1, 2, 5, 14, 15
Hair (Cut to decrease growth)	16, 17, 20, 21, 22, 25, 26, 27, 28, 29
Harvest (Grain for storage)	18, 19, 20
Harvest (Root crops)	18, 19, 20, 23, 24, 28, 29, 30
Investments (New)	11, 20
Loan (Ask for)	5, 6, 7
Massage (Relaxing)	5, 9, 19
Mow Lawn (Decrease growth)	16, 17, 18, 19, 23, 24, 25, 26, 27, 28, 29
Mow Lawn (Increase growth)	2, 5, 6, 7, 8, 9, 10, 14
Mushrooms (Pick)	14, 15, 16
Negotiate (Business for the Elderly)	1, 14
Prune for Better Fruit	15
Prune to Promote Healing	16, 17, 18
Wean Children	14, 15, 16, 17, 18, 19, 20
Wood Floors (Installing)	16, 17, 18
Write Letters or Contracts	1, 5, 14, 28

Activity	Animals (Neuter or spay)	Animals (Sell or buy)	Automobile (Buy)	Brewing	Build (foundation)	Business (Conducting for Self an...	Business (Start new)	Can Fruits and Veget...	Can Preserves	Concrete (Po...	Constru...	Con...

Activity	
Animals (Ne...	
Animals (Se...	
Automobile...	
Brewing	
Build (foun...	
Business (C...	
Business (S...	
Can Fruits...	
Can Preserv...	
Concrete (...	
Constructi...	
Consultant	
Contracts (...	
Cultivate	
Decorating	
Demolition	20, 21, 22, ...
Electronics (Buy)	7, 16, 25, 27
Entertain Guests	25, 26, 27, 28, 30
Floor Covering (Laying new)	15, 16, 17, 23, 24, 25, 26, 30
Habits (Break)	25, 26, 27
Hair (Cut to increase growth)	2, 11, 12, 13
Hair (Cut to decrease growth)	18, 19, 23, 24, 25, 26
Harvest (Grain for storage)	16, 20, 21
Harvest (Root crops)	15, 16, 17, 20, 21, 22, 25, 26, 27
Investments (New)	10, 20
Loan (Ask for)	3, 4, 30, 31
Massage (Relaxing)	25, 30
Mow Lawn (Decrease growth)	16, 20, 21, 23, 24, 25, 26
Mow Lawn (Increase growth)	2, 3, 4, 5, 6, 7, 11, 12, 13, 31
Mushrooms (Pick)	14, 15, 16
Negotiate (Business for the Elderly)	3, 16, 26, 30
Prune for Better Fruit	
Prune to Promote Healing	15
Wean Children	11, 12, 13, 14, 15, 16, 17
Wood Floors (Installing)	15
Write Letters or Contracts	2, 3, 11, 16, 30

	August
	, 8, 10, 29
	1, 22, 23
	15, 16, 25, 26
...d Others)	4, 8, 19, 24
	1, 10, 29
...bles	15, 16, 25
	20, 21, 25
...ur)	20, 21, 27
...tion (Begin new)	1, 4, 8, 10, 19, 24, 25, 29
...ultants (Begin work with)	1, 5, 9, 10, 15, 18, 20, 23, 25, 27, 29, 31
Contracts (Bid on)	1, 5, 9, 10, 29, 31
Cultivate	22, 23, 26, 27, 28
Decorating	3, 4, 5, 12, 13, 30, 31
Demolition	17, 18, 26, 27
Electronics (Buy)	12, 22, 23, 31
Entertain Guests	19, 20, 23
Floor Covering (Laying new)	19, 20, 21, 22, 23, 26, 27, 28
Habits (Break)	22, 23, 24, 26, 27
Hair (Cut to increase growth)	7, 8, 9, 10
Hair (Cut to decrease growth)	14, 15, 19, 20, 21, 22, 23, 26
Harvest (Grain for storage)	17, 18
Harvest (Root crops)	13, 17, 18, 21, 22, 23, 26, 27
Investments (New)	8, 19
Loan (Ask for)	
Massage (Relaxing)	3, 24
Mow Lawn (Decrease growth)	17, 18, 19, 20, 21, 22, 23, 26, 27
Mow Lawn (Increase growth)	1, 2, 3, 4, 7, 8, 9, 10, 11, 12, 29, 30, 31
Mushrooms (Pick)	12, 13, 14
Negotiate (Business for the Elderly)	8, 27
Prune for Better Fruit	
Prune to Promote Healing	
Wean Children	7, 8, 9, 10, 11, 12, 13, 14
Wood Floors (Installing)	
Write Letters or Contracts	1, 12, 22, 26, 27

Activity	September
Animals (Neuter or spay)	
Animals (Sell or buy)	2, 6, 11
Automobile (Buy)	18, 19
Brewing	21, 22
Build (foundation)	
Business (Conducting for Self and Others)	2, 7, 17, 22
Business (Start new)	6
Can Fruits and Vegetables	21, 22
Can Preserves	16, 17, 21, 22
Concrete (Pour)	16, 17, 23
Construction (Begin new)	6, 7, 17, 21, 22, 25
Consultants (Begin work with)	5, 6, 11, 16, 21, 22, 25, 27
Contracts (Bid on)	5, 6, 11, 14
Cultivate	23, 24, 25, 26
Decorating	1, 8, 9, 10, 27, 28
Demolition	13, 14, 23, 24
Electronics (Buy)	8, 18, 27
Entertain Guests	16, 18, 23, 28
Floor Covering (Laying new)	15, 16, 17, 18, 19, 23, 24, 25, 26, 27
Habits (Break)	23, 24
Hair (Cut to increase growth)	3, 4, 5, 6, 7, 10, 11
Hair (Cut to decrease growth)	15, 16, 17, 18, 19, 22
Harvest (Grain for storage)	13, 14, 15, 18, 19
Harvest (Root crops)	13, 14, 15, 18, 19, 20, 23, 24
Investments (New)	7, 17
Loan (Ask for)	
Massage (Relaxing)	23, 28
Mow Lawn (Decrease growth)	13, 14, 15, 16, 17, 18, 19, 23, 25
Mow Lawn (Increase growth)	3, 4, 5, 6, 7, 8, 9, 29
Mushrooms (Pick)	11, 12, 13
Negotiate (Business for the Elderly)	4, 9, 19
Prune for Better Fruit	
Prune to Promote Healing	
Wean Children	4, 5, 6, 7, 8, 9, 10
Wood Floors (Installing)	
Write Letters or Contracts	8, 18, 23

Activity	October
Animals (Neuter or spay)	28, 29, 30, 31
Animals (Sell or buy)	2, 7, 8, 30
Automobile (Buy)	15, 17, 23
Brewing	18, 19
Build (foundation)	
Business (Conducting for Self and Others)	1, 6, 17, 22, 31
Business (Start new)	3, 30
Can Fruits and Vegetables	18, 19
Can Preserves	13, 14, 18, 19
Concrete (Pour)	13, 14, 21
Construction (Begin new)	1, 3, 6, 17, 18, 22, 30, 31
Consultants (Begin work with)	1, 3, 7, 8, 13, 18, 22, 23, 27, 30
Contracts (Bid on)	1, 3, 7, 8, 27, 30
Cultivate	20, 21, 22, 23, 24
Decorating	5, 6, 7
Demolition	11, 20, 21
Electronics (Buy)	5, 7, 15
Entertain Guests	15, 16, 17, 18
Floor Covering (Laying new)	12, 13, 14, 15, 16, 20, 21, 22, 23, 24, 25, 26
Habits (Break)	20, 21, 22
Hair (Cut to increase growth)	1, 2, 3, 4, 7, 8, 9, 28, 29, 30, 31
Hair (Cut to decrease growth)	12, 13, 14, 15, 16, 20
Harvest (Grain for storage)	12, 15, 16, 17
Harvest (Root crops)	12, 15, 16, 17, 20, 21
Investments (New)	6, 17
Loan (Ask for)	
Massage (Relaxing)	7, 18
Mow Lawn (Decrease growth)	12, 13, 14, 15, 16, 20, 21, 22, 23, 24, 25
Mow Lawn (Increase growth)	1, 2, 3, 4, 5, 6, 10, 28, 29, 30, 31
Mushrooms (Pick)	10, 11, 12
Negotiate (Business for the Elderly)	2, 21, 29
Prune for Better Fruit	26
Prune to Promote Healing	
Wean Children	1, 2, 3, 4, 5, 6, 7, 28, 29, 30, 31
Wood Floors (Installing)	
Write Letters or Contracts	1, 5, 15, 20, 27, 28

Activity	November
Animals (Neuter or spay)	24, 25
Animals (Sell or buy)	1, 4, 7, 27
Automobile (Buy)	1, 11, 13
Brewing	14, 15, 23
Build (foundation)	
Business (Conducting for Self and Others)	5, 15, 20, 29
Business (Start new)	27
Can Fruits and Vegetables	14, 15, 23, 24
Can Preserves	11, 14, 15, 23, 24
Concrete (Pour)	11, 17, 18
Construction (Begin new)	14, 15, 18, 20, 27, 29
Consultants (Begin work with)	1, 4, 7, 9, 14, 17, 18, 22, 26, 27, 30
Contracts (Bid on)	1, 4, 7, 9, 26, 27, 30
Cultivate	18, 19, 20
Decorating	1, 2, 3, 29, 30
Demolition	16, 17, 24, 25
Electronics (Buy)	1, 11, 22, 29, 30
Entertain Guests	9, 10, 11, 13, 14, 15, 17, 22
Floor Covering (Laying new)	11, 12, 13, 16, 17, 18, 19, 20, 21, 22
Habits (Break)	
Hair (Cut to increase growth)	4, 5, 25, 26, 27, 28
Hair (Cut to decrease growth)	9, 10, 11, 12, 13, 16, 24
Harvest (Grain for storage)	12, 16, 17, 18
Harvest (Root crops)	11, 12, 13, 16, 17, 18
Investments (New)	5, 15
Loan (Ask for)	9
Massage (Relaxing)	17, 22
Mow Lawn (Decrease growth)	11, 12, 16, 17, 18, 19, 20, 21
Mow Lawn (Increase growth)	1, 2, 3, 7, 9, 26, 27, 29, 30
Mushrooms (Pick)	9, 10, 11
Negotiate (Business for the Elderly)	3, 13, 26
Prune for Better Fruit	22, 23, 24
Prune to Promote Healing	
Wean Children	1, 2, 3, 25, 26, 27, 28, 29, 30
Wood Floors (Installing)	
Write Letters or Contracts	1, 11, 16, 24, 29

Activity	December
Animals (Neuter or spay)	22, 23
Animals (Sell or buy)	1, 7, 28
Automobile (Buy)	8, 11
Brewing	12, 13, 21
Build (foundation)	1, 28
Business (Conducting for Self and Others)	4, 15, 20, 29
Business (Start new)	
Can Fruits and Vegetables	12, 13, 21
Can Preserves	12, 13, 21
Concrete (Pour)	14, 15
Construction (Begin new)	4, 11, 15, 20, 24
Consultants (Begin work with)	1, 4, 6, 11, 13, 15, 18, 22, 24, 27, 28
Contracts (Bid on)	1, 4, 6, 27, 28
Cultivate	17, 18
Decorating	1, 8, 9, 10, 26, 27, 28
Demolition	13, 14, 22, 23
Electronics (Buy)	8, 18, 26, 27
Entertain Guests	6, 7, 8, 11, 12
Floor Covering (Laying new)	13, 14, 15, 16, 17, 18, 19, 20
Habits (Break)	
Hair (Cut to increase growth)	1, 2, 6, 7, 8, 9
Hair (Cut to decrease growth)	13, 22, 23, 24, 25, 28, 29, 30
Harvest (Grain for storage)	14, 15
Harvest (Root crops)	10, 13, 14, 15, 22, 23
Investments (New)	4, 15
Loan (Ask for)	6, 7, 8
Massage (Relaxing)	7, 27
Mow Lawn (Decrease growth)	13, 14, 15, 16, 17, 18, 19, 22, 23
Mow Lawn (Increase growth)	3, 4, 5, 6, 7, 8, 9, 25, 26, 27, 31
Mushrooms (Pick)	9, 10, 11
Negotiate (Business for the Elderly)	15, 28
Prune for Better Fruit	20, 21, 22, 23
Prune to Promote Healing	24
Wean Children	1, 22, 23, 24, 25, 26, 27, 28
Wood Floors (Installing)	24
Write Letters or Contracts	8, 13, 22, 26

2010 © Cecilia Lim. Image from BigStockPhoto.com

Choose the Best Time for Your Activities

When rules for elections refer to "favorable" and "unfavorable" aspects to your Sun or other planets, please refer to the Favorable and Unfavorable Days Tables and Lunar Aspectarian for more information. You'll find instructions beginning on page 129 and the tables beginning on page 136.

The material in this section came from several sources including: *The New A to Z Horoscope Maker and Delineator* by Llewellyn George (Llewellyn, 1999), *Moon Sign Book* (Llewellyn, 1945), and *Electional Astrology* by Vivian Robson (Slingshot Publishing, 2000). Robson's book was originally published in 1937.

Advertise (Internet)
The Moon should be conjunct, sextile, or trine Mercury or Uranus and in the sign of Gemini, Capricorn, or Aquarius.

Advertise (Print)

Write ads on a day favorable to your Sun. The Moon should be conjunct, sextile, or trine Mercury or Venus. Avoid hard aspects to Mars and Saturn. Ad campaigns produce the best results when the Moon is well aspected in Gemini (to enhance communication) or Capricorn (to build business).

Animals

Take home new pets when the day is favorable to your Sun, or when the Moon is trine, sextile, or conjunct Mercury, Venus, or Jupiter, or in the sign of Virgo or Pisces. However, avoid days when the Moon is either square or opposing the Sun, Mars, Saturn, Uranus, Neptune, or Pluto. When selecting a pet, have the Moon well aspected by the planet that rules the animal. Cats are ruled by the Sun, dogs by Mercury, birds by Venus, horses by Jupiter, and fish by Neptune. Buy large animals when the Moon is in Sagittarius or Pisces and making favorable aspects to Jupiter or Mercury. Buy animals smaller than sheep when the Moon is in Virgo with favorable aspects to Mercury or Venus.

Animals (Breed)

Animals are easiest to handle when the Moon is in Taurus, Cancer, Libra, or Pisces, but try to avoid the Full Moon. To encourage healthy births, animals should be mated so births occur when the Moon is increasing in Taurus, Cancer, Pisces, or Libra. Those born during a semi-fruitful sign (Taurus and Capricorn) will produce leaner meat. Libra yields beautiful animals for showing and racing.

Animals (Declaw)

Declaw cats in the dark of the Moon. Avoid the week before and after the Full Moon and the sign of Pisces.

Animals (Neuter or spay)

Have livestock and pets neutered or spayed when the Moon is in Sagittarius, Capricorn, or Pisces, after it has passed through Scorpio, the sign that rules reproductive organs. Avoid the week before and after the Full Moon.

Animals (Sell or buy)

In either buying or selling, it is important to keep the Moon and Mercury free from any aspect to Mars. Aspects to Mars will create discord and increase the likelihood of wrangling over price and quality. The Moon should be passing from the first quarter to full and sextile or trine Venus or Jupiter. When buying racehorses, let the Moon be in an air sign. The Moon should be in air signs when you buy birds. If the birds are to be pets, let the Moon be in good aspect to Venus.

Animals (Train)

Train pets when the Moon is in Virgo or trine to Mercury.

Animals (Train dogs to hunt)

Let the Moon be in Aries in conjunction with Mars, which makes them courageous and quick to learn. But let Jupiter also be in aspect to preserve them from danger in hunting.

Automobiles

When buying an automobile, select a time when the Moon is conjunct, sextile, or trine to Mercury, Saturn, or Uranus and in the sign of Gemini or Capricorn. Avoid times when Mercury is in retrograde motion.

Baking Cakes

Your cakes will have a lighter texture if you see that the Moon is in Gemini, Libra, or Aquarius and in good aspect to Venus or Mercury. If you are decorating a cake or confections are being made, have the Moon placed in Libra.

Beauty Treatments (Massage, etc.)

See that the Moon is in Taurus, Cancer, Leo, Libra, or Aquarius and in favorable aspect to Venus. In the case of plastic surgery, aspects to Mars should be avoided, and the Moon should not be in the sign ruling the part to be operated on.

Borrow (Money or goods)

See that the Moon is not placed between 15 degrees Libra and 15 degrees Scorpio. Let the Moon be waning and in Leo, Scorpio (16 to 30 degrees), Sagittarius, or Pisces. Venus should be in good aspect to the Moon, and the Moon should not be square, opposing, or conjunct either Saturn or Mars.

Brewing

Start brewing during the third or fourth quarter, when the Moon is in Cancer, Scorpio, or Pisces.

Build (Start foundation)

Turning the first sod for the foundation marks the beginning of the building. For best results, excavate the site when the Moon is in the first quarter of a fixed sign and making favorable aspects to Saturn.

Business (Start new)

When starting a business, have the Moon be in Taurus, Virgo, or Capricorn and increasing. The Moon should be sextile or trine Jupiter or Saturn, but avoid oppositions or squares. The planet ruling the business should be well aspected, too.

Buy Goods

Buy during the third quarter, when the Moon is in Taurus for quality or in a mutable sign (Gemini, Sagittarius, Virgo, or Pisces) for savings. Good aspects to Venus or the Sun are desirable. If you are buying for yourself, it is good if the day is favorable for your Sun sign. You may also apply rules for buying specific items.

Canning

Can fruits and vegetables when the Moon is in either the third or fourth quarter and in the water sign Cancer or Pisces. Preserves and jellies use the same quarters and the signs Cancer, Pisces, or Taurus.

Clothing

Buy clothing on a day that is favorable for your Sun sign and when Venus or Mercury is well aspected. Avoid aspects to Mars and Saturn. Buy your clothing when the Moon is in Taurus if you want to remain satisfied. Do not buy clothing or jewelry when the Moon is in Scorpio or Aries. See that the Moon is sextile or trine the Sun during the first or second quarters.

Collections

Try to make collections on days when your Sun is well aspected. Avoid days when the Moon is opposing or square Mars or Saturn. If possible, the Moon should be in a cardinal sign (Aries, Cancer, Libra, or Capricorn). It is more difficult to collect when the Moon is in Taurus or Scorpio.

Concrete

Pour concrete when the Moon is in the third quarter of the fixed sign Taurus, Leo, or Aquarius.

Construction (Begin new)

The Moon should be sextile or trine Jupiter. According to Hermes, no building should be begun when the Moon is in Scorpio or Pisces. The best time to begin building is when the Moon is in Aquarius.

Consultants (Work with)

The Moon should be conjunct, sextile, or trine Mercury or Jupiter.

2009 © Arpad Nagy-Bagoly. Image from BigStockPhoto.com

Contracts (Bid on)

The Moon should be in Gemini or Capricorn and either the Moon or Mercury should be conjunct, sextile, or trine Jupiter.

Copyrights/Patents

The Moon should be conjunct, trine, or sextile either Mercury or Jupiter.

Coronations and Installations

Let the Moon be in Leo and in favorable aspect to Venus, Jupiter, or Mercury. The Moon should be applying to these planets.

Cultivate

Cultivate when the Moon is in a barren sign and waning, ideally the fourth quarter in Aries, Gemini, Leo, Virgo, or Aquarius. The third quarter in the sign of Sagittarius will also work.

Cut Timber

Timber cut during the waning Moon does not become worm-eaten; it will season well and not warp, decay, or snap during burning. Cut when the Moon is in Taurus, Gemini, Virgo, or Capricorn—especially in August. Avoid the water signs. Look for favorable aspects to Mars.

Decorating or Home Repairs

Have the Moon waxing and in the sign of Libra, Gemini, or Aquarius. Avoid squares or oppositions to either Mars or Saturn. Venus in good aspect to Mars or Saturn is beneficial.

Demolition

Let the waning Moon be in Leo, Sagittarius, or Aries.

Dental and Dentists

Visit the dentist when the Moon is in Virgo, or pick a day marked favorable for your Sun sign. Mars should be marked sextile, conjunct, or trine; avoid squares or oppositions to Saturn, Uranus, or Jupiter.

Teeth are best removed when the Moon is in Gemini, Virgo, Sagittarius, or Pisces and during the first or second quarter. Avoid the Full Moon! The day should be favorable for your lunar cycle, and Mars and Saturn should be marked conjunct, trine, or sextile. Fillings should be done in the third or fourth quarters in the sign of Taurus, Leo, Scorpio, or Pisces. The same applies for dentures.

Dressmaking

William Lilly wrote in 1676: "Make no new clothes, or first put them on when the Moon is in Scorpio or afflicted by Mars, for they will be apt to be torn and quickly worn out." Design, repair, and sew clothes in the first and second quarters of Taurus, Leo, or Libra on a day marked favorable for your Sun sign. Venus, Jupiter, and Mercury should be favorably aspected, but avoid hard aspects to Mars or Saturn.

Egg-setting (see p. 161)

Eggs should be set so chicks will hatch during fruitful signs. To set eggs, subtract the number of days given for incubation or gestation from the fruitful dates. Chickens incubate in twenty-one days, turkeys and geese in twenty-eight days.

A freshly laid egg loses quality rapidly if it is not handled properly. Use plenty of clean litter in the nests to reduce the number of dirty or cracked eggs. Gather eggs daily in mild weather and at least two times daily in hot or cold weather. The eggs should be placed in a cooler immediately after gathering and stored at 50 to 55 degrees Fahrenheit. Do not store eggs with foods or products that give off pungent odors since eggs may absorb the odors.

Eggs saved for hatching purposes should not be washed. Only clean and slightly soiled eggs should be saved for hatching. Dirty eggs should not be incubated. Eggs should be stored in a cool place with the large ends up. It is not advisable to store the eggs longer than one week before setting them in an incubator.

Electricity and Gas (Install)
The Moon should be in a fire sign, and there should be no squares, oppositions, or conjunctions with Uranus (ruler of electricity), Neptune (ruler of gas), Saturn, or Mars. Hard aspects to Mars can cause fires.

Electronics (Buying)
Choose a day when the Moon is in an air sign (Gemini, Libra, Aquarius) and well aspected by Mercury and/or Uranus when buying electronics.

Electronics (Repair)
The Moon should be sextile or trine Mars or Uranus and in a fixed sign (Taurus, Leo, Scorpio, Aquarius).

Entertain Friends
Let the Moon be in Leo or Libra and making good aspects to Venus. Avoid squares or oppositions to either Mars or Saturn by the Moon or Venus.

Eyes and Eyeglasses

Have your eyes tested and glasses fitted on a day marked favorable for your Sun sign, and on a day that falls during your favorable lunar cycle. Mars should not be in aspect with the Moon. The same applies for any treatment of the eyes, which should also be started during the Moon's first or second quarter.

Fence Posts

Set posts when the Moon is in the third or fourth quarter of the fixed sign Taurus or Leo.

Fertilize and Compost

Fertilize when the Moon is in a fruitful sign (Cancer, Scorpio, Pisces). Organic fertilizers are best when the Moon is waning. Use chemical fertilizers when the Moon is waxing. Start compost when the Moon is in the fourth quarter in a water sign.

Find Hidden Treasure

Let the Moon be in good aspect to Jupiter or Venus. If you erect a horoscope for this election, place the Moon in the Fourth House.

Find Lost Articles

Search for lost articles during the first quarter and when your Sun sign is marked favorable. Also check to see that the planet ruling the lost item is trine, sextile, or conjunct the Moon. The Moon rules household utensils; Mercury rules letters and books; and Venus rules clothing, jewelry, and money.

Fishing

During the summer months, the best time of the day to fish is from sunrise to three hours after and from two hours before sunset until one hour after. Fish do not bite in cooler months until the air is warm, from noon to 3 pm. Warm, cloudy days are good. The most favorable winds are from the south and southwest. Easterly winds are unfavorable. The best days of the month for fishing are when the Moon changes quarters, especially if the change occurs on a day when the Moon is in a water sign (Cancer, Scorpio, Pisces). The best period in any month is the day after the Full Moon.

Friendship

The need for friendship is greater when the Moon is in Aquarius or when Uranus aspects the Moon. Friendship prospers when Venus or Uranus is trine, sextile, or conjunct the Moon. The Moon in Gemini facilitates the chance meeting of acquaintances and friends.

Grafting or Budding

Grafting is the process of introducing new varieties of fruit on less desirable trees. For this process you should use the increasing phase of the Moon in fruitful signs such as Cancer, Scorpio, or Pisces. Capricorn may be used, too. Cut your grafts while trees are dormant, from December to March. Keep them in a cool, dark place, not too dry or too damp. Do the grafting before the sap starts to flow and while the Moon is waxing, preferably while it is in Cancer, Scorpio, or Pisces. The type of plant should determine both cutting and planting times.

Habit (Breaking)

To end an undesirable habit, and this applies to ending everything from a bad relationship to smoking, start on a day when the Moon is in the fourth quarter and in the barren sign of Gemini, Leo, or Aquarius. Aries, Virgo, and Capricorn may be suitable as well, depending on the habit you want to be rid of. Make sure that your lunar cycle is favorable. Avoid lunar aspects to Mars or Jupiter. However, favorable aspects to Pluto are helpful.

Haircuts

Cut hair when the Moon is in Gemini, Sagittarius, Pisces, Taurus, or Capricorn, but not in Virgo. Look for favorable aspects to

Venus. For faster growth, cut hair when the Moon is increasing in Cancer or Pisces. To make hair grow thicker, cut when the Moon is full in the signs of Taurus, Cancer, or Leo. If you want your hair to grow more slowly, have the Moon be decreasing in Aries, Gemini, or Virgo, and have the Moon square or opposing Saturn.

Permanents, straightening, and hair coloring will take well if the Moon is in Taurus or Leo and trine or sextile Venus. Avoid hair treatments if Mars is marked as square or in opposition, especially if heat is to be used. For permanents, a trine to Jupiter is helpful. The Moon also should be in the first quarter. Check the lunar cycle for a favorable day in relation to your Sun sign.

Harvest Crops

Harvest root crops when the Moon is in a dry sign (Aries, Leo, Sagittarius, Gemini, Aquarius) and waning. Harvest grain for storage just after the Full Moon, avoiding Cancer,

2009 © Mykhailo Kovtoniuk. Image from BigStockPhoto.com

Scorpio, or Pisces. Harvest in the third and fourth quarters in dry signs. Dry crops in the third quarter in fire signs.

Health

A diagnosis is more likely to be successful when the Moon is in Aries, Cancer, Libra, or Capricorn and less so when in Gemini, Sagittarius, Pisces, or Virgo. Begin a recuperation program when the Moon is in a cardinal or fixed sign and the day is favorable to your Sun sign. Enter hospitals at these times, too. For surgery, see "Surgical Procedures." Buy medicines when the Moon is in Virgo or Scorpio.

Home (Buy new)

If you desire a permanent home, buy when the New Moon is in a fixed sign—Taurus or Leo—for example. Each sign will affect your decision in a different way. A house bought when the Moon is in Taurus is likely to be more practical and have a country look—right down to the split-rail fence. A house purchased when the Moon is in Leo will more likely be a real showplace.

If you're buying for speculation and a quick turnover, be certain that the Moon is in a cardinal sign (Aries, Cancer, Libra, Capricorn). Avoid buying when the Moon is in a fixed sign (Leo, Scorpio, Aquarius, Taurus).

Home (Make repairs)

In all repairs, avoid squares, oppositions, or conjunctions to the planet ruling the place or thing to be repaired. For example, bathrooms are ruled by Scorpio and Cancer. You would not want to start a project in those rooms when the Moon or Pluto is receiving hard aspects. The front entrance, hall, dining room, and porch are ruled by the Sun. So you would want to avoid times when Saturn or Mars are square, opposing, or conjunct the Sun. Also, let the Moon be waxing.

Home (Sell)

Make a strong effort to list your property for sale when the Sun is marked favorable in your sign and in good aspect to Jupiter. Avoid adverse aspects to as many planets as possible.

Home Furnishings (Buy new)

Saturn days (Saturday) are good for buying, and Jupiter days (Thursday) are good for selling. Items bought on days when Saturn is well aspected tend to wear longer and purchases tend to be more conservative.

Job (Start new)
Jupiter and Venus should be sextile, trine, or conjunct the Moon. A day when your Sun is receiving favorable aspects is preferred.

Legal Matters
Good Moon-Jupiter aspects improve the outcome in legal decisions. To gain damages through a lawsuit, begin the process during the increasing Moon. To avoid paying damages, a court date during the decreasing Moon is desirable. Good Moon-Sun aspects strengthen your chance of success. A well-aspected Moon in Cancer or Leo, making good aspects to the Sun, brings the best results in custody cases. In divorce cases, a favorable Moon-Venus aspect is best.

Loan (Ask for)
A first and second quarter phase favors the lender, the third and fourth quarters favor the borrower. Good aspects of Jupiter and Venus to the Moon are favorable to both, as is having the Moon in Leo or Taurus.

Machinery, Appliances, or Tools (Buy)
Tools, machinery, and other implements should be bought on days when your lunar cycle is favorable and when Mars and Uranus are trine, sextile, or conjunct the Moon. Any quarter of the Moon is suitable. When buying gas or electrical appliances, the Moon should be in Aquarius.

Make a Will
Let the Moon be in a fixed sign (Taurus, Leo, Scorpio, or Aquarius) to ensure permanence. If the Moon is in a cardinal sign (Aries, Cancer, Libra, or Capricorn), the will could be altered. Let the Moon be waxing—increasing in light—and in good aspect to Saturn, Venus, or Mercury. In case the will is made in an emergency during illness and the Moon is slow in motion, void-of-course,

combust, or under the Sun's beams, the testator will die and the will remain unaltered. There is some danger that it will be lost or stolen, however.

Marriage

The best time for marriage to take place is when the Moon is increasing, but not yet full. Good signs for the Moon to be in are Taurus, Cancer, Leo, or Libra.

The Moon in Taurus produces the most steadfast marriages, but if the partners later want to separate, they may have a difficult time. Make sure that the Moon is well aspected, especially to Venus or Jupiter. Avoid aspects to Mars, Uranus, or Pluto and the signs Aries, Gemini, Virgo, Scorpio, or Aquarius.

The values of the signs are as follows:

- Aries is not favored for marriage
- Taurus from 0 to 19 degrees is good, the remaining degrees are less favorable
- Cancer is unfavorable unless you are marrying a widow
- Leo is favored, but it may cause one party to deceive the other as to his or her money or possessions
- Virgo is not favored except when marrying a widow
- Libra is good for engagements but not for marriage
- Scorpio from 0 to 15 degrees is good, but the last 15 degrees are entirely unfortunate. The woman may be fickle, envious, and quarrelsome
- Sagittarius is neutral
- Capricorn, from 0 to 10 degrees, is difficult for marriage; however, the remaining degrees are favorable, especially when marrying a widow
- Aquarius is not favored
- Pisces is favored, although marriage under this sign can incline a woman to chatter a lot

These effects are strongest when the Moon is in the sign. If the Moon and Venus are in a cardinal sign, happiness between the couple may not continue long.

On no account should the Moon apply to Saturn or Mars, even by good aspect.

Medical Treatment for the Eyes

Let the Moon be increasing in light and motion and making favorable aspects to Venus or Jupiter and be unaspected by Mars. Keep the Moon out of Taurus, Capricorn, or Virgo. If an aspect between the Moon and Mars is unavoidable, let it be separating.

Medical Treatment for the Head

If possible, have Mars and Saturn free of hard aspects. Let the Moon be in Aries or Taurus, decreasing in light, in conjunction or aspect with Venus or Jupiter and free of hard aspects. The Sun should not be in any aspect to the Moon.

Medical Treatment for the Nose

Let the Moon be in Cancer, Leo, or Virgo and not aspecting Mars or Saturn and also not in conjunction with a retrograde or weak planet.

2009 © Maria Yfanti. Image from BigStockPhoto.com

Mining

Saturn rules mining.

Begin work when Saturn is marked conjunct, trine, or sextile. Mine for gold when the Sun is marked conjunct, trine, or sextile. Mercury rules quicksilver, Venus rules copper, Jupiter rules tin, Saturn rules lead and coal, Uranus rules radioactive elements, Neptune rules oil, the Moon rules water. Mine for these items when the ruling planet is marked conjunct, trine, or sextile.

Move to New Home

If you have a choice, and sometimes you don't, make sure that Mars is not aspecting the Moon. Move on a day favorable to your Sun sign or when the Moon is conjunct, sextile, or trine the Sun.

Mow Lawn

Mow in the first and second quarters (waxing phase) to increase growth and lushness, and in the third and fourth quarters (waning phase) to decrease growth.

Negotiate

When you are choosing a time to negotiate, consider what the meeting is about and what you want to have happen. If it is agreement or compromise between two parties that you desire, have the Moon be in the sign of Libra. When you are making contracts, it is best to have the Moon in the same element. For example, if your concern is communication, then elect a time when the Moon is in an air sign. If, on the other hand, your concern is about possessions, an earth sign would be more appropriate. Fixed signs are unfavorable, with the exception of Leo; so are cardinal signs, except for Capricorn. If you are negotiating the end of something, use the rules that apply to ending habits.

Occupational Training

When you begin training, see that your lunar cycle is favorable that day and that the planet ruling your occupation is marked conjunct or trine.

Paint

Paint buildings during the waning Libra or Aquarius Moon. If the weather is hot, paint when the Moon is in Taurus. If the weather is cold, paint when the Moon is in Leo. Schedule the painting to start in the fourth quarter as the wood is drier and paint will penetrate wood better. Avoid painting around the New

Moon, though, as the wood is likely to be damp, making the paint subject to scalding when hot weather hits it. If the temperature is below 70 degrees Fahrenheit, it is not advisable to paint while the Moon is in Cancer, Scorpio, or Pisces as the paint is apt to creep, check, or run.

Party (Host or attend)

A party timed so the Moon is in Gemini, Leo, Libra, or Sagittarius, with good aspects to Venus and Jupiter, will be fun and well attended. There should be no aspects between the Moon and Mars or Saturn.

Pawn

Do not pawn any article when Jupiter is receiving a square or opposition from Saturn or Mars or when Jupiter is within 17 degrees of the Sun, for you will have little chance to redeem the items.

Pick Mushrooms

Mushrooms, one of the most promising traditional medicines in the world, should be gathered at the Full Moon.

Plant

Root crops, like carrots and potatoes, are best if planted in the sign Taurus or Capricorn. Beans, peas, tomatoes, peppers, and other fruit-bearing plants are best if planted in a sign that supports seed growth. Leaf plants, like lettuce, broccoli, or cauliflower, are best planted when the Moon is in a water sign.

It is recommended that you transplant during a decreasing Moon, when forces are streaming into the lower part of the plant. This helps root growth.

Promotion (Ask for)

Choose a day favorable to your Sun sign. Mercury should be marked conjunct, trine, or sextile. Avoid days when Mars or Saturn is aspected.

Prune

Prune during the third and fourth quarter of a Scorpio Moon to retard growth and to promote better fruit. Prune when the Moon is in cardinal Capricorn to promote healing.

Reconcile with People

If the reconciliation be with a woman, let Venus be strong and well aspected. If elders or superiors are involved, see that Saturn is receiving good aspects; if the reconciliation is between young people or between an older and younger person, see that Mercury is well aspected.

Romance

There is less control of when a romance starts, but romances begun under an increasing Moon are more likely to be permanent or satisfying, while those begun during the decreasing Moon tend to transform the participants. The tone of the relationship can be guessed from the sign the Moon is in. Romances begun with the Moon in Aries may be impulsive. Those begun in Capricorn will take greater effort to bring to a desirable conclusion, but they may be very rewarding. Good aspects between the Moon and Venus will have a positive influence on the relationship. Avoid unfavorable aspects to Mars, Uranus, and Pluto. A decreasing Moon, particularly the fourth quarter, facilitates ending a relationship and causes the least pain.

Roof a Building

Begin roofing a building during the third or fourth quarter, when the Moon is in Aries or Aquarius. Shingles laid during the New Moon have a tendency to curl at the edges.

Sauerkraut

The best-tasting sauerkraut is made just after the Full Moon in the fruitful signs of Cancer, Scorpio, or Pisces.

2010 © Alisa Kufarova. Image from BigStockPhoto.com

Select a Child's Sex

Count from the last day of menstruation to the first day of the next cycle and divide the interval between the two dates in half. Pregnancy in the first half produces females, but copulation should take place with the Moon in a feminine sign. Pregnancy in the latter half, up to three days before the beginning of menstruation, produces males, but copulation should take place with the Moon in a masculine sign. The three-day period before the next period again produces females.

Sell or Canvass

Begin these activities during a day favorable to your Sun sign. Otherwise, sell on days when Jupiter, Mercury, or Mars is trine, sextile, or conjunct the Moon. Avoid days when Saturn is square or opposing the Moon, for that always hinders business and causes discord. If the Moon is passing from the first quarter to full, it is best to have the Moon swift in motion and in good aspect with Venus and/or Jupiter.

Sign Papers

Sign contracts or agreements when the Moon is increasing in a fruitful sign and on a day when the Moon is making favorable aspects to Mercury. Avoid days when Mars, Saturn, or Neptune are square or opposite the Moon.

Spray and Weed

Spray pests and weeds during the fourth quarter when the Moon is in the barren sign Leo or Aquarius and making favorable aspects to Pluto. Weed during a waning Moon in a barren sign.

Staff (Fire)

Have the Moon in the third or fourth quarter, but not full. The Moon should not be square any planets.

Staff (Hire)

The Moon should be in the first or second quarter, and preferably in the sign of Gemini or Virgo. The Moon should be conjunct, trine, or sextile Mercury or Jupiter.

Stocks (Buy)

The Moon should be in Taurus or Capricorn, and there should be a sextile or trine to Jupiter or Saturn.

Surgical Procedures

Blood flow, like ocean tides, appears to be related to Moon phases. To reduce hemorrhage after a surgery, schedule it within one week before or after a New Moon. Schedule surgery to occur during the increase of the Moon if possible, as wounds heal better and vitality is greater than during the decrease of the Moon. Avoid surgery within one week before or after the Full Moon. Select a date when the Moon is past the sign governing the part of the body involved in the operation. For example, abdominal operations should be done when the Moon is in Sagittarius,

Capricorn, or Aquarius. The further removed the Moon sign is from the sign ruling the afflicted part of the body, the better.

For successful operations, avoid times when the Moon is applying to any aspect of Mars. (This tends to promote inflammation and complications.) See the Lunar Aspectarian on odd pages 137–159 to find days with negative Mars aspects and positive Venus and Jupiter aspects. Never operate with the Moon in the same sign as a person's Sun sign or Ascendant. Let the Moon be in a fixed sign and avoid square or opposing aspects. The Moon should not be void-of-course. Cosmetic surgery should be done in the increase of the Moon, when the Moon is not square or in opposition to Mars. Avoid days when the Moon is square or opposing Saturn or the Sun.

Travel (Air)

Start long trips when the Moon is making favorable aspects to the Sun. For enjoyment, aspects to Jupiter are preferable; for visiting, look for favorable aspects to Mercury. To prevent accidents, avoid squares or oppositions to Mars, Saturn, Uranus, or Pluto. Choose a day when the Moon is in Sagittarius or Gemini and well aspected to Mercury, Jupiter, or Uranus. Avoid adverse aspects of Mars, Saturn, or Uranus.

Visit

On setting out to visit a person, let the Moon be in aspect with any retrograde planet, for this ensures that the person you're visiting will be at home. If you desire to stay a long time in a place, let the Moon be in good aspect to Saturn. If you desire to leave the place quickly, let the Moon be in a cardinal sign.

Wean Children

To wean a child successfully, do so when the Moon is in Sagittarius, Capricorn, Aquarius, or Pisces—signs that do not rule vital human organs. By observing this astrological rule, much trouble for parents and child may be avoided.

Weight (Reduce)

If you want to lose weight, the best time to get started is when the Moon is in the third or fourth quarter and in the barren sign of Virgo. Review the section on How to Use the Moon Tables and Lunar Aspectarian beginning on page 136 to help you select a date that is favorable to begin your weight-loss program.

Wine and Drink Other Than Beer

Start brewing when the Moon is in Pisces or Taurus. Sextiles or trines to Venus are favorable, but avoid aspects to Mars or Saturn.

Write

Write for pleasure or publication when the Moon is in Gemini. Mercury should be making favorable aspects to Uranus and Neptune.

2010 © Jordan Edgcomb. Image from BigStockPhoto.com

How to Use the Moon Tables and Lunar Aspectarian

Timing activities is one of the most important things you can do to ensure success. In many Eastern countries, timing by the planets is so important that practically no event takes place without first setting up a chart for it. Weddings have occurred in the middle of the night because the influences were best then. You may not want to take it that far, but you can still make use of the influences of the Moon whenever possible. It's easy and it works!

Llewellyn's Moon Sign Book has information to help you plan just about any activity: weddings, fishing, making purchases, cutting your hair, traveling, and more. We provide the guidelines you need to pick the best day out of the several from which you have to choose. The Moon Tables are the *Moon Sign Book's* primary method for choosing dates. Following are instructions, examples, and directions on how to read the Moon

Tables. More advanced information on using the tables containing the Lunar Aspectarian and favorable and unfavorable days (found on odd-numbered pages opposite the Moon Tables), Moon void-of-course and retrograde information to choose the dates best for you is also included.

The Five Basic Steps

Step 1: Directions for Choosing Dates

Look up the directions for choosing dates for the activity that you wish to begin, then go to step 2.

Step 2: Check the Moon Tables

You'll find two tables for each month of the year beginning on page 136. The Moon Tables (on the left-hand pages) include the day, date, and sign the Moon is in; the element and nature of the sign; the Moon's phase; and when it changes sign or phase. If there is a time listed after a date, that time is the time when the Moon moves into that zodiac sign. Until then, the Moon is considered to be in the sign for the previous day.

The abbreviation Full signifies Full Moon and New signifies New Moon. The times listed with dates indicate when the Moon changes sign. The times listed after the phase indicate when the Moon changes phase.

Turn to the month you would like to begin your activity. You will be using the Moon's sign and phase information most often when you begin choosing your own dates. Use the Time Zone Map on page 164 and the Time Zone Conversions table on page 165 to convert time to your own time zone.

When you find dates that meet the criteria for the correct Moon phase and sign for your activity, you may have completed the process. For certain simple activities, such as getting a haircut, the phase and sign information is all that is needed. If the directions for your activity include information on certain lunar aspects, however, you should consult the Lunar Aspectarian. An example of this would be if the directions told you not to perform a certain activity when the Moon is square (Q) Jupiter.

Step 3: Check the Lunar Aspectarian

On the pages opposite the Moon Tables you will find tables containing the Lunar Aspectarian and Favorable and Unfavorable Days. The Lunar Aspectarian gives the aspects (or angles) of the Moon to other planets. Some aspects are favorable, while others are not. To use the Lunar Aspectarian, find the planet that the directions list as favorable for your activity, and run down the column to the date desired. For example, you should avoid aspects to Mars if you are planning surgery. So you would look for Mars across the top and then run down that column looking for days where there are no aspects to Mars (as signified by empty boxes). If you want to find a favorable aspect (sextile (X) or trine (T)) to Mercury, run your finger down the column under Mercury until you find an X or T. Adverse aspects to planets are squares (Q) or oppositions (O). A conjunction (C) is sometimes beneficial, sometimes not, depending on the activity or planets involved.

Step 4: Favorable and Unfavorable Days

The tables listing favorable and unfavorable days are helpful when you want to choose your personal best dates because your Sun sign is taken into consideration. The twelve Sun signs are listed on the right side of the tables. Once you have determined which days meet your criteria for phase, sign, and aspects, you can determine whether or not those days are positive for you by checking the favorable and unfavorable days for your Sun sign.

To find out if a day is positive for you, find your Sun sign and then look down the column. If it is marked F, it is very favorable. The Moon is in the same sign as your Sun on a favorable day. If it is marked f, it is slightly favorable; U is very unfavorable; and u means slightly unfavorable. A day marked very unfavorable (U) indicates that the Moon is in the sign opposing your Sun.

Once you have selected good dates for the activity you are about to begin, you can go straight to "Using What You've Learned," beginning on the next page. To learn how to fine-tune your selections even further, read on.

Step 5: Void-of-Course Moon and Retrogrades

This last step is perhaps the most advanced portion of the procedure. It is generally considered poor timing to make decisions, sign important papers, or start special activities during a Moon void-of-course period or during a Mercury retrograde. Once you have chosen the best date for your activity based on steps one through four, you can check the Void-of-Course tables, beginning on page 76, to find out if any of the dates you have chosen have void periods.

The Moon is said to be void-of-course after it has made its last aspect to a planet within a particular sign, but before it has moved into the next sign. Put simply, the Moon is "resting" during the void-of-course period, so activities initiated at this time generally don't come to fruition. You will notice that there are many void periods during the year, and it is nearly impossible to avoid all of them. Some people choose to ignore these altogether and do not take them into consideration when planning activities.

Next, you can check the Retrograde Planets tables on page 160 to see what planets are retrograde during your chosen date(s).

A planet is said to be retrograde when it appears to move backward in the sky as viewed from the Earth. Generally, the farther a planet is away from the Sun, the longer it can stay retrograde. Some planets will retrograde for several months at a time. Avoiding retrogrades is not as important in lunar planning as avoiding the Moon void-of-course, with the exception of the planet Mercury.

Mercury rules thought and communication, so it is advisable not to sign important papers, initiate important business or legal work, or make crucial decisions during these times. As with the Moon void-of-course, it is difficult to avoid all planetary retrogrades when beginning events, and you may choose to ignore this step of the process. Following are some examples using some or all of the steps outlined above.

Using What You've Learned

Let's say it's a new year and you want to have your hair cut. It's thin and you would like it to look fuller, so you find the directions for hair care and you see that for thicker hair you should cut hair while the Moon is Full and in the sign of Taurus, Cancer, or Leo. You should avoid the Moon in Aries, Gemini, or Virgo. Look at the January Moon Table on page 136. You see that the Full Moon is on January 19 at 4:21 pm. The Moon moved into the sign of Leo at 5:16 pm that day and remains in Leo until January 21 at 6:10 pm, so January 19–21 meets both the phase and sign criteria.

Let's move on to a more difficult example using the sign and phase of the Moon. You want to buy a permanent home. After checking the instructions for purchasing a house: "Home (Buy new)" on page 118, you see that you should buy a home when the Moon is in Taurus, Cancer, or Leo. You need to get a loan, so you should also look under "Loan (Ask for)" on page 119. Here it says that the third and fourth quarters favor the borrower (you). You are going to buy the house in October so go to page 154. The Moon is in the third quarter October 11–19. The Moon is in Cancer from 9:38 pm on October 17 until October 20 at 6:06 am. The best days for obtaining a loan would be October 17–19, while the Moon is in Cancer.

Just match up the best sign and phase (quarter) to come up with the best date. With all activities, be sure to check the favorable and unfavorable days for your Sun sign in the table adjoining the Lunar Aspectarian. If there is a choice between several dates, pick the one most favorable for you. Because buying a home is an important business decision, you may also wish to see if the Moon is void or if Mercury is retrograde during these dates.

Now let's look at an example that uses signs, phases, and aspects. Our example is starting new home construction. We will use the month of April. Look under "Build (Start foundation)" on page 110 and you'll see that the Moon should be in the first quarter of Taurus or Leo. You should select a time when the Moon is not making unfavorable aspects to Saturn. (Conjunctions are usually considered good if they are not to Mars, Saturn, or Neptune.) Look in the April Moon Table. You will see that the Moon is in the first quarter April 3–11. The Moon is in Taurus from 7:46 pm on April 4 until April 7 at 7:22 am. Now, look to the April Lunar Aspectarian. We see that there are no squares or oppositions to Saturn April 4–7. These are good dates to start a foundation.

A Note About Time and Time Zones

All tables in the *Moon Sign Book* use Eastern Time. You must calculate the difference between your time zone and the Eastern Time Zone. Please refer to the Time Zone Conversions chart on 165 for help with time conversions. The sign the Moon is in at midnight is the sign shown in the Aspectarian and Favorable and Unfavorable Days tables.

How Does the Time Matter?

Due to the three-hour time difference between the East and West Coasts of the United States, those of you living on the East Coast may be, for example, under the influence of a Virgo Moon, while those of you living on the West Coast will still have a Leo Moon influence.

We follow a commonly held belief among astrologers: whatever sign the Moon is in at the start of a day—12:00 am Eastern

Time—is considered the dominant influence of the day. That sign is indicated in the Moon Tables. If the date you select for an activity shows the Moon changing signs, you can decide how important the sign change may be for your specific election and adjust your election date and time accordingly.

Use Common Sense

Some activities depend on outside factors. Obviously, you can't go out and plant when there is a foot of snow on the ground. You should adjust to the conditions at hand. If the weather was bad during the first quarter, when it was best to plant crops, do it during the second quarter while the Moon is in a fruitful sign. If the Moon is not in a fruitful sign during the first or second quarter, choose a day when it is in a semi-fruitful sign. The best advice is to choose either the sign or phase that is most favorable, when the two don't coincide.

To Summarize

First, look up the activity under the proper heading, then look for the information given in the tables. Choose the best date considering the number of positive factors in effect. If most of the dates are favorable, there is no problem choosing the one that will fit your schedule. However, if there aren't any really good dates, pick the ones with the least number of negative influences. Please keep in mind that the information found here applies in the broadest sense to the events you want to plan or are considering. To be the most effective, when you use electional astrology, you should also consider your own birth chart in relation to a chart drawn for the time or times you have under consideration. The best advice we can offer you is: read the entire introduction to each section.

January Moon Table

Date	Sign	Element	Nature	Phase
1 Sat	Sagittarius	Fire	Barren	4th
2 Sun	Sagittarius	Fire	Barren	4th
3 Mon 2:39 am	Capricorn	Earth	Semi-fruitful	4th
4 Tue	Capricorn	Earth	Semi-fruitful	New 4:03 am
5 Wed 11:08 am	Aquarius	Air	Barren	1st
6 Thu	Aquarius	Air	Barren	1st
7 Fri 9:57 pm	Pisces	Water	Fruitful	1st
8 Sat	Pisces	Water	Fruitful	1st
9 Sun	Pisces	Water	Fruitful	1st
10 Mon 10:24 am	Aries	Fire	Barren	1st
11 Tue	Aries	Fire	Barren	1st
12 Wed 10:37 pm	Taurus	Earth	Semi-fruitful	2nd 6:31 am
13 Thu	Taurus	Earth	Semi-fruitful	2nd
14 Fri	Taurus	Earth	Semi-fruitful	2nd
15 Sat 8:23 am	Gemini	Air	Barren	2nd
16 Sun	Gemini	Air	Barren	2nd
17 Mon 2:29 pm	Cancer	Water	Fruitful	2nd
18 Tue	Cancer	Water	Fruitful	2nd
19 Wed 5:16 pm	Leo	Fire	Barren	Full 4:21 pm
20 Thu	Leo	Fire	Barren	3rd
21 Fri 6:10 pm	Virgo	Earth	Barren	3rd
22 Sat	Virgo	Earth	Barren	3rd
23 Sun 6:59 pm	Libra	Air	Semi-fruitful	3rd
24 Mon	Libra	Air	Semi-fruitful	3rd
25 Tue 9:15 pm	Scorpio	Water	Fruitful	3rd
26 Wed	Scorpio	Water	Fruitful	4th 7:57 am
27 Thu	Scorpio	Water	Fruitful	4th
28 Fri 1:55 am	Sagittarius	Fire	Barren	4th
29 Sat	Sagittarius	Fire	Barren	4th
30 Sun 9:04 am	Capricorn	Earth	Semi-fruitful	4th
31 Mon	Capricorn	Earth	Semi-fruitful	4th

January Aspectarian/Favorable & Unfavorable Days

Date	Sun	Mercury	Venus	Mars	Jupiter	Saturn	Uranus	Neptune	Pluto	Aries	Taurus	Gemini	Cancer	Leo	Virgo	Libra	Scorpio	Sagittarius	Capricorn	Aquarius	Pisces
1										f		U		f	u	f		F		f	u
2		C			Q	X	Q	X		f		U		f	u	f		F		f	u
3									C	u	f		U		f	u	f		F		f
4	C			C		Q				u	f		U		f	u	f		F		f
5			X		X			X		f	u	f	U		f	u	f		F		
6						T				f	u	f	U		f	u	f		F		
7		X	Q					C		f	u	f	U		f	u	f		F		
8									X		f	u	f		U		f	u	f		F
9	X										f	u	f		U		f	u	f		F
10		Q	T	X	C		C		Q	F		f	u	f		U		f	u	f	
11						O				F		f	u	f		U		f	u	f	
12	Q	T		Q				X		F		f	u	f		U		f	u	f	
13									T		F		f	u	f		U		f	u	f
14	T										F		f	u	f		U		f	u	f
15				T	X		X	Q		f		F		f	u	f		U		f	u
16			O			T				f		F		f	u	f		U		f	u
17					Q		Q	T		f		F		f	u	f		U		f	u
18		O			Q				O	u	f		F		f	u	f		U		f
19	O			O	T		T			u	f		F		f	u	f		U		f
20			T			X				f	u	f		F		f	u	f		U	
21									O	f	u	f		F		f	u	f		U	
22		T	Q						T		f	u	f		F		f	u	f		U
23					O		O				f	u	f		F		f	u	f		U
24	T	Q		T	C				Q	U		f	u	f		F		f	u	f	
25			X					T		U		f	u	f		F		f	u	f	
26	Q			Q					X		U		f	u	f		F		f	u	f
27		X					T	Q			U		f	u	f		F		f	u	f
28	X			X	T					f		U		f	u	f		F		f	u
29			C			X				f		U		f	u	f		F		f	u
30				Q		Q	X	C		u	f		U		f	u	f		F		f
31						Q				u	f		U		f	u	f		F		f

137

February Moon Table

Date	Sign	Element	Nature	Phase
1 Tue 6:21 pm	Aquarius	Air	Barren	4th
2 Wed	Aquarius	Air	Barren	New 9:31 pm
3 Thu	Aquarius	Air	Barren	1st
4 Fri 5:24 am	Pisces	Water	Fruitful	1st
5 Sat	Pisces	Water	Fruitful	1st
6 Sun 5:45 pm	Aries	Fire	Barren	1st
7 Mon	Aries	Fire	Barren	1st
8 Tue	Aries	Fire	Barren	1st
9 Wed 6:22 am	Taurus	Earth	Semi-fruitful	1st
10 Thu	Taurus	Earth	Semi-fruitful	1st
11 Fri 5:20 pm	Gemini	Air	Barren	2nd 2:18 am
12 Sat	Gemini	Air	Barren	2nd
13 Sun	Gemini	Air	Barren	2nd
14 Mon 12:48 am	Cancer	Water	Fruitful	2nd
15 Tue	Cancer	Water	Fruitful	2nd
16 Wed 4:14 am	Leo	Fire	Barren	2nd
17 Thu	Leo	Fire	Barren	2nd
18 Fri 4:39 am	Virgo	Earth	Barren	Full 3:36 am
19 Sat	Virgo	Earth	Barren	3rd
20 Sun 4:01 am	Libra	Air	Semi-fruitful	3rd
21 Mon	Libra	Air	Semi-fruitful	3rd
22 Tue 4:29 am	Scorpio	Water	Fruitful	3rd
23 Wed	Scorpio	Water	Fruitful	3rd
24 Thu 7:46 am	Sagittarius	Fire	Barren	4th 6:26 pm
25 Fri	Sagittarius	Fire	Barren	4th
26 Sat 2:32 pm	Capricorn	Earth	Semi-fruitful	4th
27 Sun	Capricorn	Earth	Semi-fruitful	4th
28 Mon	Capricorn	Earth	Semi-fruitful	4th

February Aspectarian/Favorable & Unfavorable Days

Date	Sun	Mercury	Venus	Mars	Jupiter	Saturn	Uranus	Neptune	Pluto	Aries	Taurus	Gemini	Cancer	Leo	Virgo	Libra	Scorpio	Sagittarius	Capricorn	Aquarius	Pisces
1		C			X		X			u	f		U		f	u	f		F		f
2	C			C						f	u	f		U		f	u	f		F	
3						T				f	u	f		U		f	u	f		F	
4			X					C	X		f	u	f		U		f	u	f		F
5											f	u	f		U		f	u	f		F
6				C		C					f	u	f		U		f	u	f		F
7		X	Q						Q	F		f	u	f		U		f	u	f	
8	X			X	O					F		f	u	f		U		f	u	f	
9			T					X	T		F		f	u	f		U		f	u	f
10		Q		Q							F		f	u	f		U		f	u	f
11	Q						X	Q			F		f	u	f		U		f	u	f
12		T			X					f		F		f	u	f		U		f	u
13	T			T		T	Q	T		f		F		f	u	f		U		f	u
14			O		Q				O	u	f		F		f	u	f		U		f
15						Q				u	f		F		f	u	f		U		f
16					T		T			f	u	f		F		f	u	f		U	
17		O		O	X					f	u	f		F		f	u	f		U	
18	O						O	T			f	u	f		F		f	u	f		U
19			T								f	u	f		F		f	u	f		U
20				O		O		Q		U		f	u	f		F		f	u	f	
21			Q		C					U		f	u	f		F		f	u	f	
22	T	T		T				T	X	U		f	u	f		F		f	u	f	
23			X								U		f	u	f		F		f	u	f
24	Q	Q		Q	T		T	Q		f		U		f	u	f		F		f	u
25						X				f		U		f	u	f		F		f	u
26				X			Q	X		f		U		f	u	f		F		f	u
27	X	X			Q	Q			C	u	f		U		f	u	f		F		f
28			C				X			u	f		U		f	u	f		F		f

139

March Moon Table

Date	Sign	Element	Nature	Phase
1 Tue 12:14 am	Aquarius	Air	Barren	4th
2 Wed	Aquarius	Air	Barren	4th
3 Thu 11:47 am	Pisces	Water	Fruitful	4th
4 Fri	Pisces	Water	Fruitful	New 3:46 pm
5 Sat	Pisces	Water	Fruitful	1st
6 Sun 12:14 am	Aries	Fire	Barren	1st
7 Mon	Aries	Fire	Barren	1st
8 Tue 12:52 pm	Taurus	Earth	Semi-fruitful	1st
9 Wed	Taurus	Earth	Semi-fruitful	1st
10 Thu	Taurus	Earth	Semi-fruitful	1st
11 Fri 12:31 am	Gemini	Air	Barren	1st
12 Sat	Gemini	Air	Barren	2nd 6:45 pm
13 Sun 10:29 am	Cancer	Water	Fruitful	2nd
14 Mon	Cancer	Water	Fruitful	2nd
15 Tue 3:33 pm	Leo	Fire	Barren	2nd
16 Wed	Leo	Fire	Barren	2nd
17 Thu 4:53 pm	Virgo	Earth	Barren	2nd
18 Fri	Virgo	Earth	Barren	2nd
19 Sat 4:03 pm	Libra	Air	Semi-fruitful	Full 2:10 pm
20 Sun	Libra	Air	Semi-fruitful	3rd
21 Mon 3:17 pm	Scorpio	Water	Fruitful	3rd
22 Tue	Scorpio	Water	Fruitful	3rd
23 Wed 4:45 pm	Sagittarius	Fire	Barren	3rd
24 Thu	Sagittarius	Fire	Barren	3rd
25 Fri 9:57 pm	Capricorn	Earth	Semi-fruitful	3rd
26 Sat	Capricorn	Earth	Semi-fruitful	4th 8:07 am
27 Sun	Capricorn	Earth	Semi-fruitful	4th
28 Mon 7:00 am	Aquarius	Air	Barren	4th
29 Tue	Aquarius	Air	Barren	4th
30 Wed 6:38 pm	Pisces	Water	Fruitful	4th
31 Thu	Pisces	Water	Fruitful	4th

March Aspectarian/Favorable & Unfavorable Days

Date	Sun	Mercury	Venus	Mars	Jupiter	Saturn	Uranus	Neptune	Pluto	Aries	Taurus	Gemini	Cancer	Leo	Virgo	Libra	Scorpio	Sagittarius	Capricorn	Aquarius	Pisces
1					X					f	u	f		U		f	u	f		F	
2						T				f	u	f		U		f	u	f		F	
3									C		f	u	f		U		f	u	f		F
4	C			C				X			f	u	f		U		f	u	f		F
5		C					C				f	u	f		U		f	u	f		F
6			X		C				Q	F		f	u	f		U		f	u	f	
7						O				F		f	u	f		U		f	u	f	
8								X		F		f	u	f		U		f	u	f	
9			Q	X					T		F		f	u	f		U		f	u	f
10	X							Q			F		f	u	f		U		f	u	f
11		X	T		X		X			f		F		f	u	f		U		f	u
12	Q			Q		T				f		F		f	u	f		U		f	u
13						Q	T	O		u	f		F		f	u	f		U		f
14		Q		T	Q	Q				u	f		F		f	u	f		U		f
15	T						T			u	f		F		f	u	f		U		f
16		T	O		T	X				f	u	f		F		f	u	f		U	
17								O		f	u	f		F		f	u	f		U	
18			O						T		f	u	f		F		f	u	f		U
19	O						O				f	u	f		F		f	u	f		U
20		O			O	C			Q	U		f	u	f		F		f	u	f	
21			T					T		U		f	u	f		F		f	u	f	
22									X		U		f	u	f		F		f	u	f
23	T		Q	T			T	Q			U		f	u	f		F		f	u	f
24					T	X				f		U		f	u	f		F		f	u
25		T	X	Q			Q	X		f		U		f	u	f		F		f	u
26	Q								C	u	f		U		f	u	f		F		f
27		Q		X	Q	Q				u	f		U		f	u	f		F		f
28	X						X			f	u	f		U		f	u	f		F	
29					X	T				f	u	f		U		f	u	f		F	
30		X							C	f	u	f		U		f	u	f		F	
31			C					X			f	u	f		U		f	u	f		F

April Moon Table

Date	Sign	Element	Nature	Phase
1 Fri	Pisces	Water	Fruitful	4th
2 Sat 7:16 am	Aries	Fire	Barren	4th
3 Sun	Aries	Fire	Barren	New 10:32 am
4 Mon 7:46 pm	Taurus	Earth	Semi-fruitful	1st
5 Tue	Taurus	Earth	Semi-fruitful	1st
6 Wed	Taurus	Earth	Semi-fruitful	1st
7 Thu 7:22 am	Gemini	Air	Barren	1st
8 Fri	Gemini	Air	Barren	1st
9 Sat 5:02 pm	Cancer	Water	Fruitful	1st
10 Sun	Cancer	Water	Fruitful	1st
11 Mon 11:37 pm	Leo	Fire	Barren	2nd 8:05 am
12 Tue	Leo	Fire	Barren	2nd
13 Wed	Leo	Fire	Barren	2nd
14 Thu 2:40 am	Virgo	Earth	Barren	2nd
15 Fri	Virgo	Earth	Barren	2nd
16 Sat 2:59 am	Libra	Air	Semi-fruitful	2nd
17 Sun	Libra	Air	Semi-fruitful	Full 10:44 pm
18 Mon 2:19 am	Scorpio	Water	Fruitful	3rd
19 Tue	Scorpio	Water	Fruitful	3rd
20 Wed 2:50 am	Sagittarius	Fire	Barren	3rd
21 Thu	Sagittarius	Fire	Barren	3rd
22 Fri 6:24 am	Capricorn	Earth	Semi-fruitful	3rd
23 Sat	Capricorn	Earth	Semi-fruitful	3rd
24 Sun 1:59 pm	Aquarius	Air	Barren	4th 10:47 pm
25 Mon	Aquarius	Air	Barren	4th
26 Tue	Aquarius	Air	Barren	4th
27 Wed 12:57 am	Pisces	Water	Fruitful	4th
28 Thu	Pisces	Water	Fruitful	4th
29 Fri 1:33 pm	Aries	Fire	Barren	4th
30 Sat	Aries	Fire	Barren	4th

April Aspectarian/Favorable & Unfavorable Days

Date	Sun	Mercury	Venus	Mars	Jupiter	Saturn	Uranus	Neptune	Pluto	Aries	Taurus	Gemini	Cancer	Leo	Virgo	Libra	Scorpio	Sagittarus	Capricorn	Aquarius	Pisces
1											f	u	f		U		f	u	f		F
2				C			C		Q	F		f	u	f		U		f	u	f	
3	C				C	O				F		f	u	f		U		f	u	f	
4		C						X		F		f	u	f		U		f	u	f	
5			X						T		F		f	u	f		U		f	u	f
6											F		f	u	f		U		f	u	f
7				X			X	Q		f		F		f	u	f		U		f	u
8	X	X	Q		X	T				f		F		f	u	f		U		f	u
9								Q	T	f		F		f	u	f		U		f	u
10				Q		Q			O	u	f		F		f	u	f		U		f
11	Q	Q	T		Q					u	f		F		f	u	f		U		f
12			T			X	T			f	u	f		F		f	u	f		U	
13	T	T			T					f	u	f		F		f	u	f		U	
14								O	T		f	u	f		F		f	u	f		U
15		O									f	u	f		F		f	u	f		U
16			O		C	O			Q	U		f	u	f		F		f	u	f	
17	O	O			O					U		f	u	f		F		f	u	f	
18								T	X		U		f	u	f		F		f	u	f
19											U		f	u	f		F		f	u	f
20			T			T	Q			f		U		f	u	f		F		f	u
21		T			T	T	X			f		U		f	u	f		F		f	u
22	T		Q			Q	X	C		u	f		U		f	u	f		F		f
23		Q			Q	Q	Q			u	f		U		f	u	f		F		f
24	Q		X				X			u	f		U		f	u	f		F		f
25		X				T				f	u	f		U		f	u	f		F	
26			X	X						f	u	f		U		f	u	f		F	
27	X							C	X		f	u	f		U		f	u	f		F
28											f	u	f		U		f	u	f		F
29							C				f	u	f		U		f	u	f		F
30		C	C			O			Q	F		f	u	f		U		f	u	f	

May Moon Table

Date	Sign	Element	Nature	Phase
1 Sun	Aries	Fire	Barren	4th
2 Mon 1:58 am	Taurus	Earth	Semi-fruitful	4th
3 Tue	Taurus	Earth	Semi-fruitful	New 2:51 am
4 Wed 1:09 pm	Gemini	Air	Barren	1st
5 Thu	Gemini	Air	Barren	1st
6 Fri 10:32 pm	Cancer	Water	Fruitful	1st
7 Sat	Cancer	Water	Fruitful	1st
8 Sun	Cancer	Water	Fruitful	1st
9 Mon 5:35 am	Leo	Fire	Barren	1st
10 Tue	Leo	Fire	Barren	2nd 4:33 pm
11 Wed 9:59 am	Virgo	Earth	Barren	2nd
12 Thu	Virgo	Earth	Barren	2nd
13 Fri 11:56 am	Libra	Air	Semi-fruitful	2nd
14 Sat	Libra	Air	Semi-fruitful	2nd
15 Sun 12:31 pm	Scorpio	Water	Fruitful	2nd
16 Mon	Scorpio	Water	Fruitful	2nd
17 Tue 1:22 pm	Sagittarius	Fire	Barren	Full 7:09 am
18 Wed	Sagittarius	Fire	Barren	3rd
19 Thu 4:16 pm	Capricorn	Earth	Semi-fruitful	3rd
20 Fri	Capricorn	Earth	Semi-fruitful	3rd
21 Sat 10:32 pm	Aquarius	Air	Barren	3rd
22 Sun	Aquarius	Air	Barren	3rd
23 Mon	Aquarius	Air	Barren	3rd
24 Tue 8:24 am	Pisces	Water	Fruitful	4th 2:52 pm
25 Wed	Pisces	Water	Fruitful	4th
26 Thu 8:36 pm	Aries	Fire	Barren	4th
27 Fri	Aries	Fire	Barren	4th
28 Sat	Aries	Fire	Barren	4th
29 Sun 9:02 am	Taurus	Earth	Semi-fruitful	4th
30 Mon	Taurus	Earth	Semi-fruitful	4th
31 Tue 7:56 pm	Gemini	Air	Barren	4th

May Aspectarian/Favorable & Unfavorable Days

Date	Sun	Mercury	Venus	Mars	Jupiter	Saturn	Uranus	Neptune	Pluto	Aries	Taurus	Gemini	Cancer	Leo	Virgo	Libra	Scorpio	Sagittarus	Capricorn	Aquarius	Pisces
1				C	C					F		f	u	f		U	f	u	f		
2								X	T		F		f	u	f		U	f	u	f	
3	C										F		f	u	f		U	f	u	f	
4								X	Q		F		f	u	f		U	f	u	f	
5						T						F		f	u	f		U	f	u	f
6		X	X	X	X			T				F		f	u	f		U	f	u	f
7						Q	Q		O	f			F		f	u	f		U	f	u
8	X	Q	Q		Q					f			F		f	u	f		U	f	u
9			Q				T			u	f			F		f	u	f		U	f
10	Q	T				X				u	f			F		f	u	f		U	f
11			T	T	T			O	T	f	u	f			F		f	u	f		U
12	T									f	u	f			F		f	u	f		U
13							O		Q	U	f	u	f			F		f	u	f	
14						C				U	f	u	f			F		f	u	f	
15		O	O	O	O			T		U	f	u	f			F		f	u	f	
16									X		U	f	u	f			F		f	u	f
17	O							T	Q		U	f	u	f			F		f	u	f
18					X					f		U	f	u	f			F		f	u
19				T				Q	X	f		U	f	u	f			F		f	u
20		T	T	T	Q				C	u	f		U	f	u	f			F		f
21	T				Q					u	f		U	f	u	f			F		f
22		Q	Q	Q		T	X			f	u	f		U	f	u	f			F	
23										f	u	f		U	f	u	f			F	
24	Q				X			C	X		f	u	f		U	f	u	f			F
25		X	X	X							f	u	f		U	f	u	f			F
26											f	u	f		U	f	u	f			F
27	X					O	C		Q	F		f	u	f		U	f	u	f		
28										F		f	u	f		U	f	u	f		
29					C			X	T		F		f	u	f		U	f	u	f	
30			C	C							F		f	u	f		U	f	u	f	
31		C							Q		F		f	u	f		U	f	u	f	

145

June Moon Table

Date	Sign	Element	Nature	Phase
1 Wed	Gemini	Air	Barren	New 5:03 pm
2 Thu	Gemini	Air	Barren	1st
3 Fri 4:36 am	Cancer	Water	Fruitful	1st
4 Sat	Cancer	Water	Fruitful	1st
5 Sun 11:03 am	Leo	Fire	Barren	1st
6 Mon	Leo	Fire	Barren	1st
7 Tue 3:33 pm	Virgo	Earth	Barren	1st
8 Wed	Virgo	Earth	Barren	2nd 10:11 pm
9 Thu 6:31 pm	Libra	Air	Semi-fruitful	2nd
10 Fri	Libra	Air	Semi-fruitful	2nd
11 Sat 8:33 pm	Scorpio	Water	Fruitful	2nd
12 Sun	Scorpio	Water	Fruitful	2nd
13 Mon 10:38 pm	Sagittarius	Fire	Barren	2nd
14 Tue	Sagittarius	Fire	Barren	2nd
15 Wed	Sagittarius	Fire	Barren	Full 4:14 pm
16 Thu 1:59 am	Capricorn	Earth	Semi-fruitful	3rd
17 Fri	Capricorn	Earth	Semi-fruitful	3rd
18 Sat 7:47 am	Aquarius	Air	Barren	3rd
19 Sun	Aquarius	Air	Barren	3rd
20 Mon 4:45 pm	Pisces	Water	Fruitful	3rd
21 Tue	Pisces	Water	Fruitful	3rd
22 Wed	Pisces	Water	Fruitful	3rd
23 Thu 4:24 am	Aries	Fire	Barren	4th 7:48 am
24 Fri	Aries	Fire	Barren	4th
25 Sat 4:53 pm	Taurus	Earth	Semi-fruitful	4th
26 Sun	Taurus	Earth	Semi-fruitful	4th
27 Mon	Taurus	Earth	Semi-fruitful	4th
28 Tue 3:56 am	Gemini	Air	Barren	4th
29 Wed	Gemini	Air	Barren	4th
30 Thu 12:13 pm	Cancer	Water	Fruitful	4th

June Aspectarian/Favorable & Unfavorable Days

Date	Sun	Mercury	Venus	Mars	Jupiter	Saturn	Uranus	Neptune	Pluto	Aries	Taurus	Gemini	Cancer	Leo	Virgo	Libra	Scorpio	Sagittarius	Capricorn	Aquarius	Pisces
1	C					T	X			f		F		f	u	f		U		f	u
2										f		F		f	u	f		U		f	u
3					X	Q	Q	T	O	u	f		F		f	u	f		U		f
4				X						u	f		F		f	u	f		U		f
5		X	X		Q	T				f	u	f		F		f	u	f		U	
6	X				Q	X				f	u	f		F		f	u	f		U	
7			Q		T				O	f	u	f		F		f	u	f		U	
8	Q	Q						T			f	u	f		F		f	u	f		U
9			T	T							f	u	f		F		f	u	f		U
10						C	O		Q	U		f	u	f		F		f	u	f	
11	T	T			O			T		U		f	u	f		F		f	u	f	
12								X			U		f	u	f		F		f	u	f
13				O							U		f	u	f		F		f	u	f
14			O		X	T	Q			f		U		f	u	f		F		f	u
15	O	O								f		U		f	u	f		F		f	u
16					T	Q	Q	X	C	u	f		U		f	u	f		F		f
17										u	f		U		f	u	f		F		f
18					T	Q	X			f	u	f		U		f	u	f		F	
19		T				T				f	u	f		U		f	u	f		F	
20	T			Q	X			C		f	u	f		U		f	u	f		F	
21		T	Q						X		f	u	f		U		f	u	f		F
22											f	u	f		U		f	u	f		F
23	Q			X		C			Q	F		f	u	f		U		f	u	f	
24		Q	X		O					F		f	u	f		U		f	u	f	
25								X		F		f	u	f		U		f	u	f	
26	X				C				T		F		f	u	f		U		f	u	f
27		X									F		f	u	f		U		f	u	f
28			C			X	Q			f		F		f	u	f		U		f	u
29				T						f		F		f	u	f		U		f	u
30			C	X		Q	T		O	f		F		f	u	f		U		f	u

July Moon Table

Date	Sign	Element	Nature	Phase
1 Fri	Cancer	Water	Fruitful	New 4:54 am
2 Sat 5:43 pm	Leo	Fire	Barren	1st
3 Sun	Leo	Fire	Barren	1st
4 Mon 9:15 pm	Virgo	Earth	Barren	1st
5 Tue	Virgo	Earth	Barren	1st
6 Wed 11:54 pm	Libra	Air	Semi-fruitful	1st
7 Thu	Libra	Air	Semi-fruitful	1st
8 Fri	Libra	Air	Semi-fruitful	2nd 2:29 am
9 Sat 2:31 am	Scorpio	Water	Fruitful	2nd
10 Sun	Scorpio	Water	Fruitful	2nd
11 Mon 5:47 am	Sagittarius	Fire	Barren	2nd
12 Tue	Sagittarius	Fire	Barren	2nd
13 Wed 10:14 am	Capricorn	Earth	Semi-fruitful	2nd
14 Thu	Capricorn	Earth	Semi-fruitful	2nd
15 Fri 4:30 pm	Aquarius	Air	Barren	Full 2:40 am
16 Sat	Aquarius	Air	Barren	3rd
17 Sun	Aquarius	Air	Barren	3rd
18 Mon 1:13 am	Pisces	Water	Fruitful	3rd
19 Tue	Pisces	Water	Fruitful	3rd
20 Wed 12:25 pm	Aries	Fire	Barren	3rd
21 Thu	Aries	Fire	Barren	3rd
22 Fri	Aries	Fire	Barren	3rd
23 Sat 12:58 am	Taurus	Earth	Semi-fruitful	4th 1:02 am
24 Sun	Taurus	Earth	Semi-fruitful	4th
25 Mon 12:34 pm	Gemini	Air	Barren	4th
26 Tue	Gemini	Air	Barren	4th
27 Wed 9:11 pm	Cancer	Water	Fruitful	4th
28 Thu	Cancer	Water	Fruitful	4th
29 Fri	Cancer	Water	Fruitful	4th
30 Sat 2:16 am	Leo	Fire	Barren	New 2:40 pm
31 Sun	Leo	Fire	Barren	1st

July Aspectarian/Favorable & Unfavorable Days

Date	Sun	Mercury	Venus	Mars	Jupiter	Saturn	Uranus	Neptune	Pluto	Aries	Taurus	Gemini	Cancer	Leo	Virgo	Libra	Scorpio	Sagittarus	Capricorn	Aquarius	Pisces
1	C					Q				u	f		F		f	u	f		U		f
2		C								u	f		F		f	u	f		U		f
3			X		Q	X	T			f	u	f		F		f	u	f		U	
4			X					O		f	u	f		F		f	u	f		U	
5	X			Q	T				T		f	u	f		F		f	u	f		U
6											f	u	f		F		f	u	f		U
7		X	Q	T		C	O		Q	U		f	u	f		F		f	u	f	
8	Q									U		f	u	f		F		f	u	f	
9		Q	T		O			T	X		U		f	u	f		F		f	u	f
10	T										U		f	u	f		F		f	u	f
11							T	Q		f		U		f	u	f		F		f	u
12		T		O		X				f		U		f	u	f		F		f	u
13					T		Q	X	C	u	f		U		f	u	f		F		f
14			O		Q					u	f		U		f	u	f		F		f
15	O									u	f		U		f	u	f		F		f
16					Q	T	X			f	u	f		U		f	u	f		F	
17		O		T						f	u	f		U		f	u	f		F	
18				X				C	X	f	u	f		U		f	u	f			F
19			T	Q						f	u	f		U		f	u	f			F
20	T					C			Q	f	u	f		U		f	u	f			F
21					O					F	f	u	f		U		f	u	f		
22		T	Q	X						F	f	u	f		U		f	u	f		
23	Q				C			X	T		F		f	u	f		U		f	u	f
24											F		f	u	f		U		f	u	f
25	X	Q	X					X	Q		F		f	u	f		U		f	u	f
26						T				f		F		f	u	f		U		f	u
27		X		C				T		f		F		f	u	f		U		f	u
28					X	Q	Q		O	u	f		F		f	u	f		U		f
29										u	f		F		f	u	f		U		f
30	C		C		Q	X	T			f	u	f		F		f	u	f		U	
31										f	u	f		F		f	u	f		U	

August Moon Table

Date	Sign	Element	Nature	Phase
1 Mon 4:41 am	Virgo	Earth	Barren	1st
2 Tue	Virgo	Earth	Barren	1st
3 Wed 6:04 am	Libra	Air	Semi-fruitful	1st
4 Thu	Libra	Air	Semi-fruitful	1st
5 Fri 7:57 am	Scorpio	Water	Fruitful	1st
6 Sat	Scorpio	Water	Fruitful	2nd 7:08 am
7 Sun 11:21 am	Sagittarius	Fire	Barren	2nd
8 Mon	Sagittarius	Fire	Barren	2nd
9 Tue 4:38 pm	Capricorn	Earth	Semi-fruitful	2nd
10 Wed	Capricorn	Earth	Semi-fruitful	2nd
11 Thu 11:47 pm	Aquarius	Air	Barren	2nd
12 Fri	Aquarius	Air	Barren	2nd
13 Sat	Aquarius	Air	Barren	Full 2:58 pm
14 Sun 8:54 am	Pisces	Water	Fruitful	3rd
15 Mon	Pisces	Water	Fruitful	3rd
16 Tue 8:01 pm	Aries	Fire	Barren	3rd
17 Wed	Aries	Fire	Barren	3rd
18 Thu	Aries	Fire	Barren	3rd
19 Fri 8:36 am	Taurus	Earth	Semi-fruitful	3rd
20 Sat	Taurus	Earth	Semi-fruitful	3rd
21 Sun 8:53 pm	Gemini	Air	Barren	4th 5:54 pm
22 Mon	Gemini	Air	Barren	4th
23 Tue	Gemini	Air	Barren	4th
24 Wed 6:31 am	Cancer	Water	Fruitful	4th
25 Thu	Cancer	Water	Fruitful	4th
26 Fri 12:09 pm	Leo	Fire	Barren	4th
27 Sat	Leo	Fire	Barren	4th
28 Sun 2:13 pm	Virgo	Earth	Barren	New 11:04 pm
29 Mon	Virgo	Earth	Barren	1st
30 Tue 2:25 pm	Libra	Air	Semi-fruitful	1st
31 Wed	Libra	Air	Semi-fruitful	1st

August Aspectarian/Favorable & Unfavorable Days

Date	Sun	Mercury	Venus	Mars	Jupiter	Saturn	Uranus	Neptune	Pluto	Aries	Taurus	Gemini	Cancer	Leo	Virgo	Libra	Scorpio	Sagittarius	Capricorn	Aquarius	Pisces
1		C		X	T			O	T		f	u	f		F		f	u	f		U
2											f	u	f		F		f	u	f		U
3			X	Q			O		Q	U		f	u	f		F		f	u	f	
4	X					C				U		f	u	f		F		f	u	f	
5		X		T	O			T	X		U		f	u	f		F		f	u	f
6	Q		Q								U		f	u	f		F		f	u	f
7		Q					T	Q		f		U		f	u	f		F		f	u
8	T		T			X				f		U		f	u	f		F		f	u
9		T						X		f		U		f	u	f		F		f	u
10				O	T	Q	Q		C	u	f		U		f	u	f		F		f
11										u	f		U		f	u	f		F		f
12				Q		X				f	u	f		U		f	u	f		F	
13	O		O			T				f	u	f		U		f	u	f		F	
14		O						C	X	f	u	f		U		f	u	f			F
15				T	X					f	u	f		U		f	u	f			F
16										f	u	f		U		f	u	f			F
17				Q	O	C		Q		F		f	u	f		U		f	u	f	
18		T								F		f	u	f		U		f	u	f	
19	T		T					X	T		F		f	u	f		U		f	u	f
20				X	C						F		f	u	f		U		f	u	f
21	Q	Q	Q					Q			F		f	u	f		U		f	u	f
22						X				f		F		f	u	f		U		f	u
23		X				T				f		F		f	u	f		U		f	u
24	X		X				Q	T	O	u	f		F		f	u	f		U		f
25			C	X	Q					u	f		F		f	u	f		U		f
26						T				u	f		F		f	u	f		U		f
27		C		Q	X					f	u	f		F		f	u	f		U	
28	C							O	T	f	u	f		F		f	u	f		U	
29			C	X	T						f	u	f		F		f	u	f		U
30							O		Q		f	u	f		F		f	u	f		U
31		X		Q		C				U		f	u	f		F		f	u	f	

September Moon Table

Date	Sign	Element	Nature	Phase
1 Thu 2:48 pm	Scorpio	Water	Fruitful	1st
2 Fri	Scorpio	Water	Fruitful	1st
3 Sat 5:03 pm	Sagittarius	Fire	Barren	1st
4 Sun	Sagittarius	Fire	Barren	2nd 1:39 pm
5 Mon 10:03 pm	Capricorn	Earth	Semi-fruitful	2nd
6 Tue	Capricorn	Earth	Semi-fruitful	2nd
7 Wed	Capricorn	Earth	Semi-fruitful	2nd
8 Thu 5:42 am	Aquarius	Air	Barren	2nd
9 Fri	Aquarius	Air	Barren	2nd
10 Sat 3:26 pm	Pisces	Water	Fruitful	2nd
11 Sun	Pisces	Water	Fruitful	2nd
12 Mon	Pisces	Water	Fruitful	Full 5:27 am
13 Tue 2:49 am	Aries	Fire	Barren	3rd
14 Wed	Aries	Fire	Barren	3rd
15 Thu 3:25 pm	Taurus	Earth	Semi-fruitful	3rd
16 Fri	Taurus	Earth	Semi-fruitful	3rd
17 Sat	Taurus	Earth	Semi-fruitful	3rd
18 Sun 4:06 am	Gemini	Air	Barren	3rd
19 Mon	Gemini	Air	Barren	3rd
20 Tue 2:53 pm	Cancer	Water	Fruitful	4th 9:39 am
21 Wed	Cancer	Water	Fruitful	4th
22 Thu 9:55 pm	Leo	Fire	Barren	4th
23 Fri	Leo	Fire	Barren	4th
24 Sat	Leo	Fire	Barren	4th
25 Sun 12:49 am	Virgo	Earth	Barren	4th
26 Mon	Virgo	Earth	Barren	4th
27 Tue 12:51 am	Libra	Air	Semi-fruitful	New 7:09 am
28 Wed	Libra	Air	Semi-fruitful	1st
29 Thu 12:05 am	Scorpio	Water	Fruitful	1st
30 Fri	Scorpio	Water	Fruitful	1st

September Aspectarian/Favorable & Unfavorable Days

Date	Sun	Mercury	Venus	Mars	Jupiter	Saturn	Uranus	Neptune	Pluto	Aries	Taurus	Gemini	Cancer	Leo	Virgo	Libra	Scorpio	Sagittarus	Capricorn	Aquarius	Pisces
1								T	X	U		f	u	f		F		f	u	f	
2	X		X	O							U		f	u	f		F		f	u	f
3		Q	T				T	Q			U		f	u	f		F		f	u	f
4	Q		Q		X					f		U		f	u	f		F		f	u
5		T						X		f		U		f	u	f		F		f	u
6				T		Q			C	u	f		U		f	u	f		F		f
7	T		T	O		Q				u	f		U		f	u	f		F		f
8							X			f	u	f		U		f	u	f		F	
9				Q	T					f	u	f		U		f	u	f		F	
10		O							C	f	u	f		U		f	u	f		F	
11					X				X		f	u	f		U		f	u	f		F
12	O		O	T							f	u	f		U		f	u	f		F
13						C		Q		F		f	u	f		U		f	u	f	
14					O					F		f	u	f		U		f	u	f	
15			Q					X		F		f	u	f		U		f	u	f	
16		T			C			T			F		f	u	f		U		f	u	f
17	T										F		f	u	f		U		f	u	f
18			T	X			X	Q		f		F		f	u	f		U		f	u
19		Q				T				f		F		f	u	f		U		f	u
20	Q						Q	T		f		F		f	u	f		U		f	u
21		Q			X	Q			O	u	f		F		f	u	f		U		f
22	X	X								u	f		F		f	u	f		U		f
23			X	C	Q		T			f	u	f		F		f	u	f		U	
24					X			O		f	u	f		F		f	u	f		U	
25				T				T			f	u	f		F		f	u	f		U
26											f	u	f		F		f	u	f		U
27	C	C		X		O		Q		U		f	u	f		F		f	u	f	
28		C			C			T		U		f	u	f		F		f	u	f	
29			Q	O				X			U		f	u	f		F		f	u	f
30								Q			U		f	u	f		F		f	u	f

October Moon Table

Date	Sign	Element	Nature	Phase
1 Sat 12:42 am	Sagittarius	Fire	Barren	1st
2 Sun	Sagittarius	Fire	Barren	1st
3 Mon 4:16 am	Capricorn	Earth	Semi-fruitful	2nd 11:15 pm
4 Tue	Capricorn	Earth	Semi-fruitful	2nd
5 Wed 11:18 am	Aquarius	Air	Barren	2nd
6 Thu	Aquarius	Air	Barren	2nd
7 Fri 9:13 pm	Pisces	Water	Fruitful	2nd
8 Sat	Pisces	Water	Fruitful	2nd
9 Sun	Pisces	Water	Fruitful	2nd
10 Mon 8:57 am	Aries	Fire	Barren	2nd
11 Tue	Aries	Fire	Barren	Full 10:06 pm
12 Wed 9:35 pm	Taurus	Earth	Semi-fruitful	3rd
13 Thu	Taurus	Earth	Semi-fruitful	3rd
14 Fri	Taurus	Earth	Semi-fruitful	3rd
15 Sat 10:15 am	Gemini	Air	Barren	3rd
16 Sun	Gemini	Air	Barren	3rd
17 Mon 9:38 pm	Cancer	Water	Fruitful	3rd
18 Tue	Cancer	Water	Fruitful	3rd
19 Wed	Cancer	Water	Fruitful	4th 11:30 pm
20 Thu 6:06 am	Leo	Fire	Barren	4th
21 Fri	Leo	Fire	Barren	4th
22 Sat 10:40 am	Virgo	Earth	Barren	4th
23 Sun	Virgo	Earth	Barren	4th
24 Mon 11:49 am	Libra	Air	Semi-fruitful	4th
25 Tue	Libra	Air	Semi-fruitful	4th
26 Wed 11:08 am	Scorpio	Water	Fruitful	New 3:56 pm
27 Thu	Scorpio	Water	Fruitful	1st
28 Fri 10:45 am	Sagittarius	Fire	Barren	1st
29 Sat	Sagittarius	Fire	Barren	1st
30 Sun 12:39 pm	Capricorn	Earth	Semi-fruitful	1st
31 Mon	Capricorn	Earth	Semi-fruitful	1st

October Aspectarian/Favorable & Unfavorable Days

Date	Sun	Mercury	Venus	Mars	Jupiter	Saturn	Uranus	Neptune	Pluto	Aries	Taurus	Gemini	Cancer	Leo	Virgo	Libra	Scorpio	Sagittarus	Capricorn	Aquarius	Pisces
1	X	X		T			T			f		U		f	u	f		F		f	u
2			X			X				f		U		f	u	f		F		f	u
3	Q				T		Q	X	C	u	f		U		f	u	f		F		f
4		Q			Q					u	f		U		f	u	f		F		f
5			Q				X			f	u	f		U		f	u	f		F	
6	T			O	Q					f	u	f		U		f	u	f		F	
7		T	T			T		C		f	u	f		U		f	u	f		F	
8					X				X		f	u	f		U		f	u	f		F
9											f	u	f		U		f	u	f		F
10							C	Q		F		f	u	f		U		f	u	f	
11	O			T						F		f	u	f		U		f	u	f	
12	O					O		X		F		f	u	f		U		f	u	f	
13			O	C					T		F		f	u	f		U		f	u	f
14				Q							F		f	u	f		U		f	u	f
15							X	Q		f		F		f	u	f		U		f	u
16			X							f		F		f	u	f		U		f	u
17	T					T		T		f		F		f	u	f		U		f	u
18		T	T		X		Q		O	u	f		F		f	u	f		U		f
19	Q				Q					u	f		F		f	u	f		U		f
20				Q		T				f	u	f		F		f	u	f		U	
21		Q	Q	C		X				f	u	f		F		f	u	f		U	
22	X				T			O	T		f	u	f		F		f	u	f		U
23		X	X								f	u	f		F		f	u	f		U
24						O		Q		U		f	u	f		F		f	u	f	
25				X	C					U		f	u	f		F		f	u	f	
26	C				O			T	X		U		f	u	f		F		f	u	f
27		C	Q								U		f	u	f		F		f	u	f
28			C			T		Q		f		U		f	u	f		F		f	u
29						X				f		U		f	u	f		F		f	u
30				T	T		Q	X	C	f		U		f	u	f		F		f	u
31	X									u	f		U		f	u	f		F		f

November Moon Table

Date	Sign	Element	Nature	Phase
1 Tue 6:08 pm	Aquarius	Air	Barren	1st
2 Wed	Aquarius	Air	Barren	2nd 12:38 pm
3 Thu	Aquarius	Air	Barren	2nd
4 Fri 3:18 am	Pisces	Water	Fruitful	2nd
5 Sat	Pisces	Water	Fruitful	2nd
6 Sun 2:02 pm	Aries	Fire	Barren	2nd
7 Mon	Aries	Fire	Barren	2nd
8 Tue	Aries	Fire	Barren	2nd
9 Wed 2:45 am	Taurus	Earth	Semi-fruitful	2nd
10 Thu	Taurus	Earth	Semi-fruitful	Full 3:16 pm
11 Fri 3:10 pm	Gemini	Air	Barren	3rd
12 Sat	Gemini	Air	Barren	3rd
13 Sun	Gemini	Air	Barren	3rd
14 Mon 2:19 am	Cancer	Water	Fruitful	3rd
15 Tue	Cancer	Water	Fruitful	3rd
16 Wed 11:17 am	Leo	Fire	Barren	3rd
17 Thu	Leo	Fire	Barren	3rd
18 Fri 5:19 pm	Virgo	Earth	Barren	4th 10:09 am
19 Sat	Virgo	Earth	Barren	4th
20 Sun 8:16 pm	Libra	Air	Semi-fruitful	4th
21 Mon	Libra	Air	Semi-fruitful	4th
22 Tue 8:58 pm	Scorpio	Water	Fruitful	4th
23 Wed	Scorpio	Water	Fruitful	4th
24 Thu 8:57 pm	Sagittarius	Fire	Barren	4th
25 Fri	Sagittarius	Fire	Barren	New 1:10 am
26 Sat 10:05 pm	Capricorn	Earth	Semi-fruitful	1st
27 Sun	Capricorn	Earth	Semi-fruitful	1st
28 Mon	Capricorn	Earth	Semi-fruitful	1st
29 Tue 2:02 am	Aquarius	Air	Barren	1st
30 Wed	Aquarius	Air	Barren	1st

November Aspectarian/Favorable & Unfavorable Days

Date	Sun	Mercury	Venus	Mars	Jupiter	Saturn	Uranus	Neptune	Pluto	Aries	Taurus	Gemini	Cancer	Leo	Virgo	Libra	Scorpio	Sagittarius	Capricorn	Aquarius	Pisces
1		X	X			Q	X			u	f		U		f	u	f		F		f
2	Q				Q					f	u	f		U		f	u	f		F	
3				O		T		C		f	u	f		U		f	u	f		F	
4		Q	Q		X				X		f	u	f		U		f	u	f		F
5	T										f	u	f		U		f	u	f		F
6						C					f	u	f		U		f	u	f		F
7		T	T						Q	F		f	u	f		U		f	u	f	
8						O		X		F		f	u	f		U		f	u	f	
9				T	C				T		F		f	u	f		U		f	u	f
10	O										F		f	u	f		U		f	u	f
11				Q			X	Q			F		f	u	f		U		f	u	f
12		O	O							f		F		f	u	f		U		f	u
13						T		T		f		F		f	u	f		U		f	u
14				X	X		Q		O	u	f		F		f	u	f		U		f
15	T									u	f		F		f	u	f		U		f
16						Q	Q	T		f	u	f		F		f	u	f		U	
17		T	T							f	u	f		F		f	u	f		U	
18	Q				T	X		O		f	u	f		F		f	u	f		U	
19				C					T		f	u	f		F		f	u	f		U
20	X	Q	Q				O				f	u	f		F		f	u	f		U
21									Q	U		f	u	f		F		f	u	f	
22		X	X		C			T		U		f	u	f		F		f	u	f	
23				X	O				X		U		f	u	f		F		f	u	f
24						T	Q				U		f	u	f		F		f	u	f
25	C			Q						f		U		f	u	f		F		f	u
26		C	C			X	Q	X		f		U		f	u	f		F		f	u
27				T	T				C	u	f		U		f	u	f		F		f
28						Q				u	f		U		f	u	f		F		f
29	X			Q			X			f	u	f		U		f	u	f		F	
30		X								f	u	f		U		f	u	f		F	

December Moon Table

Date	Sign	Element	Nature	Phase
1 Thu 9:45 am	Pisces	Water	Fruitful	1st
2 Fri	Pisces	Water	Fruitful	2nd 4:52 am
3 Sat 8:51 pm	Aries	Fire	Barren	2nd
4 Sun	Aries	Fire	Barren	2nd
5 Mon	Aries	Fire	Barren	2nd
6 Tue 9:34 am	Taurus	Earth	Semi-fruitful	2nd
7 Wed	Taurus	Earth	Semi-fruitful	2nd
8 Thu 9:52 pm	Gemini	Air	Barren	2nd
9 Fri	Gemini	Air	Barren	2nd
10 Sat	Gemini	Air	Barren	Full 9:36 am
11 Sun 8:26 am	Cancer	Water	Fruitful	3rd
12 Mon	Cancer	Water	Fruitful	3rd
13 Tue 4:48 pm	Leo	Fire	Barren	3rd
14 Wed	Leo	Fire	Barren	3rd
15 Thu 10:58 pm	Virgo	Earth	Barren	3rd
16 Fri	Virgo	Earth	Barren	3rd
17 Sat	Virgo	Earth	Barren	4th 7:48 pm
18 Sun 3:06 am	Libra	Air	Semi-fruitful	4th
19 Mon	Libra	Air	Semi-fruitful	4th
20 Tue 5:33 am	Scorpio	Water	Fruitful	4th
21 Wed	Scorpio	Water	Fruitful	4th
22 Thu 7:03 am	Sagittarius	Fire	Barren	4th
23 Fri	Sagittarius	Fire	Barren	4th
24 Sat 8:47 am	Capricorn	Earth	Semi-fruitful	New 1:06 pm
25 Sun	Capricorn	Earth	Semi-fruitful	1st
26 Mon 12:14 pm	Aquarius	Air	Barren	1st
27 Tue	Aquarius	Air	Barren	1st
28 Wed 6:45 pm	Pisces	Water	Fruitful	1st
29 Thu	Pisces	Water	Fruitful	1st
30 Fri	Pisces	Water	Fruitful	1st
31 Sat 4:48 am	Aries	Fire	Barren	1st

December Aspectarian/Favorable & Unfavorable Days

Date	Sun	Mercury	Venus	Mars	Jupiter	Saturn	Uranus	Neptune	Pluto	Aries	Taurus	Gemini	Cancer	Leo	Virgo	Libra	Scorpio	Sagittarius	Capricorn	Aquarius	Pisces
1			X		X	T		C	X		f	u	f		U		f	u	f		F
2	Q	Q		O							f	u	f		U		f	u	f		F
3							C				f	u	f		U		f	u	f		F
4	T	T	Q						Q	F		f	u	f		U		f	u	f	
5										F		f	u	f		U		f	u	f	
6					C	O		X	T		F		f	u	f		U		f	u	f
7			T	T							F		f	u	f		U		f	u	f
8							X	Q			F		f	u	f		U		f	u	f
9		O		Q						f		F		f	u	f		U		f	u
10	O									f		F		f	u	f		U		f	u
11					X	T	Q	T	O	u	f		F		f	u	f		U		f
12			O	X						u	f		F		f	u	f		U		f
13		T			Q	Q	T			u	f		F		f	u	f		U		f
14										f	u	f		F		f	u	f		U	
15	T				T	X		O		f	u	f		F		f	u	f		U	
16		Q						T			f	u	f		F		f	u	f		U
17	Q		T	C							f	u	f		F		f	u	f		U
18		X					O		Q	U		f	u	f		F		f	u	f	
19										U		f	u	f		F		f	u	f	
20	X		Q		O	C		T	X		U		f	u	f		F		f	u	f
21				X							U		f	u	f		F		f	u	f
22		C	X			T		Q		f		U		f	u	f		F		f	u
23			Q							f		U		f	u	f		F		f	u
24	C				T	X	Q	X	C	u	f		U		f	u	f		F		f
25				T						u	f		U		f	u	f		F		f
26					Q	Q	X			u	f		U		f	u	f		F		f
27		X	C							f	u	f		U		f	u	f		F	
28					X	T		C		f	u	f		U		f	u	f		F	
29	X								X		f	u	f		U		f	u	f		F
30		Q		O							f	u	f		U		f	u	f		F
31								C	Q	F		f	u	f		U		f	u	f	

2011 Retrograde Planets

Planet	Begin	Eastern	Pacific	End	Eastern	Pacific
Saturn	01/25/11		**10:10 pm**	06/12/11	11:51 pm	**8:51 pm**
	01/26/11	1:10 am				
Mercury	03/30/11	4:48 pm	**1:48 pm**	04/23/11	6:04 am	**3:04 am**
Pluto	04/09/11	4:50 am	**1:50 am**	09/16/11	2:24 pm	**11:24 am**
Neptune	06/03/11	3:27 am	**12:27 am**	11/09/11	1:54 pm	**10:54 am**
Uranus	07/09/11	8:35 pm	**5:35 pm**	12/09/11		**11:04 pm**
				12/10/11	2:04 am	
Mercury	08/02/11	11:50 pm	**8:50 pm**	08/26/11	6:03 pm	**3:03 pm**
Jupiter	08/30/11	5:17 am	**2:17 am**	12/25/11	5:08 pm	**2:08 pm**
Mercury	11/23/11		**11:19 pm**	12/13/11	8:43 pm	**5:43 pm**
	11/24/11	2:19 am				

Eastern Time in plain type, **Pacific Time in bold type**

Egg-Setting Dates

To Have Eggs by this Date	Sign	Qtr.	Date to Set Eggs
Jan 7, 9:57 pm–Jan 10, 10:24 am	Pisces	1st	Dec 17, 2010
Jan 12, 10:37 pm–Jan 15, 8:23 am	Taurus	2nd	Dec 22, 2010
Jan 17, 2:29 pm–Jan 19, 4:21 pm	Cancer	2nd	Dec 27, 2010
Feb 4, 5:24 am–Feb 6, 5:45 pm	Pisces	1st	Jan 14, 2011
Feb 9, 6:22 am–Feb 11, 5:20 pm	Taurus	1st	Jan 19
Feb 14, 12:48 am–Feb 16, 4:14 am	Cancer	2nd	Jan 24
Mar 4, 3:46 pm–Mar 6, 12:14 am	Pisces	1st	Feb 11
Mar 8, 12:52 pm–Mar 11, 12:31 am	Taurus	1st	Feb 15
Mar 13, 10:29 am–Mar 15, 3:33 pm	Cancer	2nd	Feb 20
Apr 4, 7:46 pm–Apr 7, 7:22 am	Taurus	1st	Mar 14
Apr 9, 5:02 pm–Apr 11, 11:37 pm	Cancer	1st	Mar 19
Apr 16, 2:59 am–Apr 17, 10:44 pm	Libra	2nd	Mar 26
May 3, 2:51 am–May 4, 1:09 pm	Taurus	1st	Apr 12
May 6, 10:32 pm–May 9, 5:35 am	Cancer	1st	Apr 15
May 13, 11:56 am–May 15, 12:31 pm	Libra	2nd	Apr 22
Jun 3, 4:36 am–Jun 5, 11:03 am	Cancer	1st	May 13
Jun 9, 6:31 pm–Jun 11, 8:33 pm	Libra	2nd	May 19
Jul 1, 4:54 am–Jul 2, 5:43 pm	Cancer	1st	Jun 10
Jul 6, 11:54 pm–Jul 9, 2:31 am	Libra	1st	Jun 15
Aug 3, 6:04 am–Aug 5, 7:57 am	Libra	1st	Jul 13
Aug 30, 2:25 pm–Sep 1, 2:48 pm	Libra	1st	Aug 09
Sep 10, 3:26 pm–Sep 12, 5:27 am	Pisces	2nd	Aug 20
Sep 27, 7:09 am–Sep 29, 12:05 am	Libra	1st	Sep 06
Oct 7, 9:13 pm–Oct 10, 8:57 am	Pisces	2nd	Sep 16
Nov 4, 3:18 am–Nov 6, 2:02 pm	Pisces	2nd	Oct 14
Nov 9, 2:45 am–Nov 10, 3:16 pm	Taurus	2nd	Oct 19
Dec 1, 9:45 am–Dec 3, 8:51 pm	Pisces	1st	Nov 10
Dec 6, 9:34 am–Dec 8, 9:52 pm	Taurus	2nd	Nov 15
Dec 28, 6:45 pm–Dec 31, 4:48 am	Pisces	1st	Dec 07

Dates to Hunt and Fish

Date	Quarter	Sign
Jan 7, 9:57 pm–Jan 10, 10:24 am	1st	Pisces
Jan 17, 2:29 pm–Jan 19, 5:16 pm	2nd	Cancer
Jan 25, 9:15 pm–Jan 28, 1:55 am	3rd	Scorpio
Feb 4, 5:24 am–Feb 6, 5:45 pm	1st	Pisces
Feb 14, 12:48 am–Feb 16, 4:14 am	2nd	Cancer
Feb 22, 4:29 am–Feb 24, 7:46 am	3rd	Scorpio
Feb 24, 7:46 am–Feb 26, 2:32 pm	3rd	Sagittarius
Mar 3, 11:47 am–Mar 6, 12:14 am	4th	Pisces
Mar 13, 10:29 am–Mar 15, 3:33 pm	2nd	Cancer
Mar 21, 3:17 pm–Mar 23, 4:45 pm	3rd	Scorpio
Mar 23, 4:45 pm–Mar 25, 9:57 pm	3rd	Sagittarius
Mar 30, 6:38 pm–Apr 2, 7:16 am	4th	Pisces
Apr 9, 5:02 pm–Apr 11, 11:37 pm	1st	Cancer
Apr 18, 2:19 am–Apr 20, 2:50 am	3rd	Scorpio
Apr 20, 2:50 am–Apr 22, 6:24 am	3rd	Sagittarius
Apr 27, 12:57 am–Apr 29, 1:33 pm	4th	Pisces
May 6, 10:32 pm–May 9, 5:35 am	1st	Cancer
May 15, 12:31 pm–May 17, 1:22 pm	2nd	Scorpio
May 17, 1:22 pm–May 19, 4:16 pm	3rd	Sagittarius
May 24, 8:24 am–May 26, 8:36 pm	3rd	Pisces
Jun 3, 4:36 am–Jun 5, 11:03 am	1st	Cancer
Jun 11, 8:33 pm–Jun 13, 10:38 pm	2nd	Scorpio
Jun 13, 10:38 pm–Jun 16, 1:59 am	2nd	Sagittarius
Jun 20, 4:45 pm–Jun 23, 4:24 am	3rd	Pisces
Jun 23, 4:24 am–Jun 25, 4:53 pm	3rd	Aries
Jun 30, 12:13 pm–Jul 2, 5:43 pm	4th	Cancer
Jul 9, 2:31 am–Jul 11, 5:47 am	2nd	Scorpio
Jul 11, 5:47 am–Jul 13, 10:14 am	2nd	Sagittarius
Jul 18, 1:13 am–Jul 20, 12:25 pm	3rd	Pisces
Jul 20, 12:25 pm–Jul 23, 12:58 am	3rd	Aries
Jul 27, 9:11 pm–Jul 30, 2:16 am	4th	Cancer
Aug 5, 7:57 am–Aug 7, 11:21 am	1st	Scorpio
Aug 7, 11:21 am–Aug 9, 4:38 pm	2nd	Sagittarius
Aug 14, 8:54 am–Aug 16, 8:01 pm	3rd	Pisces
Aug 16, 8:01 pm–Aug 19, 8:36 am	3rd	Aries
Aug 24, 6:31 am–Aug 26, 12:09 pm	4th	Cancer
Sep 1, 2:48 pm–Sep 3, 5:03 pm	1st	Scorpio
Sep 10, 3:26 pm–Sep 13, 2:49 am	2nd	Pisces
Sep 13, 2:49 am–Sep 15, 3:25 am	3rd	Aries
Sep 20, 2:53 pm–Sep 22, 9:55 pm	4th	Cancer
Sep 29, 12:05 am–Oct 1, 12:42 am	1st	Scorpio
Oct 7, 9:13 pm–Oct 10, 8:57 am	2nd	Pisces
Oct 10, 8:57 am–Oct 12, 9:35 pm	2nd	Aries
Oct 17, 9:38 pm–Oct 20, 6:06 am	3rd	Cancer
Oct 26, 11:08 am–Oct 28, 10:45 am	4th	Scorpio
Nov 4, 3:18 am–Nov 6, 2:02 pm	2nd	Pisces
Nov 14, 2:19 am–Nov 16, 11:17 am	3rd	Cancer
Nov 22, 8:58 pm–Nov 24, 8:57 pm	4th	Scorpio
Dec 1, 9:45 am–Dec 3, 8:51 pm	1st	Pisces
Dec 3, 8:51 pm–Dec 6, 9:34 am	2nd	Aries
Dec 11, 8:26 am–Dec 13, 4:48 pm	3rd	Cancer
Dec 20, 5:33 am–Dec 22, 7:03 am	4th	Scorpio
Dec 28, 6:45 pm–Dec 31, 4:48 am	1st	Pisces

Dates to Destroy Weeds and Pests

From		To		Sign	Qtr.
Jan 19	5:16 pm	Jan 21	6:10 pm	Leo	3rd
Jan 21	6:10 pm	Jan 23	6:59 pm	Virgo	3rd
Jan 28	1:55 am	Jan 30	9:04 am	Sagittarius	4th
Feb 1	6:21 pm	Feb 2	9:31 pm	Aquarius	4th
Feb 18	3:36 am	Feb 18	4:39 am	Leo	3rd
Feb 18	4:39 am	Feb 20	4:01 am	Virgo	3rd
Feb 24	7:46 am	Feb 24	6:26 pm	Sagittarius	3rd
Feb 24	6:26 pm	Feb 26	2:32 pm	Sagittarius	4th
Mar 1	12:14 am	Mar 3	11:47 am	Aquarius	4th
Mar 19	2:10 pm	Mar 19	4:03 pm	Virgo	3rd
Mar 23	4:45 pm	Mar 25	9:57 pm	Sagittarius	3rd
Mar 28	7:00 am	Mar 30	6:38 pm	Aquarius	4th
Apr 2	7:16 am	Apr 3	10:32 am	Aries	4th
Apr 20	2:50 am	Apr 22	6:24 am	Sagittarius	3rd
Apr 24	1:59 am	Apr 24	10:47 pm	Aquarius	3rd
Apr 24	10:47 pm	Apr 27	12:57 am	Aquarius	4th
Apr 29	1:33 pm	May 2	1:58 am	Aries	4th
May 17	1:22 pm	May 19	4:16 pm	Sagittarius	3rd
May 21	10:32 pm	May 24	8:24 am	Aquarius	3rd
May 26	8:36 pm	May 29	9:02 am	Aries	4th
May 31	7:56 pm	Jun 1	5:03 pm	Gemini	4th
Jun 15	4:14 pm	Jun 16	1:59 am	Sagittarius	3rd
Jun 18	7:47 am	Jun 20	4:45 pm	Aquarius	3rd
Jun 23	4:24 am	Jun 23	7:48 am	Aries	3rd
Jun 23	7:48 am	Jun 25	4:53 pm	Aries	4th
Jun 28	3:56 am	Jun 30	12:13 pm	Gemini	4th
Jul 15	4:30 pm	Jul 18	1:13 am	Aquarius	3rd
Jul 20	12:25 pm	Jul 23	12:58 am	Aries	3rd
Jul 25	12:34 pm	Jul 27	9:11 pm	Gemini	4th
Jul 30	2:16 am	Jul 30	2:40 pm	Leo	4th
Aug 13	2:58 pm	Aug 14	8:54 am	Aquarius	3rd
Aug 16	8:01 pm	Aug 19	8:36 am	Aries	3rd
Aug 21	8:53 pm	Aug 24	6:31 am	Gemini	4th
Aug 26	12:09 pm	Aug 28	2:13 pm	Leo	4th
Aug 28	2:13 pm	Aug 28	11:04 pm	Virgo	4th
Sep 13	2:49 am	Sep 15	3:25 pm	Aries	3rd
Sep 18	4:06 am	Sep 20	9:39 am	Gemini	3rd
Sep 20	9:39 am	Sep 20	2:53 pm	Gemini	4th
Sep 22	9:55 pm	Sep 25	12:49 am	Leo	4th
Sep 25	12:49 am	Sep 27	12:51 am	Virgo	4th
Oct 11	10:06 pm	Oct 12	9:35 pm	Aries	3rd
Oct 15	10:15 am	Oct 17	9:38 pm	Gemini	3rd
Oct 20	6:06 am	Oct 22	10:40 am	Leo	4th
Oct 22	10:40 am	Oct 24	11:49 am	Virgo	4th
Nov 11	3:10 pm	Nov 14	2:19 am	Gemini	3rd
Nov 16	11:17 am	Nov 18	10:09 am	Leo	3rd
Nov 18	10:09 am	Nov 18	5:19 pm	Leo	4th
Nov 18	5:19 pm	Nov 20	8:16 pm	Virgo	4th
Nov 24	8:57 pm	Nov 25	1:10 am	Sagittarius	4th
Dec 10	9:36 am	Dec 11	8:26 am	Gemini	3rd
Dec 13	4:48 pm	Dec 15	10:58 pm	Leo	3rd
Dec 15	10:58 pm	Dec 17	7:48 pm	Virgo	3rd
Dec 17	7:48 pm	Dec 18	3:06 am	Virgo	4th
Dec 22	7:03 am	Dec 24	8:47 am	Sagittarius	4th

Time Zone Map

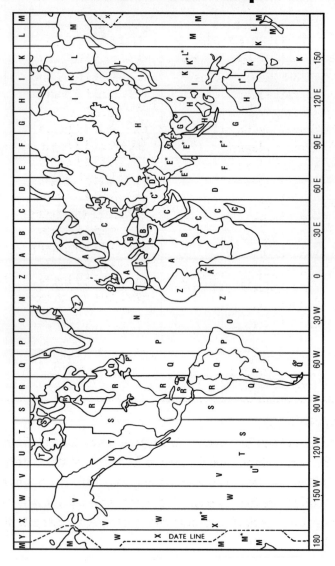

Time Zone Conversions

(R) EST—Used in book
(S) CST—Subtract 1 hour
(T) MST—Subtract 2 hours
(U) PST—Subtract 3 hours
(V) Subtract 4 hours
(V*) Subtract 4½ hours
(U*) Subtract 3½ hours
(W) Subtract 5 hours
(X) Subtract 6 hours
(Y) Subtract 7 hours
(Q) Add 1 hour
(P) Add 2 hours
(P*) Add 2½ hours
(O) Add 3 hours
(N) Add 4 hours
(Z) Add 5 hours
(A) Add 6 hours
(B) Add 7 hours
(C) Add 8 hours
(C*) Add 8½ hours

(D) Add 9 hours
(D*) Add 9½ hours
(E) Add 10 hours
(E*) Add 10½ hours
(F) Add 11 hours
(F*) Add 11½ hours
(G) Add 12 hours
(H) Add 13 hours
(I) Add 14 hours
(I*) Add 14½ hours
(K) Add 15 hours
(K*) Add 15½ hours
(L) Add 16 hours
(L*) Add 16½ hours
(M) Add 17 hours
(M*) Add 18 hours
(P*) Add 2½ hours

Important!

All times given in the *Moon Sign Book* are set in Eastern Time. The conversions shown here are for standard times only. Use the time zone conversions map and table to calculate the difference in your time zone. You must make the adjustment for your time zone and adjust for Daylight Saving Time where applicable.

Weather, Economic & Lunar Forecasts

2010 © JinYoung Lee. Image from BigStockPhoto.com

2010 © Jeff Davies. Image from BigStockPhoto.com

Forecasting the Weather

By Kris Brandt Riske

Astrometeorology—astrological weather forecasting—reveals seasonal and weekly weather trends based on the cardinal ingresses (Summer and Winter Solstices, and Spring and Autumn Equinoxes) and the four monthly lunar phases. The planetary alignments and the longitudes and latitudes they influence have the strongest effect, but the zodiacal signs are also involved in creating weather conditions.

The components of a thunderstorm, for example, are heat, wind, and electricity. A Mars-Jupiter configuration generates the necessary heat and Mercury adds wind and electricity. A severe thunderstorm, and those that produce tornados, usually involve Mercury, Mars, Uranus, or Neptune. The zodiacal signs add their energy to the planetary mix to increase or decrease the chance of weather phenomena and their severity.

In general, the fire signs (Aries, Leo, Sagittarius) indicate heat and dryness, both of which peak when Mars, the planet with a similar nature, is in these signs. Water signs (Cancer, Scorpio, Pisces) are conducive to precipitation, and air signs (Gemini, Libra, Aquarius) to cool temperatures and wind. Earth signs (Taurus, Virgo, Capricorn) vary from wet to dry, heat to cold. The signs and their prevailing weather conditions are listed here:

Aries: Heat, dry, wind
Taurus: Moderate temperatures, precipitation
Gemini: Cool temperatures, wind, dry
Cancer: Cold, steady precipitation
Leo: Heat, dry, lightning
Virgo: Cold, dry, windy
Libra: Cool, windy, fair
Scorpio: Extreme temperatures, abundant precipitation
Sagittarius: Warm, fair, moderate wind
Capricorn: Cold, wet, damp
Aquarius: Cold, dry, high pressure, lightning
Pisces: Wet, cool, low pressure

Take note of the Moon's sign at each lunar phase. It reveals the prevailing weather conditions for the next six to seven days. The same is true of Mercury and Venus. These two influential weather planets transit the entire zodiac each year, unless retrograde patterns add their influence.

Planetary Influences

People relied on astrology to forecast weather for thousands of years. They were able to predict drought, floods, and temperature variations through interpreting planetary alignments. In recent years there has been a renewed interest in astrometeorology. A weather forecast can be composed for any date—tomorrow, next week, or a thousand years in the future. According to astrometeorology, each planet governs certain weather phenomena. When certain planets are aligned with other planets, weather—precipitation, cloudy or clear skies, tornados, hurricanes, and other conditions—are generated.

Sun and Moon

The Sun governs the constitution of the weather and, like the Moon, it serves as a trigger for other planetary configurations that result in weather events. When the Sun is prominent in a cardinal ingress or lunar phase chart, the area is often warm and sunny. The Moon can bring or withhold moisture, depending upon its sign placement.

Mercury

Mercury is also a triggering planet, but its main influence is wind direction and velocity. In its stationary periods, Mercury reflects high winds, and its influence is always prominent in major weather events, such as hurricanes and tornados, when it tends to lower the temperature.

Venus

Venus governs moisture, clouds, and humidity. It brings warming trends that produce sunny, pleasant weather if in positive aspect to other planets. In some signs—Libra, Virgo, Gemini, Sagittarius—Venus is drier. It is at its wettest when placed in Cancer, Scorpio, Pisces, or Taurus.

Mars

Mars is associated with heat, drought, and wind, and can raise the temperature to record-setting levels when in a fire sign (Aries, Leo, Sagittarius). Mars ios also the planet that provides the spark that generates thunderstorms and is prominent in tornado and hurricane configurations.

Jupiter

Jupiter, a fair-weather planet, tends toward higher temperatures when in Aries, Leo, or Sagittarius. It is associated with high-pressure systems and is a contributing factor at times to dryness. Storms are often amplified by Jupiter.

Saturn

Saturn is associated with low-pressure systems, cloudy to over-cast skies, and excessive precipitation. Temperatures drop when Saturn is involved. Major winter storms always have a strong Saturn influence, as do storms that produce a slow, steady downpour for hours or days.

Uranus

Like Jupiter, Uranus indicates high-pressure systems. It reflects descending cold air and, when prominent, is responsible for a jet stream that extends far south. Uranus can bring drought in winter, and it is involved in thunderstorms, tornados, and hurricanes.

Neptune

Neptune is the wettest planet. It signals low-pressure systems and is dominant when hurricanes are in the forecast. When Neptune is strongly placed, flood danger is high. It's often associated with winter thaws. Temperatures, humidity, and cloudiness increase where Neptune influences weather.

Pluto

Pluto is associated with weather extremes, as well as unseasonably warm temperatures and drought. It reflects the high winds involved in major hurricanes, storms, and tornados.

2010 © Christina DeRidder. Image from BigStockPhoto.com

Temperatures Fall When Sun and Saturn Align

By Bruce Scofield

Today, when we turn to the news for weather forecasts, we often find them accurate for only a few days ahead, sometimes even less. In the past, weather forecasts were made years in advance by astrologers. Such forecasts were found—and still are, like those you find in this *Moon Sign Book*—in a special type of publication: the annual "farmer's" almanac. These almanacs, written by a number of authors over the centuries, have been among the most widely published writings of all time. They have been popular in both England and New England since the sixteenth century.

Until recently, nearly all farmer's almanacs contained weather forecasts based on geocentric planetary alignments called aspects. Typically, aspects in the zodiac by 0, 60, 90, 120 and 180 degrees were considered the most potent, these being the Ptolemaic aspects: conjunction, sextile, square/quadrature, trine, and opposition, respectively. In the tradition of almanac weather forecasting, the various geocentric aspects between the planets, Sun, and Moon were each associated with meteorological phenomena including heat, cold, rain, winds, and storms. One established family of alignments for predicting cold weather are the aspects between the Sun and Saturn. Here's what a sampling of astrologers from the past 750 years had to say about the Sun and Saturn in aspect:

Guido Bonatti (1210–1295): Whenever Saturn is joined to the Sun, the heat is remitted and the cold increased, which alone may be a sufficient testimony of the truth of astrology (*The Astrologer's Guide*).

Leonarde Digges (1520–1559): The conjunction, quadrature, or opposition of Saturn with the Sunne, chiefly in colde signs, snow, dark weather, haile, rayne, thunder, and cold days (*A Prognostication Everlasting*).

Johannes Kepler (1571–1630): The effect of this [Sun-Saturn] conjunction is quite general and gives nature at least an opportunity to cause turbulence in the air . . . this purifies the air, brings freezes, snow and rain. [Astrologers] . . . observe when Saturn stands opposite the Sun in the summertime, when no other planet is aspecting the Sun, and observe that the weather is cool and rainy (*Tertius Interventiens*, Theses 135 and 45).

John Goad (1616–1687): [Saturn and Sun] produce cold and frost and misty weather, clouds, and dark air with snow (*Astrometeorlogica*, p. 275).

Thomas Wilsford (seventeenth century): Saturn and Sun, in conjunction, square, or opposition, do cause generally rain, hail, and cold weather, both before and after, especially in the water signs, or in Sagittarius or Capricorn, and is called *Apertio Pota-rum*, or opening the Cataracts of Heaven. Particularly their effects in spring are cold showers; in summer, much thunder and storms of hail; in autumn, rain and cold; in winter, snow or moist, dark, and cloudy weather, and oftentimes frost (*Nature's Secrets*).

Ebenezer Sibly (1752–1799): Saturn and the Sun in conjunc-tion, quartile, or opposition is *Apertio Potarum*, especially if it happens in a moist constellation; for then, in the spring time, it threatens dark and heavy clouds; in summer, hail, thunder, and remission of heat; in autumn, rain and cold; in winter, frost and cloudy weather (*Illustration of the Astrological and Occult Sciences*).

Alfred John Pearce (1840–1923): Saturn's action, when con-figured with the Sun, is to condense aqueous vapour, to lower the temperature of the air, and to excite tempests. When the atmosphere happens to be quiescent under Saturn's ascendancy, it is often dark and foggy. When Saturn crosses the equator, the atmosphere is greatly disturbed and such effects last for several months (*The Text Book of Astrology*).

This compilation of historical sources shows that in addition to cold, frost, snow, hail, rain, thunder, fog, and dark clouds were also associated with the various aspects between the Sun and Saturn. Below is a table organizing the descriptions of the above authors, which shows that all agree on an association of cold with the Sun-Saturn aspects.

Source	Cold	Frost	Snow	Hail	Rain	Thunder	Fog	Dark Clouds
Bonatti	x							
Digges	x			x	x	x		x
Kepler	x	x	x		x			
Goad	x	x			x			
Wilsford	x	x	x	x	x	x		x
Sibley	x	x	x	x	x	x		x
Pearce	x						x	x

In times where no instruments (thermometers, barometers, etc.) were available to quantify weather data, meteorologists had to resort to descriptive language. In *Tertitus Interveniens*, essentially a discussion and debate between a skeptical doctor, a questioning scientist, and an astrologer, Kepler brings his arguments in favor of astrology to a climax by presenting a seventeen-year diary documenting the weather around the time of Sun-Saturn conjunctions. In the section of the diary below, Kepler lists the year and the dates, and then records his weather observations.

1599, 13th and 14th October in Libra. On the 12th, rain, cold. The 13th overcast, cold. The 14th cold, sunshine. From that time on the Sun and Moon appeared red through a heavy, smoke-like, low-lying material, in such a way that the high mountain tops protruded from it, as from fog. This became a general condition.

1600, the 24th and 25th of October in the beginning of Scorpio, in Prague. The 24th, rain and sunshine. The 25th, cold wind, freezing; the freeze lasted almost to the end of the month.

1601, the 5th & 6th of November, conjunction of Saturn, Sun and Mercury, the 1st wintry cold, 2nd strong wind, 3rd & 4th snow, 5th and 6th rain.

1602, the 17th of November at the end of Scorpio. The 16th fog, overcast. 17th fog, cold, then pleasant. 18th wintry cold, pleasant, because of a cold wind.

(*Tertius Interveniens*, Thesis 134, p. 196)

A half-century later, an amateur researcher named John Goad followed up on Kepler's study. He published his results in a massive book on astrology and weather forecasting, called *Astrometeorologica, or Aphorisms and Discourses of the Bodies Celestial, their Natures and Influences*, where he presented sections of his own weather diary that illustrated the effects of the individual planetary aspects. His diary listed the day of the month followed by a qualitative description of the weather. Here is a part of his daily record for the Sun-Saturn conjunction of October 25, 1660.

21. Frost, black thick clouds in S. Sun occ., clear and fair. E.N.
22. Frost, clear, some wind. N.E.
23. Cloudy, windy, Nly, fair 9 m. N.
24. Fair, windy. S.W.
25. Cold, windy, cloudy; frequent clouds in S.SW. NE.
26. Clouds curdled, close day. W.
27. Dry, cold wdy, Hail and R. 1 p. a shower 3 p.
28. Rain after mids. Cloudy.
29. Curdled clouds. N.

Some years ago, I decided to do some of my own investigating. First I obtained a listing of daily temperatures from the Shaler Meteorological Station at Harvard Forest, Petersham, Massachusetts, which has data from 1964 to 2002. Then, using SolarFire™ astrological software from Astrolabe, I computed the exact date of each of the Sun-Saturn Ptolemaic aspects, beginning with the conjunction. Then, from the database, I took twenty-one-day samples of daily weather centered on the day the aspect was exact. Finally, the daily mean of all the twenty-one-day records centered on the Sun-Saturn aspect was calculated for the entire thirty-nine-year period under study.

What I found was interesting. Of the Ptolemaic aspects, the one that stood out more than the others in indicating colder temperatures on or near the date of exactness was the opposition. Below is a graph showing this result. In this graph, the temperature dipped about a degree centigrade starting a few days before the aspect became exact, bottomed out the day before the aspect, and then rose rapidly, about 2 degrees, over the next few days. A similar effect was also found for the first square (equivalent to the first quarter of the Moon) but within a narrower temperature range. Here, the lowest temperature was also the day before the exact aspect. The other aspects were not as focused.

These results got me thinking that maybe a cooling effect has something to do with the distance between the Earth and

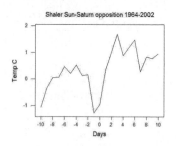

Saturn. When the Sun and Saturn are in opposition, geocentrically, the Sun is on one side of the Earth and Saturn on the other, which means the Earth is closest to Saturn then. The planets orbit in ellipses, not circles, and distances vary over time. These results suggested to me that during those times when the Earth is farthest from the Sun and Saturn was closest to Earth, there should be an even stronger effect. Saturn is at perigee (closest to Earth) in early July and so I retrieved the one opposition in my dataset that occurred then. I also reorganized my dataset so that the temperatures could be shown relative to the mean for the entire study period, so zero on the y-axis in the graph below is the mean. What the graph reveals is striking. At four days before the opposition became exact, the temperature began to fall, more than 10 degrees in just two days! The bottom was reached two days before the exact aspect and then the temperature began to climb again. What is one to make of this? Perhaps the behavior of temperatures relative to the aspect conforms to the old rule in astrology that states that forming aspects are more intense than separating ones.

I next decided to test whether Sun-Saturn oppositions and conjunctions were enhanced in any way if they occurred within two days of a New or Full Moon. There were fourteen such events in the database and the plot is shown below. Notice that the average temperature drops about 3 degrees in the days leading up to the exact aspect and bottoms out right on that day!

I next tested the parallel, not really an aspect, but a condition when two planets are at the same declination; that is, the same distance north or south of the equator. My results below show initial cold temperatures, a rise and then a drop two days before the exact aspect, but then another rise that begins even before the aspect closes. I then took the seven oppositions in the study period that were less than 3 degrees of declination, which means they occurred very close to the equinoxes. The results show a pronounced drop to a bottom on the day the parallel was exact!

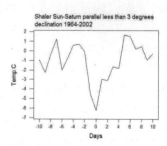

These results appear to indicate that oppositions between the Sun and Saturn do seem to coincide with falling temperatures, and more so when the two planets are close to each other. These effects are enhanced when the Full or New Moon falls near the same day as the Sun-Saturn opposition. Further, the parallel, especially under 3 degrees, shows a strong effect on the day the aspect is exact. All of this suggests to me that there is some kind of a gravitational influence involving Sun and Saturn, perhaps an atmospheric tide where the atmosphere is pulled out at low latitudes, just like the ocean tides. But when this happens, the atmosphere near the poles is flattened out and this could move cold air southward, down from Canada into New England. Another hint supporting this idea is that the oppositions with low declination, which occur near to the equinoxes, are at right angles to the poles of the Earth, making the tug on the polar air very precise.

In 2011, the Sun opposes Saturn on April 3. This is also the day of the New Moon. Perhaps this will mark a very cold period, but we should also consider that Jupiter is nearby as well and this, as some of my studies has shown, can modify the basic Sun-Saturn rule. It is possible that there could be cold with strong winds (Jupiter) or much precipitation. And it is possible the effects will be strongest a day or two before the aspect is exact. We shall see.

Atmospheric tides modulated by Saturn is just a speculation on what might be happening during a Sun-Saturn aspect. Certainly the effects would differ from place to place, but here in New England, it does seem to "work." But all of this is just an introduction to an interesting and complex astrological phenomenon. I have since taken my study much further along and to different climes, which I plan to report on in the future.

References

Bonatti, Guido. *The Astrologer's Guide.* Ed. William Lilly. n.p., 1675.

Digges, Leonarde. *A Prognostication Everlasting.* London, 1605.

Goad, John. *Astrometeorologica, or Aphorism and Discourses of the Bodies Celestial, their Natures and Influences.* London: J. Rawlins, 1686.

Henninger, S. K., Jr. *A Handbook of Renaissance Meteorology.* Durham, NC: Duke University Press, 1960.

Kepler, Johannes. *Concerning the More Certain Fundamentals of Astrology.* New York: Holmes Publishing Group, 1987.

————. *Tertius Interveniens*. In *Kepler's Astrology,* trans. Ken Negus. Amherst, MA: Earth Heart Publications, 2008.

Pearce, Alfred John. *The Text Book of Astrology*. Phoenix, AZ: American Federation of Astrology, 2006.

Sibley, Ebenezer. *Illustration of the Occult Sciences*. London, 1791.

Wilsford, Thomas. *Nature's Secrets*. London, 1665.

About the Author

Bruce Scofield is a practicing astrologer who has maintained a private practice as an astrological consultant and conference speaker for over forty years. He is the author of seven books and hundreds of articles on astrology. He has served on the education committee of the National Council for Geocosmic Research since 1979 and was that organization's national education director between 1998 and 2003. He holds a master's degree in history and a Ph.D. in geosciences, and currently teaches at Kepler College and at the University of Massachusetts. Bruce Scofield and Barry Orr maintain a website, www.onereed.com, that contains articles and an online calculation program on Mesoamerican (Maya and Aztec) astrology.

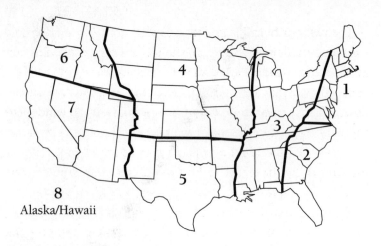

Weather Forecast for 2011

By Kris Brandt Riske

Winter 2011

The northeastern part of the country (zone 1) will be prone to low-pressure systems and resulting abundant downfall, as well as more cloudy days and temperatures below seasonal. Southern areas of the zone will also see cold temperatures as a result of descending cold air, which could trigger ice storms. Parts of zone 2 (Georgia and Florida) can expect more precipitation along with an increased number of cloudy days as a result of weather systems moving southeast from Canada.

Northeastern areas of zone 3 will also experience increased cold Arctic air and low-pressure fronts with high winds. This area is also prone to periodic thaws with flood potential. Central areas of zone 3 will have more days that are very cold, again as a result of Arctic air. Western areas, although not quite as cold, can still expect temperatures to dip. Precipitation will be normal to above, and southerly winds will at times bring unusually warm weather prior to a major downfall.

The vast northern Plains that comprise zone 4 will have cold weather overall, while central areas can expect precipitation normal to above and more seasonal temperatures. Eastern areas of the zone will be windy with significant storms, some with abundant downfall, very cold temperatures, and periods of high winds. The southern Plains states (zone 5) will also experience cold weather with the most abundant precipitation in central Texas. Many of the storms that traverse the Plains will enter the country from Canada as low-pressure systems originating north of Montana.

Western parts of zone 6 can expect periods of chilly weather, but conditions will be more seasonal in central and eastern areas, where abundant downfall will be more the norm than the exception. Northeastern areas of zone 7 will experience periods of very cold temperatures along with high winds and abundant moisture in the mountains. Central areas of zone 7 will be mostly seasonal, while western parts of the zone can expect cool, cloudy weather and periods of abundant downfall.

Winter in Alaska will be generally seasonal, with more cloudiness, major storms, and precipitation in central parts of the state. Western and central parts of Hawaii will see above-normal precipitation and cooler temperatures at times, and eastern areas of the state will be generally seasonal.

January 4–11, New Moon
Zone 1: The zone is windy and cloudy with precipitation and seasonal temperatures.

Zone 2: Much of the zone sees precipitation and wind with seasonal temperatures.

Zone 3: Temperatures are seasonal to below as cloudy, windy skies bring precipitation (some abundant) across the zone.

Zone 4: A front brings precipitation, some abundant, to northwestern parts of the zone and advancing into the western Plains; temperatures are cold but more seasonal in eastern areas, which also see precipitation.

Zone 5: The zone is cold as Arctic air slips south, bringing precipitation to western and central areas; eastern parts of the zone are windy and more seasonal with variable cloudiness.

Zone 6: Western and central areas are windy with variable cloudiness and temperatures seasonal to below; temperatures are more seasonal east but it is windy under fair to partly cloudy skies.

Zone 7: Northern coastal areas are windy with precipitation and fog, central parts of the zone are windy, and eastern areas see precipitation, some abundant; temperatures are seasonal to below.

Zone 8: Western and central Alaska are cold and windy with abundant snowfall in some areas; eastern parts of the state are more seasonal. Hawaii is windy and cool as a front advances, bringing precipitation.

January 12–18, 2nd Quarter Moon

Zone 1: Temperatures are seasonal to below and the zone is mostly fair and windy, with a front moving in later in the week.

Zone 2: Northern areas are windy with a chance for precipitation, central and southern areas are variably cloudy and windy with possible severe storms, and temperatures are seasonal to below.

Zone 3: Western and central parts of the zone are overcast with scattered precipitation and temperatures ranging from seasonal to below, with eastern areas seeing precipitation later in the week; southern areas may have severe thunderstorms.

Zone 4: Stormy conditions and cold temperatures accompany abundant precipitation west, central areas are more seasonal and fair to partly cloudy, and eastern areas are cloudy and seasonal.

Zone 5: Western areas are very windy and cold, with weather activity moving into central parts of the zone; seasonal temperatures and partly cloudy skies prevail in the east.

Zone 6: Western and central parts of the zone are cloudy and windy with precipitation, and eastern areas are fair; temperatures range from seasonal to below.

2010 © Marilena Morariu. Image from BigStockPhoto.com

Zone 7: Temperatures are seasonal to below and conditions are windy with precipitation west later in the week; central areas are windy and variably cloudy, and eastern parts of the zone are fair.

Zone 8: Alaska is seasonal to below and mostly fair with cloudiness and scattered precipitation central. Hawaii is fair to partly cloudy and seasonal.

January 19–26, Full Moon

Zone 1: The zone is windy and cold with precipitation later in the week as a front moves into the area.

Zone 2: The zone is cold and fair to partly cloudy.

Zone 3: Temperatures are seasonal west under partly cloudy and windy skies, northern areas see scattered precipitation, and eastern areas are cold.

Zone 4: Western areas are cloudy with precipitation, the western Plains are variably cloudy and cold, and the eastern Plains are more seasonal.

Zone 5: The zone is partly cloudy west, windy and fair central, and eastern areas see precipitation followed by clearing and colder temperatures.

Zone 6: Much of the zone is cloudy and windy, with precipitation (some abundant); temperatures are seasonal to below.

Zone 7: Coastal and central areas are cloudy with temperatures seasonal to below; some eastern areas see abundant precipitation.

Zone 8: Western Alaska is windy with a front that advances into central areas under overcast skies and temperatures are seasonal to below; eastern areas are more seasonal. Hawaii sees variable cloudiness and cooler temperatures in eastern areas.

January 26–February 1, 3rd Quarter Moon

Zone 1: The zone is mostly fair; temperatures seasonal to below.

Zone 2: Northern areas are fair to partly cloudy, and central and southern are seasonal with more clouds and a chance of precipitation.

Zone 3: The zone is mostly fair with more cloudiness and scattered precipitation east; temperatures warm as the week unfolds.

Zone 4: Precipitation prevails to the west, and central and eastern parts of the zone are fair to partly cloudy with a chance for precipitation; temperatures are seasonal to below.

Zone 5: Western skies are windy with scattered precipitation that moves eastward into central areas of the zone, and eastern areas are partly cloudy; temperatures are seasonal to below.

Zone 6: Weather activity moves across much of the zone, bringing precipitation that could be heavy at higher elevations, while easternmost areas are fair to partly cloudy.

Zone 7: Northern coastal areas are cloudy with precipitation; southern coastal, central, and eastern parts of the zone have a chance for precipitation.

Zone 8: Eastern Alaska is cold with precipitation, and western and central areas are fair to partly cloudy with below-seasonal temperatures. Hawaii is mostly fair and seasonal with clouds and showers developing later in the week west and central.

February 2–10, New Moon

Zone 1: The zone sees cold temperatures, high winds, and precipitation (some abundant).

Zone 2: Much of the zone is cold with precipitation, including the potential for an ice storm.

Zone 3: Western skies are fair, and central and eastern areas see precipitation, some abundant, followed by cold temperatures.

Zone 4: Central areas are windy and cold with variable cloudiness and a chance for precipitation, eastern areas are fair, and western skies are fair to partly cloudy with a chance for precipitation later in the week; temperatures are seasonal to below.

Zone 5: Temperatures are seasonal and skies are fair west, with variable cloudiness and wind in central and eastern areas.

Zone 6: Much of the zone sees precipitation, some abundant; temperatures range from seasonal to below.

Zone 7: Northern coastal precipitation moves eastward, bringing abundant downfalls to some central areas, while eastern parts of the zone have a chance for precipitation; temperatures are seasonal to below.

Zone 8: Central Alaska is windy and overcast with precipitation that moves into eastern areas; temperatures are much colder west with precipitation. Hawaii is seasonal to below with variable cloudiness, and central areas are windy.

February 11–17, 2nd Quarter Moon

Zone 1: Cold and windy with fair to partly cloudy skies.

Zone 2: Much of the zone is windy and seasonal, with fair skies north and some cloudiness south.

Zone 3: Cloudiness prevails across the zone with cooler temperatures west.

Zone 4: Western areas see precipitation followed by colder temperatures, and clouds increase in the Plains as weather activity moves into the area with the potential for abundant snowfall.

Zone 5: Skies are fair to partly cloudy with more clouds central and east; temperatures are seasonal to below.

Zone 6: Western parts of the zone are fair to partly cloudy with a chance for precipitation, and central and eastern areas are cold with precipitation.

Zone 7: The zone is generally fair and windy with temperatures seasonal to below.

Zone 8: Central and western Alaska are very cold with precipitation, and eastern parts of the state are mostly fair and seasonal. Hawaii is fair west and central, with precipitation in the east; temperatures are seasonal to above.

February 18–23, Full Moon

Zone 1: Windy conditions prevail across much of the zone with variable cloudiness.

Zone 2: Northern areas are windy and fair to partly cloudy, while central and southern areas are cloudy with precipitation (some abundant) and strong thunderstorms with tornado potential.

Zone 3: The zone is windy as a front brings precipitation, some abundant; southern areas could see strong thunderstorms with tornado potential; temperatures are seasonal to below.

Zone 4: Fair to partly cloudy skies across the zone accompany seasonal temperatures, but eastern areas are colder and windy.

Zone 5: Western skies are fair, and central and eastern areas see some cloudiness with a chance for precipitation.

Zone 6: Fair to partly cloudy skies precede a front that moves into coastal areas at week's end with potential for significant precipitation; central and eastern areas are fair to partly cloudy and seasonal.

Zone 7: Western and central areas are windy with variable cloudiness, and eastern areas are cloudy with a chance for precipitation; temperatures are seasonal.

Zone 8: Alaska's temperatures are seasonal to below and skies are fair to partly cloudy. Hawaii is mostly fair and seasonal.

February 24–March 3, 3rd Quarter Moon

Zone 1: Seasonal temperatures accompany partly cloudy skies north and scattered precipitation south.

Zone 2: The zone is mostly fair to partly cloudy with more clouds and precipitation in some southern and central areas.

Zone 3: Much of the zone is windy, southern areas see strong thunderstorms with tornado potential, and western areas have a chance for precipitation.

Zone 4: The zone is fair to partly cloudy and windy with scattered precipitation; temperatures range from seasonal to below.

Zone 5: Most of the zone is fair to partly cloudy, but eastern areas see precipitation (some abundant) later in the week; temperatures are seasonal to below.

Zone 6: Western precipitation moves into central areas, followed by colder temperatures, and eastern parts of the zone are windy with some cloudiness; temperatures seasonal to below.

Zone 7: Northern coastal and central areas of the zone see precipitation, with the rest of the zone mostly fair and windy; temperatures are seasonal to below.

Zone 8: Western Alaska sees high winds and precipitation, which moves into central areas of the zone; eastern areas also see precipitation, followed by clear skies. Hawaii is mostly fair and seasonal with a chance for scattered showers west and central.

March 4–11, New Moon

Zone 1: The zone is seasonal with fair to partly cloudy skies and precipitation south later in the week.

Zone 2: Seasonal temperatures accompany precipitation across much of the zone.

Zone 3: Western skies are fair to partly cloudy, central and eastern areas see precipitation, and temperatures are seasonal.

Zone 4: Western areas are very windy, and the rest of the zone is variably cloudy with precipitation east.

Zone 5: The zone is variably cloudy with scattered precipitation central and east.

Zone 6: Much of the zone is windy with temperatures seasonal to below.

Zone 7: Northern coastal areas see scattered precipitation with increasing cloudiness in all but eastern areas, which brings precipitation to northern parts of the zone; eastern areas are fair to partly cloudy.

Zone 8: Western and central Alaska are cloudy with precipitation and eastern areas are mostly fair; temperatures are seasonal to below. Hawaii is variably cloudy and seasonal with western areas seeing showers later in the week.

March 12–18, 2nd Quarter Moon

Zone 1: Northern areas are cold with a chance for precipitation; temperatures are not as cold to the south, which sees scattered precipitation.

Zone 2: The zone has a chance for precipitation and temperatures are seasonal.

Zone 3: Western areas have a chance for thunderstorms, which could be strong, and central areas may see precipitation, but the zone is generally fair to partly cloudy and seasonal.

Zone 4: Northwestern areas see precipitation later in the week, and the zone is very windy and mostly fair to partly cloudy.

Zone 5: Fair to partly cloudy skies and temperatures ranging from seasonal to above prevail across the zone, and eastern areas could see strong thunderstorms.

Zone 6: Western and central parts of the zone see precipitation and clouds increase to the east later in the week; temperatures are seasonal to below.

Zone 7: Variable cloudiness prevails to the west with precipitation in northern coastal areas that moves east, bringing abundant downfall to some areas, primarily north; temperatures are seasonal to below.

Zone 8: Central Alaska is cloudy with precipitation (some abundant), and western and eastern areas are mostly fair; temperatures are seasonal to below. Hawaii is fair to partly cloudy with temperatures ranging from seasonal to above.

Spring 2011

Despite the arrival of spring, winter will persist in northern areas of zone 1, with very cold temperatures. Southern areas of the zone will be more seasonal but also chilly. In zone 2, temperatures will also be seasonal to below, and inland locations in the Carolinas will see more cloudy, damp weather with potential for abundant precipitation.

Low-pressure systems will bring abundant precipitation to central and northeastern areas of zone 3. Areas from Indiana south to Alabama will see periods of severe thunderstorms as well as precipitation ranging from seasonal to above. Southwestern areas of the zone will also be prone to severe thunderstorms.

In zone 4, storm systems will enter the United States in mid-Montana and western Minnesota, moving south. Planetary alignments also indicate temperatures below normal in western and central parts of the zone, which could affect crops in the form of periods of abundant precipitation and cloudy skies. Eastern areas will see more seasonal temperatures along with strong to severe thunderstorms with tornado potential. Zone 5, although generally more seasonal, will also experience temperatures below normal with abundant precipitation at times. Eastern areas have an increased chance for severe thunderstorms and tornados.

Overall, zone 6 will see more than the usual amount of precipitation along with cool temperatures. To the south, central areas of zone 7 will see elevated precipitation levels, and eastern areas will be windy and seasonal. Western areas of zone 7 will be warmer than normal and generally fair, especially to the south.

Temperatures in central Alaska will be seasonal to below, as this area is prone to low-pressure systems and abundant precipitation.

Western Alaska will be cold with precipitation from normal to above, and eastern parts of the state will be seasonal. Eastern Alaska will be windy, and periods of fair weather will alternate with those producing abundant precipitation.

March 19–25, Full Moon

Zone 1: Southern areas are overcast with precipitation that moves into the north; temperatures are seasonal to below.

Zone 2: Cloudy skies bring precipitation across much of the zone with temperatures seasonal to below.

Zone 3: Cold air dips south in western areas of the zone, bringing precipitation; eastern areas are cloudy but more seasonal with precipitation.

Zone 4: Temperatures are seasonal to below under variably cloudy skies west and central, and eastern areas see cooler temperatures and precipitation.

Zone 5: The zone is variably cloudy, and rising temperatures and

2010 © Victor Zastol'skiy. Image from BigStockPhoto.com

wind central and east could trigger strong thunderstorms with tornado potential.

Zone 6: Western and central areas of the zone see precipitation with the heaviest downfall central, and eastern areas are fair.

Zone 7: Mostly cloudy skies west and central yield precipitation, while eastern areas are fair and windy with a chance for precipitation; temperatures are seasonal but warmer in the desert.

Zone 8: Alaska is fair to partly cloudy with temperatures seasonal to below. Hawaii is seasonal with mostly fair skies.

March 26–April 2, 3rd Quarter Moon

Zone 1: Northern skies are fair with more clouds south, where it is windy with scattered precipitation.

Zone 2: The zone is cloudy with precipitation, some locally heavy in the central and southern areas.

Zone 3: Western areas are fair and cold, and central and eastern areas are cloudy with seasonal temperatures and potential for significant precipitation.

Zone 4: Temperatures are seasonal to below with coldest temperatures under fair eastern skies; western areas are fair, and central parts of the zone are windy and cloudy.

Zone 5: The zone is variably cloudy and windy, with scattered precipitation and thunderstorms central and east.

Zone 6: Western areas are windy, and much of the zone sees precipitation under variably cloudy skies with potential for significant downfall in central areas.

Zone 7: Western areas are windy with precipitation that moves into central parts of the zone, with potential for abundant downfall in the mountains, and eastern areas are partly cloudy; temperatures are seasonal to below.

Zone 8: Western Alaska sees precipitation followed by much colder temperatures, central areas see scattered precipitation, and eastern areas are fair and seasonal. Hawaii is windy with scattered showers across much of the state, and temperatures are seasonal.

April 3–10, New Moon

Zone 1: The zone sees precipitation followed by clearing and colder temperatures.

Zone 2: Cloudy skies prevail across much of the zone with potential for significant downfall; temperatures are seasonal to below.

Zone 3: Western areas see thunderstorms, central and eastern areas have scattered precipitation, and a low-pressure system could yield significant precipitation in northeastern areas; temperatures are seasonal to below.

Zone 4: Precipitation concentrates on central and eastern areas of the zone with variable cloudiness and potential for strong thunderstorms, while western areas are fair to partly cloudy; temperatures range from seasonal to below.

Zone 5: Eastern areas see strong thunderstorms with tornado potential, central areas have a chance for precipitation, and western areas are mostly fair; temperatures are seasonal to below.

Zone 6: Eastern areas see precipitation (some abundant), which moves into central areas under increasingly cloudy skies, while eastern parts of the zone are partly cloudy with scattered precipitation; temperatures are seasonal to below.

Zone 7: Northern areas of western and central parts of the zone see precipitation, and southern and eastern areas are mostly fair; temperatures range from seasonal to above.

Zone 8: Precipitation in western and central Alaska is heaviest west, and eastern areas see precipitation followed by clearing and colder temperatures. Hawaii is fair to partly cloudy with scattered showers and seasonal temperatures.

April 11–16, 2nd Quarter Moon

Zone 1: The zone is windy under fair to partly cloudy skies with scattered precipitation and temperatures ranging from seasonal to below.

Zone 2: Central and southern parts of the zone have a chance for showers, and the zone is fair to partly cloudy and seasonal.

Zone 3: Western areas see thunderstorms, some strong with tornado potential, central areas are fair, and eastern areas are fair to partly cloudy with scattered precipitation; temperatures are seasonal.

Zone 4: Western areas are very windy, and the Plains see increasing clouds and precipitation; temperatures are seasonal to below.

Zone 5: Temperatures are seasonal to below, central and eastern areas have potential for strong thunderstorms and tornados, and western areas are fair and windy.

Zone 6: Western and central parts of the zone are windy with precipitation, and eastern areas are fair to partly cloudy; temperatures are seasonal to below.

Zone 7: Central areas see precipitation, which is scattered west, eastern areas are fair, and temperatures are seasonal to above.

Zone 8: Alaska sees precipitation with high winds central and east; temperatures are seasonal to below. Hawaii is fair to partly cloudy and seasonal with a chance for showers central and east.

April 17–23, Full Moon

Zone 1: Cloudy northern skies yield abundant precipitation in some areas, southern areas are variably cloudy with scattered precipitation, and temperatures are seasonal.

Zone 2: Northern areas are fair and seasonal, and southern areas are partly cloudy with scattered precipitation.

Zone 3: The zone is seasonal and fair to partly cloudy, but with more cloud cover central with scattered precipitation.

Zone 4: Western areas are fair under high pressure, and central and eastern areas are cloudy, with some areas receiving abundant precipitation with flood potential.

Zone 5: Western skies are fair, and central and eastern parts of the zone are variably cloudy with precipitation heaviest in eastern areas, which could see flooding.

Zone 6: The zone is fair to partly cloudy, with more clouds east accompanied by wind and precipitation; temperatures are seasonal but cooler central and east.

Zone 7: Western and central areas are fair, eastern areas are variably cloudy with a chance for precipitation, and southeastern parts of the zone are very windy.

Zone 8: Central and eastern Alaska are cold and stormy with abundant downfall in some areas, and western areas are fair and seasonal. Hawaii sees showers and seasonal temperatures.

April 24–May 2, 3rd Quarter Moon

Zone 1: Northern areas see precipitation, skies are fair to the south, and temperatures are seasonal.

Zone 2: The zone is fair to partly cloudy and seasonal with a chance for thunderstorms central and south.

Zone 3: Skies are partly cloudy with a chance for precipitation, and temperatures are seasonal.

Zone 4: Western areas are windy and cloudy with potential for heavy downfall, central and eastern areas are variably cloudy, and temperatures are seasonal.

Zone 5: Variable cloudiness prevails across the zone with scattered thunderstorms central and east.

Zone 6: Western parts of the zone are cloudy and cool with scattered precipitation developing later in the week, while eastern areas are windy with scattered precipitation; temperatures are seasonal to below.

Zone 7: Much of the zone is cloudy with precipitation, but eastern areas are variably cloudy; temperatures are seasonal to above.

Zone 8: Eastern and western areas are fair to partly cloudy and seasonal, and central parts of Alaska are windy, cloudy, and cold with abundant precipitation in some areas. Hawaii is seasonal with showers.

May 3–9, New Moon

Zone 1: The zone is variably cloudy and windy with a chance of thunderstorms south.

Zone 2: The zone is windy with scattered thunderstorms and showers, and temperatures are seasonal to above.

Zone 3: Scattered clouds bring precipitation with a greater chance for downfall central and east along with scattered thunderstorms, some possibly strong.

Zone 4: The zone is fair to partly cloudy with a high-pressure system in the Plains, eastern areas see more cloudiness with a chance for showers, and temperatures are seasonal to above.

Zone 5: Temperatures are seasonal to above across the zone, which is fair to partly cloudy.

Zone 6: The zone is fair with temperatures ranging from seasonal to above.

Zone 7: Seasonal to above temperatures accompany fair skies.

Zone 8: Alaska is fair and seasonal, with precipitation in western areas later in the week. Hawaii is windy, fair, and seasonal.

May 10–16, 2nd Quarter Moon

Zone 1: Northern areas are partly cloudy and seasonal, and southern areas are cloudy and cool.

Zone 2: Weather is cloudy, windy, and cool in northern parts of the zone, but mostly fair in the south with a chance for scattered thunderstorms.

Zone 3: Western and central parts of the zone are fair and humid, and eastern areas are cloudy and cooler.

Zone 4: Temperatures are seasonal to above under fair to partly cloudy skies.

Zone 5: The zone is mostly fair with temperatures ranging from seasonal to above.

Zone 6: Variable clouds across the zone accompany a chance for precipitation west and central with seasonal temperatures.

Zone 7: The zone is variably cloudy with temperatures seasonal to above.

Zone 8: Alaska is cloudy west, fair central and east, and seasonal. Hawaii is fair with temperatures seasonal to above.

May 17–23, Full Moon

Zone 1: Northern areas see increasing clouds with precipitation (some abundant), and skies are fair to partly cloudy south; temperatures are seasonal to above.

Zone 2: Central and southern areas are humid and fair to partly cloudy, with more cloudiness north; zonal temperatures are seasonal to above.

Zone 3: Western parts of the zone are variably cloudy with showers, central areas are fair, and eastern areas see some cloudiness; temperatures are seasonal to above.

Zone 4: Western skies are fair, central parts of the zone are cloudy with scattered precipitation, and the eastern Plains have potential for strong scattered thunderstorms; temperatures are seasonal to above, but cooler east with more cloudiness and showers.

Zone 5: Temperatures across the zone are seasonal to above and skies are fair west, while central and eastern areas have potential for strong thunderstorms.

Zone 6: Cloudy western and central skies yield precipitation (some abundant), and eastern areas are partly cloudy; temperatures are seasonal.

Zone 7: Western parts of the zone are variably cloudy, with more cloudiness north and into central areas, and fair to partly cloudy skies east; temperatures are seasonal to above.

Zone 8: Western Alaska sees precipitation, some abundant, and then cooler temperatures, and the rest of the state is mostly fair and seasonal. Hawaii is mostly fair and seasonal, with clouds and scattered precipitation east.

May 24–31, 3rd Quarter Moon

Zone 1: Temperatures are seasonal to above and the zone is humid and mostly fair.

Zone 2: The zone is fair with temperatures seasonal to above and a chance of thunderstorms.

Zone 3: Humid conditions accompany temperatures seasonal to above, fair skies, and a chance for thunderstorms east.

Zone 4: The zone is fair to partly cloudy with temperatures ranging from seasonal to above and a chance for scattered thunderstorms in the Plains.

Zone 5: Temperatures are seasonal to above and variably cloudy with a chance for scattered thunderstorms central and east.

Zone 6: Western and central areas see precipitation, and clouds increase to the east with potential for abundant downfall; temperatures are seasonal.

Zone 7: Northern coastal areas see showers, eastern areas are partly cloudy, and other areas of the zone are mostly fair; temperatures are seasonal to above.

Zone 8: Central Alaska is overcast with high winds and abundant precipitation in some areas, western parts of the zone see precipitation, and eastern areas are fair. Hawaii is fair to partly cloudy with temperatures seasonal to above.

June 1–7, New Moon

Zone 1: The zone is fair to partly cloudy, seasonal, and windy.

Zone 2: Northern areas have a chance for showers, and southern and central areas a chance for thunderstorms.

Zone 3: Temperatures are seasonal to above and the zone is mostly fair and humid with a chance for thunderstorms.

Zone 4: Western skies are variably cloudy with a chance for precipitation, and central and eastern areas have a chance for thunderstorms, possibly strong with tornado potential; temperatures are seasonal to above.

Zone 5: Central and eastern areas are humid with scattered thunderstorms, some strong with tornado potential, and western parts of the zone are cloudy and windy with precipitation; temperatures are seasonal to above.

Zone 6: The zone is mostly fair with temperatures seasonal to above, and eastern areas are windy.

Zone 7: Temperatures seasonal to above accompany fair to partly cloudy skies.

Zone 8: Alaska is cloudy with precipitation central and east, and fair west; temperatures are seasonal. Hawaii is fair to partly cloudy with scattered precipitation and temperatures seasonal to above.

June 8–14, 2nd Quarter Moon

Zone 1: The zone is partly cloudy and seasonal with scattered rain showers.

Zone 2: Temperatures are seasonal to above, northern areas are partly cloudy, and central and southern parts of the zone are humid with scattered thunderstorms.

Zone 3: Humidity accompanies temperatures seasonal to above, and western areas have a chance for strong thunderstorms.

Zone 4: Eastern and central areas are humid with scattered thunderstorms, some strong with tornado potential, and temperatures are seasonal to above.

Zone 5: The zone is variably cloudy with temperatures seasonal to above, and scattered thunderstorms could be strong.

Zone 6: The zone is mostly fair and windy with temperatures seasonal to above.

Zone 7: Humidity rises in eastern areas, and the zone is fair and windy with temperatures seasonal to above.

Zone 8: Alaska is mostly fair and seasonal and windy west. Hawaii is breezy and seasonal with fair skies.

June 15–22, Full Moon

Zone 1: The zone is fair to partly cloudy and seasonal with a chance for showers.

Zone 2: Northern areas are fair to partly cloudy and seasonal, and central and southern areas are humid and seasonal to above with strong thunderstorms and tornado potential.

Zone 3: Scattered thunderstorms west and central could produce tornadoes, and areas to the east see more clouds with scattered showers; the zone is humid with temperatures seasonal to above.

Zone 4: Western skies are cloudy, eastern areas see thunderstorms with tornado potential, and the zone is humid and seasonal.

Zone 5: The zone is seasonal and humid, western areas are cloudy with precipitation, and central and eastern parts of the zone have a chance for scattered showers.

Zone 6: The zone is windy with variable clouds, scattered showers, and temperatures seasonal to above.

Zone 7: Fair to partly cloudy skies and windy conditions accompany temperatures seasonal to above; desert areas are hot.

Zone 8: Alaska is windy and seasonal with precipitation, some abundant in central areas. Much of Hawaii is cloudy and seasonal with showers.

Summer 2011

Weather extremes will dominate in northern areas of zone 1, mostly unseasonably cool but with periods of heat; this zone could experience hurricane effects. Southern areas will see high temperatures and abundant precipitation at times, along with strong thunderstorms, but dryness will be a trend. Zone 2 should see more precipitation and there is potential for severe thunderstorms and tornados. Planetary alignments indicate strong thunderstorm and tornado potential in central and eastern areas of zone 3, while western parts of that zone will be mostly seasonal.

Temperatures in eastern and western areas of zone 4 will range from seasonal to above, along with a tendency for dryness. Central areas, however, will be cooler with more cloudiness and precipitation. Much of zone 5, especially central areas, will see precipitation range from seasonal to above, with seasonal temperatures.

Zone 6 will be mostly seasonal but with a tendency for more low-pressure systems in eastern parts of the zone. Central areas of zone 7 will be more humid than usual, with high temperatures and potential for severe thunderstorms. Eastern areas will be hot and dry. Temperatures will be generally on the high side, with periods of dryness and wind that indicate strong potential for fires. However, the area also will see some periods that are seasonally cool with precipitation.

Western Alaska can expect temperatures below seasonal along with extended periods of cloudiness and precipitation. Central and eastern parts of the state will be generally seasonal, with eastern areas seeing above-normal precipitation. Summer temperatures in Hawaii will be seasonal to above, with precipitation

2010 © Phil Morley. Image from BigStockPhoto.com

seasonal to below. Western areas will be windy with a greater chance for precipitation.

June 23–30, 3rd Quarter Moon

Zone 1: The zone is variably cloudy with precipitation, some locally heavy to the south, and temperatures are seasonal to below.

Zone 2: The zone is cloudy, especially in coastal areas where downfall is heavy, and high winds could accompany severe thunderstorms; temperatures are seasonal to below.

Zone 3: Humidity rises across the zone, where temperatures are seasonal to above in all but eastern areas, which are cloudy and cooler with precipitation; western and central areas could see strong thunderstorms with tornado potential.

Zone 4: The zone is windy and fair to partly cloudy west with rising temperatures, the Plains see scattered precipitation and thunderstorms, and eastern areas are humid with thunderstorm potential; temperatures are seasonal to above.

Zone 5: Much of the zone is windy and humid with scattered thunderstorms, possibly strong central and east, and seasonal temperatures.

Zone 6: Western areas of the zone are fair to partly cloudy with scattered precipitation later in the week, higher elevations are seasonal but cool, and central and eastern areas are windy with precipitation, some abundant.

Zone 7: Western and central areas are seasonal with variable cloudiness and showers, some heavy in central areas, and fair and windy east with high temperatures.

Zone 8: Alaska is fair central and east, and cloudy with precipitation west; temperatures are seasonal. Hawaii is fair and warm, but becoming windy and cooler with scattered precipitation later in the week.

July 1–7, New Moon

Zone 1: The zone is variably cloudy and windy with precipitation, possibly heavy from strong thunderstorms.

Zone 2: Northern and central coastal areas could see abundant precipitation, possibly from a tropical storm or hurricane; the zone is humid, with precipitation to the south.

Zone 3: Much of the zone sees scattered thunderstorms with seasonal temperatures, but a low-pressure system in the Gulf, possibly from a tropical storm or hurricane, could yield significant precipitation.

Zone 4: The zone is seasonal to above and humid, with a chance for scattered thunderstorms, some possibly strong; clouds increase in western areas later in the week.

Zone 5: Central and eastern areas are humid, temperatures are seasonal to above, and the zone has a chance for thunderstorms.

Zone 6: Variable cloudiness accompanies scattered showers across much of the zone, with more precipitation east; temperatures are seasonal.

Zone 7: The zone is windy and fair to partly cloudy with temperatures seasonal to above, and a chance for scattered thunderstorms in the mountains.

Zone 8: Much of Alaska sees precipitation, which is heaviest in central areas; temperatures are seasonal. Hawaii is fair and seasonal.

July 8–14, 2nd Quarter Moon

Zone 1: The zone is windy with variable cloudiness, seasonal to below, and scattered thunderstorms.

Zone 2: Northern areas are cooler with precipitation, and central and southern areas are seasonal to above and humid with scattered thunderstorms.

Zone 3: Western areas are fair and seasonal, central areas see scattered thunderstorms, and eastern areas are cloudy with showers and scattered thunderstorms; humidity accompanies temperatures seasonal to above.

Zone 4: Cloudy skies west yield showers and thunderstorms in western areas, central parts of the zone are humid with a chance for precipitation, and eastern areas are mostly fair; temperatures are seasonal.

Zone 5: Western and central parts of the zone see showers and scattered thunderstorms, western skies are overcast (possibly from a tropical storm or hurricane), and eastern areas are fair to partly cloudy; temperatures are seasonal to above.

Zone 6: Eastern areas are fair to partly cloudy, and western and central areas see scattered showers and thunderstorms.

Zone 7: The zone is fair to partly cloudy with a chance for precipitation west and central; temperatures are seasonal to above, and eastern areas are hot and humid.

Zone 8: Alaska is seasonal and windy with precipitation across much of the state, but fair east. Eastern and central Hawaii sees thunderstorms and then cooler temperatures, while western parts of the state are windy with precipitation later in the week.

July 15–22, Full Moon

Zone 1: Northern areas are windy with scattered precipitation and then cooler temperatures, and southern parts of the zone are mostly seasonal.

Zone 2: The zone is variably cloudy with temperatures seasonal to above.

Zone 3: Humidity accompanies temperatures seasonal to above, but conditions become cooler with more cloudiness east; western and central areas see scattered thunderstorms.

Zone 4: Precipitation in western areas moves into central parts of the zone, and eastern areas are mostly fair; temperatures are seasonal to above.

Zone 5: Western and some central areas see precipitation, and the rest of the zone is fair; temperatures are seasonal to above.

Zone 6: Western skies are fair to partly cloudy, central and eastern areas see more clouds and wind with scattered thunderstorms; temperatures are seasonal.

Zone 7: Northern coastal areas are breezy and fair to partly cloudy, southern coastal and central areas see showers and scattered thunderstorms with possible locally heavy downpours, and eastern areas are cloudy with a chance for precipitation.

Zone 8: Central Alaska sees precipitation, and western and eastern parts of the state are mostly fair; temperatures are seasonal. Hawaii is fair to partly cloudy and seasonal, with scattered showers central and east.

July 23–29, 3rd Quarter Moon

Zone 1: The zone is seasonal to above and humid with scattered thunderstorms.

Zone 2: Temperatures are seasonal to above with showers and scattered thunderstorms.

Zone 3: The zone is seasonal, mostly fair central, variably cloudy east with scattered thunderstorms, and cloudy west with showers and scattered thunderstorms.

Zone 4: Much of the zone is seasonal to above with a chance for scattered thunderstorms, which could be strong west with tornado potential, and eastern areas see more cloudiness.

Zone 5: The zone is seasonal to above and fair to partly cloudy, with scattered thunderstorms central with tornado potential and cooler with more cloudiness east with scattered showers and thunderstorms.

Zone 6: The zone is partly cloudy west, windy with scattered thunderstorms central and east, and seasonal to above.

Zone 7: Temperatures are cooler in northern coastal areas and seasonal to above in the rest of the zone with scattered thunderstorms central and east.

Zone 8: Alaska is windy west, fair to partly cloudy, and seasonal. Hawaii is mostly fair and seasonal.

July 30–August 5, New Moon

Zone 1: Northern areas are variably cloudy with scattered precipitation, and southern areas could see heavy precipitation, possibly from a tropical storm or hurricane.

Zone 2: A tropical storm or hurricane could yield abundant precipitation in northern areas, and central and southern areas are variably cloudy and windy with showers and scattered thunderstorms, some strong.

Zone 3: Western areas see scattered thunderstorms, central areas are fair to partly cloudy, and eastern areas could have heavy precipitation and strong thunderstorms with tornado potential.

Zone 4: Much of the zone is humid with temperatures seasonal to above with showers and scattered thunderstorms, but conditions are cooler east.

Zone 5: Central and eastern areas see scattered thunderstorms, some strong, and weather is humid and seasonal to above.

Zone 6: The zone is cloudy west with precipitation, fair to partly cloudy central and east, and seasonal.

Zone 7: Western and central areas are variably cloudy with a chance for precipitation, eastern skies are fair, and temperatures are seasonal.

Zone 8: Western Alaska is windy, central and eastern areas see precipitation, and temperatures are seasonal. Hawaii is fair to partly cloudy and seasonal with scattered showers east.

August 6–12, 2nd Quarter Moon

Zone 1: Southern areas see scattered thunderstorms, some strong, and northern areas see more cloudiness with precipitation.

Zone 2: The zone sees showers and thunderstorms, some strong with tornado potential.

Zone 3: Temperatures are seasonal to above and skies are variably cloudy with a chance for scattered thunderstorms west, and precipitation (some abundant) east and central.

Zone 4: Western and central areas of the zone are fair to partly cloudy, and eastern areas are humid with a chance for scattered thunderstorms; temperatures are seasonal to above.

Zone 5: Western parts of the zone are humid with scattered precipitation, and central and eastern areas are fair to partly cloudy with higher humidity and a chance for scattered showers east.

Zone 6: The zone sees scattered showers west (some locally heavy), central areas are stormy, and eastern areas are cloudy with scattered precipitation; temperatures are seasonal to below.

Zone 7: Northern coastal areas see scattered showers, southern coastal and central areas have a chance for showers, and eastern parts of the zone are cloudy and humid with scattered precipitation; temperatures are seasonal to above.

Zone 8: Central Alaska is very windy with heavy precipitation, eastern parts of the state are fair, and western areas see precipitation; temperatures are seasonal to below. Hawaii is fair to partly cloudy with temperatures seasonal to above and increasing cloudiness later in the week.

August 13–20, Full Moon

Zone 1: The zone is seasonal and fair to partly cloudy with a chance for precipitation.

Zone 2: Variable cloudiness and seasonal temperatures across the zone accompany a chance for precipitation.

Zone 3: Western and central areas see scattered thunderstorms, eastern areas are fair to partly cloudy, and the zone is humid with temperatures seasonal to above.

Zone 4: Western and central areas are variably cloudy with precipitation, some abundant in central areas, and eastern parts of the zone are fair; temperatures are seasonal to above.

Zone 5: Western areas see scattered showers and thunderstorms, and central and eastern parts of the zone are windy with heavy precipitation in the Gulf states, possibly from a tropical storm or hurricane.

Zone 6: The zone is fair to partly cloudy and seasonal to above.

Zone 7: The zone is mostly fair and seasonal to above with a chance for scattered thunderstorms in central areas.

Zone 8: Central Alaska is stormy with precipitation (some abundant) extending into eastern areas, and western parts of the state are fair; temperatures are seasonal to below. Hawaii is humid, breezy, partly cloudy, and seasonal to above with showers east.

August 21–27, 2nd Quarter Moon

Zone 1: The zone is windy with scattered thunderstorms (some strong) and seasonal temperatures.

Zone 2: Humidity rises with temperatures that are seasonal to above, triggering scattered thunderstorms across the zone.

Zone 3: Temperatures are seasonal to above with scattered thunderstorms (some strong), and weather is more seasonal east.

Zone 4: Much of the zone is humid with showers and thunderstorms, some strong west; temperature are seasonal to above.

Zone 5: The zone is seasonal to above and humid, with thunderstorms (some strong) and heavy precipitation to the west; central and eastern areas are fair to partly cloudy.

Zone 6: Weather is mostly fair and temperatures are seasonal to above with windy skies east.

Zone 7: The zone is fair to partly cloudy with gusty winds and scattered thunderstorms central and east; temperatures are seasonal to above.

Zone 8: High winds in central Alaska accompany precipitation that advances into eastern areas; temperatures are seasonal, and western areas are mostly fair. Hawaii is windy with showers and thunderstorms; temperatures seasonal to above.

August 28–September 3, New Moon

Zone 1: The zone is fair to partly cloudy with a chance for showers south; temperatures are seasonal to above.

Zone 2: Humidity and temperatures seasonal to above accompany scattered thunderstorms, some strong with tornado potential.

Zone 3: Temperatures are seasonal, western areas have a chance for thunderstorms, and central and eastern areas see scattered showers.

Zone 4: Western areas are stormy, and central and eastern parts of the zone see scattered thunderstorms, some strong with tornado potential; temperatures are seasonal to above.

Zone 5: Temperatures are seasonal to above with scattered showers and thunderstorms, which could be strong with tornado potential in central and eastern areas.

Zone 6: The zone is fair to partly cloudy and seasonal.

Zone 7: Western and central areas are fair, and eastern areas have a chance for scattered thunderstorms; temperatures are seasonal to above.

Zone 8: Central Alaska is windy with precipitation, eastern and western areas are fair to partly cloudy, and temperatures are seasonal to below. Hawaii is seasonal and windy with precipitation.

September 4–11, 2nd Quarter Moon

Zone 1: Temperatures are seasonal to above with a chance for scattered thunderstorms south.

Zone 2: Northern and central parts of the zone see showers and scattered thunderstorms, inland and southern areas are fair to partly cloudy, and temperatures are seasonal to above.

Zone 3: Western and central areas see scattered thunderstorms, eastern areas have showers; temperatures are seasonal to above.

Zone 4: Thunderstorms across much of the zone could be severe with tornado potential, and temperatures are seasonal to above; some central areas could see heavy precipitation.

Zone 5: Thunderstorms are scattered west, and central and eastern areas could see severe storms with tornado potential, possibly the result of a tropical storm or hurricane.

Zone 6: The zone is mostly fair to partly cloudy and seasonal with a chance for precipitation west and east.

2010 © Jorge Salcedo. Image from BigStockPhoto.com

Zone 7: Eastern parts of the zone are variably cloudy with a chance for thunderstorms, while western and central areas are fair and windy with a chance for precipitation later in the week; temperatures are seasonal to above.

Zone 8: Central and eastern Alaska are windy, and much of the zone sees precipitation and temperatures seasonal to below. Western Hawaii is fair, and central and eastern areas see precipitation; temperatures are seasonal.

September 12–19, Full Moon

Zone 1: Precipitation across the zone is heaviest to the south.

Zone 2: Most of the zone sees precipitation, with the most abundant in northern areas, possibly from a tropical storm or hurricane; temperatures are seasonal to below.

Zone 3: The zone is seasonal with scattered showers and thunderstorms, with the heaviest precipitation east.

Zone 4: The zone is seasonal and variably cloudy with scattered precipitation.

Zone 5: Fair to partly cloudy skies and seasonal temperatures prevail, with a chance for precipitation.

Zone 6: The zone is fair west with precipitation in central and eastern areas; temperatures are seasonal to below.

Zone 7: Temperatures seasonal to above accompany fair to partly cloudy skies and a chance for scattered thunderstorms east.

Zone 8: Alaska's temperatures are seasonal to below with precipitation. Hawaii is variably cloudy, with wind, precipitation, and temperatures seasonal to below.

September 20–26, 3rd Quarter Moon

Zone 1: The zone is windy, seasonal, and cloudy with precipitation.

Zone 2: Northern areas are windy and much of the zone sees precipitation.

Zone 3: Eastern areas see precipitation, and the zone is windy and seasonal.

Zone 4: High winds in western and central areas accompany precipitation (some abundant), the western Plains are cloudy with precipitation, and eastern areas are fair and windy; temperatures are seasonal to below.

Zone 5: Western and central areas see precipitation, and eastern areas are cloudy with precipitation, possibly abundant as a result of a tropical storm or hurricane.

Zone 6: Temperatures are seasonal to below, central and eastern areas are fair to partly cloudy, and western parts of the zone are windy and cloudy with precipitation.

Zone 7: Northern coastal areas see scattered precipitation, and the rest of the zone is fair to partly cloudy with a chance for precipitation east; temperatures are seasonal to below.

Zone 8: Alaska sees precipitation across the state and high winds in central areas with temperatures seasonal to below. Hawaii is seasonal, western areas are windy, and central and eastern areas see scattered precipitation.

Autumn 2011

Zone 1 will be seasonal with periods of warm weather and precipitation ranging from normal to below. Wind will be a factor in central and southern areas of zone 2, which will also see some significant low-pressure systems and cold temperatures. The greatest precipitation will occur in southern parts of the zone.

Western areas of zone 3 will be windy and northern parts of the central portion of this zone will see abundant precipitation and low-pressure systems, as will much of the southern area. Overall, this zone will be seasonal to below, with an above-average number of cloudy days.

In the northern states of the Plains, weather will range from seasonal to cold to windy. Western and central areas of zone 4 will be very cold at times as Arctic air dips south. Eastern and northwestern parts of the zone will be more seasonal with average precipitation, and the Rocky Mountains and foothills areas will see some significant storms that move into central states and eastern Plains. To the south, zone 5 will also see frigid temperatures at times and wind and dryness will be a factor.

Major storms and low-pressure systems will enter the country in zone 6 and then track southeast through the mountains. This precipitation will be heaviest in central and eastern parts of the zone. In zone 7, California's weather will alternate between cold/windy/dry and cloudy/wet, with some major storms. Central and much of the eastern part of the zone will be generally dry and seasonal, with warmer temperatures in the desert. Higher elevations to the east have potential for abundant precipitation.

In zone 8, eastern Alaska will be cold and windy, central parts of the state can expect more seasonal temperatures and average to above precipitation, and western areas will be cloudy with periods of abundant precipitation. Overall, Hawaii's temperatures will be seasonal to above with precipitation normal to below.

September 27–October 2, New Moon

Zone 1: The zone is windy and seasonal to below, with some coastal areas seeing abundant precipitation, possibly from a tropical storm or hurricane.

Zone 2: Precipitation across the zone could be the result of a tropical storm or hurricane.

Zone 3: Western areas see scattered thunderstorms (some strong), and precipitation in central and eastern areas could be abundant, possibly from a tropical storm or hurricane; temperatures are seasonal but cooler northeast.

Zone 4: Western skies are fair, central areas are variably cloudy with showers, and eastern parts of the zone see scattered thunderstorms; temperatures are seasonal to above.

Zone 5: Central and western areas are fair to partly cloudy, and eastern areas have a chance for scattered thunderstorms; temperatures are seasonal to above.

Zone 6: Western areas are variably cloudy and windy, and much of the zone sees precipitation, which is heaviest in central and eastern parts of the zone; temperatures are seasonal.

Zone 7: Western and central parts of the zone are fair to partly cloudy, with showers and thunderstorms east that could yield abundant downfall; temperatures are seasonal.

Zone 8: Western and eastern Alaska are fair to partly cloudy, and central parts of the state are cloudy and windy with abundant precipitation; temperatures are seasonal to below. Hawaii sees precipitation followed by cooler temperatures.

October 3–10, 2nd Quarter Moon

Zone 1: The zone is variably cloudy and seasonal with scattered precipitation.

Zone 2: Northern parts of the zone are fair, central and southern areas see increasing clouds and precipitation, some locally heavy; temperatures are seasonal to below.

Zone 3: Much of the zone sees precipitation, which is heaviest west and central, possibly from a tropical storm or hurricane; temperatures are seasonal to below.

Zone 4: Western areas are windy with a front moving through later in the week and into central parts of the zone, while eastern areas are windy with scattered precipitation; temperatures are seasonal.

Zone 5: Conditions are breezy west, central areas see more cloudiness with precipitation later in the week, and eastern areas are fair to partly cloudy; temperatures are seasonal.

Zone 6: Precipitation in western areas moves across the zone with the highest winds east later in the week; temperatures are seasonal.

Zone 7: Northern coastal areas see showers, southern coastal areas and central parts of the zone are fair to partly cloudy, and eastern areas see scattered thunderstorms, some strong; temperatures are seasonal to above.

Zone 8: Western Alaska sees precipitation, central and eastern areas are fair to partly cloudy and windy, and temperatures are seasonal to below. Hawaii has a chance for showers and thunderstorms, and the state is variably cloudy with temperatures seasonal to below.

October 11–18, Full Moon

Zone 1: Northern skies are mostly fair, and southern areas are cloudy with precipitation.

Zone 2: Much of the zone is cloudy with potentially abundant precipitation central and south.

Zone 3: The zone is mostly cloudy with strong thunderstorms west and abundant precipitation east; temperatures are seasonal to below.

Zone 4: Rain moves across the zone into central and eastern areas, and the eastern Plains are stormy with abundant precipitation.

Zone 5: Western areas see scattered precipitation, and central and eastern parts of the zone see thunderstorms, some strong with tornado potential; temperatures are seasonal to above.

Zone 6: Western and central areas are overcast with precipitation, some abundant, and eastern parts of the zone are windy with scattered precipitation.

Zone 7: Western and central parts of the zone are cloudy with precipitation, which is heaviest central, and eastern areas are fair to partly cloudy; temperatures are seasonal.

Zone 8: Much of Alaska sees precipitation with the heaviest downfall central and east; temperatures are seasonal to below. Hawaii is windy and seasonal with precipitation.

October 19–25, 3rd Quarter Moon

Zone 1: The zone is fair to partly cloudy and windy with a chance for precipitation.

Zone 2: Windy conditions across the zone accompany thunderstorms central and south, some strong with tornado potential.

Zone 3: Western areas are windy with a chance of precipitation later in the week, southern areas in central parts of the zone see precipitation with strong thunderstorms with tornado potential, and northeastern areas are cloudy with scattered precipitation; temperatures are seasonal to below.

Zone 4: Cloudy skies and seasonal temperatures prevail across much of the zone with precipitation west (some abundant) and scattered precipitation central and east.

Zone 5: The zone is seasonal with variable cloudiness and a chance for precipitation central and east.

Zone 6: Stormy weather advances from the west into central parts of the zone, and eastern areas are fair to partly cloudy and seasonal.

Zone 7: Temperatures range from seasonal to above, eastern areas are variably cloudy with a chance for precipitation, and western and central parts of the zone are windy with scattered precipitation.

Zone 8: Central and western Alaska are windy and cold with precipitation, and eastern areas are seasonal. Hawaii is fair to partly cloudy and seasonal, but with more cloudiness and scattered precipitation east.

October 26–November 1, New Moon

Zone 1: The zone is seasonal with scattered precipitation, with a better chance for downfall north.

Zone 2: Northern areas see scattered precipitation, central and southern areas are fair to partly cloudy, and temperatures are seasonal.

Zone 3: Seasonal temperatures accompany scattered precipitation across the zone, with more downfall east.

Zone 4: Western and central areas see precipitation (some abundant), and eastern areas are partly cloudy; temperatures are seasonal to below.

Zone 5: Much of the zone sees precipitation, with heavy downfall possible central and east; temperatures are seasonal to below.

Zone 6: The zone is fair and seasonal to below.

Zone 7: Northeastern areas see more clouds and a chance for precipitation, while other parts of the zone are mostly fair and seasonal.

Zone 8: Central Alaska is cold with scattered precipitation. The rest of the state is fair and seasonal. Hawaii is mostly fair and seasonal, but precipitation east is followed by cooler temperatures.

November 2–9, 2nd Quarter Moon

Zone 1: The zone is fair with temperatures seasonal to below.

Zone 2: Seasonal conditions accompany variable cloudiness with a chance for precipitation.

Zone 3: Western skies are cloudy and windy with precipitation, central and eastern parts of the zone see variable cloudiness with a chance for precipitation, and temperatures are seasonal to below.

Zone 4: The zone is generally fair to partly cloudy with a chance for precipitation in central areas and east, where there are more clouds; temperatures are seasonal to below.

Zone 5: Eastern areas see cloudiness with a chance for precipitation, and the rest of the zone is fair to partly cloudy; temperatures are seasonal to below.

Zone 6: The zone is windy, seasonal, and mostly fair, with a chance for precipitation.

Zone 7: Fair to partly cloudy conditions prevail, with a chance for precipitation northeast, where temperatures are warmer.

Zone 8: Alaska is stormy east with precipitation, central and western parts of the state are fair to partly cloudy, and temperatures are seasonal. Hawaii is seasonal with scattered showers.

November 10–17, Full Moon

Zone 1: Temperatures are seasonal to below with scattered precipitation, and southern areas are windy with more cloudiness.

Zone 2: Skies are windy and fair to partly cloudy with scattered precipitation; temperatures are seasonal to below.

Zone 3: The zone sees scattered precipitation under partly cloudy to cloudy skies and temperatures seasonal to below.

Zone 4: Much of the zone is windy and seasonal with precipitation.

Zone 5: Precipitation (some abundant) advances across the zone; temperatures are seasonal.

Zone 6: All but eastern parts of the zone are cloudy, with precipitation west and central (some abundant); temperatures are mostly seasonal.

Zone 7: Western and central areas are partly cloudy to cloudy with precipitation, and eastern skies are variably cloudy with a chance for precipitation; temperatures are seasonal.

Zone 8: In Alaska, seasonal conditions prevail under fair skies west and east, and central parts of the state are windy with precipitation. Hawaii is fair and seasonal.

November 18–24, 3rd Quarter Moon

Zone 1: The zone is variably cloudy with temperatures seasonal to below and scattered precipitation.

Zone 2: Most of the zone is cloudy with temperatures seasonal to below and precipitation, some abundant.

Zone 3: Western skies are fair and windy, and central and eastern areas, especially to the south, are cloudy with precipitation; temperatures are seasonal to below.

Zone 4: The zone is cold and variably cloudy west and central, and more seasonal east with a chance for precipitation.

Zone 5: Eastern areas see scattered precipitation, and the rest of the zone is fair to partly cloudy; temperatures are seasonal to below.

Zone 6: Central and eastern areas see precipitation (some abundant), and skies in western parts of the zone become increasingly cloudy later in the week; temperatures are seasonal.

Zone 7: Coastal areas are fair to partly cloudy with scattered precipitation north, southern coastal and central parts of the zone are windy, and eastern areas are windy with precipitation, mainly northeast; temperatures are seasonal.

Zone 8: Western Alaska is fair, central parts of the state are windy with precipitation that moves east, and temperatures are seasonal. Hawaii is seasonal with showers.

November 25–December 1, New Moon

Zone 1: The zone is windy with precipitation, which is heaviest south; temperatures are seasonal to below.

Zone 2: Northern areas are windy with precipitation, and central and southern parts of the zone are fair to partly cloudy with scattered precipitation; temperatures are seasonal to below.

Zone 3: Western and central parts of the zone are cloudy with precipitation, eastern areas are windy, and southern sections of the zone could see strong thunderstorms; temperatures are seasonal to below.

Zone 4: High winds accompany temperatures seasonal to below with precipitation that could be abundant west and central.

Zone 5: Western skies are fair to partly cloudy, and central and eastern areas could see strong thunderstorms later in the week, with abundant downfall in central parts of the zone.

Zone 6: The zone is seasonal to below, windy west, and variably cloudy with scattered precipitation.

Zone 7: Skies are variably cloudy west and central with precipitation, and windy and partly cloudy east with precipitation later in the week; temperatures are seasonal.

Zone 8: Central parts of Alaska are cold with abundant precipitation, and western and eastern areas are mostly fair. Much of Hawaii sees precipitation with temperatures seasonal to below.

December 2–9, 2nd Quarter Moon

Zone 1: Northern areas are cloudy with precipitation, and southern areas see scattered precipitation; temperatures are seasonal to below.

Zone 2: The zone is fair to partly cloudy and seasonal to below with a chance for precipitation.

Zone 3: Variable cloudiness and scattered precipitation accompany temperatures seasonal to below.

Zone 4: Western areas and the western Plains are cloudy with precipitation (some abundant), and central and eastern areas are variably cloudy with scattered precipitation; temperatures are seasonal to below.

Zone 5: Western parts of the zone are partly cloudy and seasonal, central areas are cooler and windy with precipitation (some abundant), and eastern areas are partly cloudy with more cloudiness and precipitation later in the week.

Zone 6: Temperatures are seasonal to below and much of the zone sees precipitation, which is abundant in some central and eastern areas.

Zone 7: Precipitation, some abundant in eastern areas, accompanies temperatures seasonal to below.

Zone 8: Western and central Alaska see precipitation (some abundant), and eastern skies are fair to partly cloudy; temperatures are seasonal to below. Eastern and central Hawaii are windy with a chance for precipitation, and western areas are mostly fair; temperatures are seasonal.

December 10–16, Full Moon
Zone 1: The zone is partly cloudy and windy with temperatures seasonal to below and a chance for precipitation.

Zone 2: Northern areas are windy and partly cloudy, central and southern areas are fair to partly cloudy, and the zone is seasonal with a chance for precipitation.

Zone 3: Western areas see more cloudiness with variably cloudy skies and scattered precipitation in the rest of the zone, strong thunderstorms are possible in southern areas, and eastern areas are windy and colder.

Zone 4: The central and eastern Plains are cloudy and windy with precipitation (some abundant), western skies are partly cloudy, and eastern areas are fair and windy; temperatures are seasonal to below.

Zone 5: Western skies are partly cloudy, central parts of the zone see showers and possibly strong thunderstorms, and eastern areas are cloudy with precipitation (some abundant) later in the week; temperatures are seasonal.

Zone 6: The zone is variably cloudy with temperatures seasonal to below, western areas are windy, and eastern parts of the zone see precipitation.

Zone 7: Much of the zone is fair to partly cloudy, eastern skies are windy, and temperatures are seasonal to below.

Zone 8: Alaska is mostly fair west and central, temperatures are seasonal to below, and eastern areas see abundant precipitation. Hawaii is mostly fair and seasonal.

December 17–23, 3rd Quarter Moon

Zone 1: The zone is seasonal with precipitation, which is abundant to the south.

Zone 2: Much of the zone is windy with precipitation, with the heaviest downfall in northern coastal and central areas; temperatures are seasonal.

Zone 3: Western areas are windy and fair to partly cloudy, and central and eastern areas see precipitation, some abundant; temperatures are seasonal.

Zone 4: The zone is variably cloudy with increasing cloudiness in central areas and precipitation (some abundant) in central and eastern parts of the zone; temperatures are seasonal to below.

Zone 5: Western skies are fair, and central and eastern areas see precipitation later in the week with high winds and possible strong thunderstorms.

Zone 6: The zone is windy with precipitation (heaviest east), more cloudiness central and east, and temperatures seasonal to below.

Zone 7: Variably cloudy skies accompany windy conditions west and central, and the zone has a chance for precipitation with possible thunderstorms, some strong, in southeastern areas; temperatures are seasonal to below.

Zone 8: Western and central Alaska are windy with precipitation, which is abundant in central areas, and eastern areas see scattered precipitation; temperatures are below seasonal. Hawaii is seasonal with showers and thunderstorms across the state with more cloudiness and downfall west.

December 24–31, New Moon

Zone 1: The zone is windy with scattered precipitation and seasonal temperatures.

Zone 2: Conditions are seasonal with scattered precipitation, northern areas see more cloudiness, and thunderstorms are possible in central coastal areas.

Zone 3: The zone is cold, partly cloudy, and windy.

Zone 4: Western areas are windy with precipitation, central areas see more cloudiness and precipitation, and eastern areas are cold.

Zone 5: Western parts of the zone are windy with possible thunderstorms, and central and eastern areas are cloudy with precipitation; temperatures are seasonal to below.

Zone 6: Precipitation advances across the zone with the heaviest east, and temperatures are seasonal.

Zone 7: The zone is variably cloudy and seasonal with scattered precipitation west, windy with precipitation central and east, and thunderstorms southeast.

Zone 8: Central and eastern Alaska are windy with precipitation (some abundant), and western skies are mostly fair; temperatures are seasonal. Hawaii is cloudy and seasonal to below with precipitation across much of the state.

About the Author

Kris Brandt Riske is the executive director and a professional member of the American Federation of Astrologers (AFA), the oldest U.S. astrological organization, founded in 1938; and a member of National Council for Geocosmic Research (NCGR). She has a master's degree in journalism and a certificate of achievement in weather forecasting from Penn State. Kris is the author of several books, including: Llewellyn's Complete Book of Astrology: The Easy Way to Learn Astrology; Mapping Your Money; Mapping Your Future; *and coauthor of* Mapping Your Travels and Relocation; *and* Astrometeorology: Planetary Powers in Weather Forecasting. *She also writes for astrology publications, and does the annual weather forecast for* Llewellyn's Moon Sign Book. *In addition to astrometeorology, she specializes in predictive astrology. Kris is an avid NASCAR fan, although she'd rather be a driver than a spectator. In 2010 she started blogging, posting a weather forecast for each of the thirty-six race weekends (qualifying and race day) for NASCAR drivers and fans. Visit her blog at http://racecarweather.wordpress.com. Kris also enjoys gardening, reading, jazz, and her three cats.*

2010 © Sandra Caldwell. Image from BigStockPhoto.com

Economic Forecast for 2011

By Dorothy J. Kovach

Even skeptics are starting to realize what astrologers always knew: the ups and downs on the markets are caused not by the big boys on Wall Street, but the stars up above. Knowing the ways of the planets can give you the same edge that insiders have, because the stars rule the future. Thus, those who follow the stars improve their financial fortune, because the planets let us know when to hold 'em and when to fold 'em.

True, in recent years, the markets have whipped us around more than a roller coaster ride, but we must remember that this downturn is *not* your father's, nor your grandfather's, Great Depression. There is still money to be made out there. In fact, this is a good time to educate ourselves on markets. In this day and age, it is only the foolhardy and masochistic who hand their hard-earned money over to complete strangers without a second glance. Handing your portfolio over to fund managers without a second thought is no different than placing a bet in Las Vegas—sad but true. Despite the investment companies' commercials, the chances of making a fortune *without* an astrological strategy is about the same as the chances of winning the lottery: it can be done, but the odds are against you.

There are three things no adult should be without, and one is a basic grasp of how markets work. The second is a contrary attitude. The third is patience. Your financial well-being is up to you. Even though nobody can make you rich, there are plenty of people out there who will be more than willing to make you poor! Markets (and those who manage them) are like any other business: purely selfish. In other words, the stock market does not care about you; it's just out to make a buck. Brokers do not care about you; they care about their own pocketbooks. When it comes to money, it's every man and woman for him- or herself. Thus, education is the key to winning in this economy. Stock prices are purely subjective entities, meaning their value is completely dependent upon whatever people *think* they are worth. We have seen stocks fall well beyond their "real" value; we have also seen stocks rise well beyond their "real" value. By the end of this annual forecast, we may see a glimmer of light at the end of the long tunnel and plan our future investments for the long haul. In the meantime, it is time to educate ourselves so we can be ready when markets finally do turn around.

70 Percent of Stocks Move with the Market

The trend is your friend. In other words, if the general market is turning down, even well-run companies will go down. On the other hand, when the market is booming, all too many of those booming stocks are not worth even a fraction of what they are going for. When it comes to markets, Saturn is your friend. He is the god of patience and due diligence. Detachment is paramount for winning in the stock market. When trading, keep your head. Markets are exciting, and it is easy to get caught up in loss and gain. If you can keep your head while those around you don't, you will thrive. Lose your head, and you will lose your shirt.

The next thing to know is that there are many different kinds of "instruments" to trade. Essentially, there are two kinds of financial securities: equity and debt. When you buy stock, you get a certain amount of equity in a company; when you buy bonds, you loan money, thus becoming a creditor. Stocks get a lot of attention because they are rather melodramatic with their fluctuations; bonds are rather dull by comparison—unlike the dividends one can receive from stocks, a bond investor receives the same amount of money, even if a company is doing well. Although stocks get all the headlines, the bond market is actually far larger than the stock market.

The Internet revolutionized the way people trade. In the old days, just about all trades went through a person who was actually on the floor of the New York Stock Exchange. The NYSE was and is expensive—read: not at all friendly to the little guy. Automated markets like the NASDAQ brought markets right into our homes and (some would say) evened up the playing field.

There are four major categories of stocks: blue chips, secondary issues, growth stocks, and penny stocks. Blue chips represent the "cream of the crop" equities, like IBM. They are the companies that are the most expensive, and therefore the safest. When you invest in blue chips, you are putting your money in a relatively safe place, but you may not make a lot off your investment because of the expense. Then there are secondary issues. These are good, well-established companies that, for one reason or another, have lost some investor confidence and have fallen on hard times. In markets that are bottoming out, these are the stocks to watch, because there was never anything wrong with these companies! Wouldn't you love to have bought Apple, back in 2002, when it was hovering in the teens? As of this printing, Apple (AAPL) is now trading at $242 a share! The next category is the growth stocks, which are comprised primarily of young stocks. They have a lot of growth potential, but they are also more risky than the first two types of stock. Growth stocks are very risky, but remember our mantra: 70 percent of stocks go with the market, so when the market is recovering, these stocks can be nice bargains. Finally, there are penny stocks, which are the dark horses of the market. They are usually long shots and have pretty much no value other than their potential for future growth. These are the most speculative and most risky. Remembering our mantra, we have no reason to play with penny stocks just yet, because they are best played when the market is doing well.

Stocks and bonds are not the only kinds of funds one can trade. There are also gold, precious metals, commodities, and currencies. We do not have the space to devote to these instruments, but just figure that gold is usually seen as a bet against inflation. Gold tends to trade in the opposite direction of the stock market, but with the minting presses going full tilt as of this writing, gold has been trading right along with the market. There is also the currency market. Generally speaking, most currency traders tend to bet against the dollar, because it is customary to bet against the big boys, especially when a market is starting to recover. This is because, as the preferred currency when there is a recession, the U.S. Treasury Department can actually just print money to pick up the slack in the economy.

The Planets

In markets, the **Sun** rules all precious commodities. In business, it rules upper management. In life, it governs the blue bloods and those in the upper echelon of society. It rules gold, platinum, all precious metals, and commodities. When the Sun is prominent, gold goes up. In general, this isn't a good sign, because when gold goes up, the dollar goes down and buys less. When purchasing power diminishes, inflation is just around the corner, bringing higher prices for goods and services. The Sun tends to indicate a general distrust toward the policies and actions of the administration in power. In general, it trades consistent with real estate. When inflation is a factor, it trades side by side with stocks. Either way, the Sun is a vote against however your government is currently handling the economy. When the South Node heads toward the Sun, gold could move in an opposite direction from stocks.

The **Moon** rules the regular man and woman. It has to do with fluctuation in the markets, because the Moon is the fastest moving of all celestial entities. Therefore the Moon will always act as the main "trigger" in the marketplace. It represents the gross domestic product (GDP) of any given country. Due to her frequent movements to and fro in the heavens, the Moon is in charge of liquidity. We focus heavily on its position in the quarterly charts to determine the exchange rate. The Moon controls the London inter-bank offered rate, better known as the LIBOR, which determines the exchange rate and how willing banks are to lend to one another. Once again, due to her frequent wanderings, the Moon will also tell us how commerce will move, specifically with regards to the international and domestic shipping industries. Above all, she rules the ground beneath our feet, and thus is very much related to our home and real estate in general. The Moon is very feeling-oriented. If it is negatively placed, it can make for a bearish trend because the Moon brings worry, and worry brings the market down.

Mercury rules all manner of communication. It is the major player in any sort of commerce because it links our desires to buyers and sellers. It is especially in charge of any and all products that have to do with communications, like telecom and telephone companies. It is linked to intellectual property of all kinds and is related to the technology industry. It has a special influence on computing stocks. Mercury is also interested in travel, thus (along with the Moon) it is directly related to the ups and downs of the trucking and shipping industries. Because of this relationship, Mercury will be the first planet to show promising market upswings.

The ancients said that the Moon and Mercury control day-to-day commerce. This is valuable information for those interested in short-term investing, like day traders. This is because the Moon is considered the mind. (Many folks think Mercury is the mind, but he is not; he is the intellect.) As the saying goes, a mind is a terrible thing to waste. This is because the mind is the eyes of

2010 © Joy Prescott. Image from BigStockPhoto.com

the soul and is immortal in nature. It records all of our actions, beginning the moment we were incarnated on this plane. Its light is that which we see in our dreams. Together, the Moon and Mercury control our instinctual behavior. Never overlook these two planets, because if you trade when they are not favorably appointed in your chart, you will be more subject to whims.

Wherever **Venus** is placed in the chart will tell us what we love and admire in any given shopping season. She is so important that there can be no economic recovery without her, because she makes people confident about tomorrow—when we are confident, we consume more. Venus is all about wanting to look good. Venus represents the latest designs and, as such, is in charge of everything related to fashion. All retailing comes under Venus' jurisdiction. Venus is one of the main moneymakers of the planets. When Venus is prominently and happily placed, we make money. Venus has a lot to say about what determines value in the marketplace. She will be looked to, to determine the future costs associated with borrowing money, and thus she has an influence on interest rates.

Mars is the spark that lights any given sector on fire. He is in charge of all growth stocks. This is because Mars rules all desires, and when Mars is strong and well placed, we have a run on whatever sign represents the sector that Mars is in. For example, as of this writing Mars is situated in Leo, the sign of gold. When he was moving forward in this sign, gold went up. When he turned backward (retrograde), gold went down. In other words, when Mars is strong, sectors he represents all thrive; when weak, worry takes over and sectors represented by the sign he's in suffer. Mars has a special affinity for the automobile industry. Perhaps its not time to completely write off Detroit. Given his swift movement, we may see some new innovations there. Mars will be direct for all of 2011, bringing much smoother sailing on the equities markets. However, with Mars strong and direct, energy costs could go up this year (though not coming close to the highs of the past).

Jupiter is the planet with the Midas touch. Jupiter is the king of the bull markets, because wherever he is, you will see expansion. When Jupiter is in charge, a sense of euphoria fills the air. Jupiter is the expanding principle. He is the one who had nothing but good feelings toward everybody. He is the ultimate insider! If we only had one planet to choose to make money with, it would be Jupiter. This is because wherever he goes, the market shoots upward. Thus, it is not a bad idea to keep a close eye on Jupiter and load up on the stocks represented by the sign he is in. Generally, Jupiter works like clockwork, spending just about a year in each sign. But instead of following his normal pattern, he is moving at breakneck speed during 2011, spending time in three signs. We might think that this would be like having three separate boom periods; however, when Jupiter is moving so rapidly, we cannot count on him to fixate on any one industry this year. He will still be lucky, but we cannot count on Jupiter's golden touch in just one sector. We will want to be diversified.

Jupiter starts off the year in the wet sign of Pisces, where he is going to make quite an impact on the shipping and all transportation that crosses oceans. Placed on the fixed star Scheat, this is a red flag for the shipping industry. Scheat has been known to cause trouble on the high seas. Shipping stocks could feel the heat (or distinct lack thereof). Travel stocks do not look good right now, which may impact travel during the holidays. Be prepared for long waits at the airports as trouble from many quarters, including terrorist threats, puts a damper on the travel industry in its peak season. With Jupiter moving alongside erratic Uranus, there may be increased danger of flooding. If you live in earthquake country, have your emergency package ready—there may be trouble ahead.

Jupiter enters fiery Aries on January 22, a sign in which people can be a bit too hasty. Jupiter here wants what he wants when he wants it. His thinking is, why worry about a tomorrow that may never come? He thinks nothing of spending money he doesn't have. As celestial exuberance abounds, markets may react by overheating. Look for higher prices at the pump. When Jupiter is in the "me me me" sign, everybody thinks that they deserve more than they are getting. When pushed, he pushes back. In April, global tensions may increase the possibility of a new war erupting. When the world is on edge, military contractors reap benefits. Broken agreements could fray already tense nerves, which in turn puts mounting pressure on the dollar from many quarters. In this climate, interest rates may go up.

On June 4, Jupiter will move into fixed and stable Taurus, where he will stay for the rest of the year. Once Jupiter arrives in the most practical sign of the zodiac, markets will demand accountability. No longer will the Treasury Department be able to just print money with little or no backing. Forget get-rich-quick schemes. Solid investments will pay off in the long run for the patient. Jupiter in Taurus favors both the practical and the habitual. If double standards don't bother you, consider the vice stocks like Altria (MO) which is both addictive and pays a good dividend. Remember, the biggest problem with Jupiter in this sign is not the buying, it's the selling. When Jupiter is in Taurus, it is easier than ever to spot a bargain a mile away, but as the collector of the zodiac, Taurus may make it harder to let go. Wise investors will get in the habit of making a monthly inventory of all their holdings, and act accordingly.

Contrary to popular astrological opinion, Jupiter is not always good. When things expand too much, bubbles develop. This is when certain stocks become so popular that price has nothing at all to do with value. What goes up, must eventually come down.

This is where **Saturn** comes in. Saturn is the planet of truth. Without Saturn there would be no success, because Saturn is the reality check of the heavens. Whenever any given sector has gone up in price to the point where its cost is well above its actual value, the ringed planet Saturn comes along and brings the price crashing down with a wave of his dark wand. As you can imagine, Saturn is not always the most anticipated, nor appreciated of the planets. We generally think of Saturn as cold and heartless. After all, where he goes, all too often loss follows. However, we need Saturn, because the limitations he places on us force us to learn when "enough is enough." And thus, we learn discipline, the most necessary ingredient for success. Without Saturn, Jupiter would be left to expand infinitely, to bulldoze every tree down, mine every last drop of the Earth's resources in the name of progress, leaving a world without scruples. Where Jupiter believes anything is possible, Saturn is interested only in the cold hard facts. Where Jupiter makes promises too numerous to keep, Saturn is dutifully honest. Where Jupiter is the rich kid, used to having the sea part before him, Saturn is the kid from the wrong side of the tracks who worked tirelessly, rising to the top on his or her own merits.

This year Saturn continues his trek through Libra. Libra is the sign of fairness. Saturn in Libra is said to be one of the very best placements, because when here, Saturn's main principle is justice, not just for the few, but for all. Saturn here works to right long-standing inequities. Diplomacy is paramount during this time. With the opposition from Jupiter, political leaders should be willing to step across the aisle, perhaps again and again, so that together they can right the economic wrongs of the past. If honesty were a stock, its value would go straight up under this placement. There will be a real outcry for true democracy and a government that works for the people.

Saturn also rules debt, and we are in a lot of it. The Devil's Dictionary (www.thedevilsdictionary.com) defines *debt* as "an ingenious substitute for the chain and whip of the slave driver." At present, the national debt hovers over us like a sword of Damocles. During the "crisis" of 2008–2009, the Federal Reserve Bank poured over one trillion dollars into the system to keep the party going. A billion rhymes with a trillion, and it's not hard to glaze over just what a staggering amount of money this really is.

If we were place a trillion one dollar bills side by side, we could go around the world almost three times! It could take us to the Moon and back 200 times! Stacked one on top of the other, the mountain created would dwarf Mount Everest by over 300,000,000 feet. In terms of money, this means that if we were to spend one million dollars every single day, from the day Christ was born until now, or every day for the next two thousand years, we would still have a quarter of a trillion dollars left! Now consider this: as of this writing, the national debt stands at about $12,000,000,000,000 and rising. Even if you have no mortgage, no credit card debt, and no car payments, if you are over twenty-one, you automatically owe $40,000 thanks to the extravagance of our leaders. Saturn's position in Libra is all about balance. It doesn't take a genius to see that something has got to give.

Corporations now have more rights than people. In 2008 and 2009, one trillion dollars was spent to bail out the large banking institutions. However, although we will have to pay for it through higher taxation, the government will not tell us where our money was spent. Saturn in Libra demands accountability. As owners of these businesses, we have every right to know where our money was spent. If the capitalistic system is to survive, risk must not only have rewards; it must also have penalties.

Jupiter and Saturn

Due to their very opposing natures, Saturn and Jupiter are the most crucial factors in market forecasting because they control the financial ebb and flow that makes for whether we are "in the money" or sitting on the sidewalk selling pencils. This year, Jupiter and Saturn will be playing out their own version of Tolstoy's classic *War and Peace*. Jupiter in Aries thinks war is a necessary evil, and by midyear, he prepares to deploy troops. Along comes Saturn dangling a white flag, asking, "Just how far can our military be stretched?" By propping up markets beyond fair value while shipping our best industries abroad and fighting one endless and expensive war after another, our leaders have been hammering nails into the coffin that was once America's middle class. As people finally tire of paying for seemingly endless wars, look for global tensions to mount.

Markets thrive on graft. Saturn in Libra is synonymous with regulation. Regulation slashes Jupiter's devil-may-care attitude. Good as they are, honor and justice are not growth industries, but while Saturn is here, they are necessary to restore value. In essence, Saturn acts as a watchdog, reforming the mess the *laissez-faire* leaders left us with. People may demand fair trade, not world trade. Where enthusiasm meets populism, we all too often see sideways market, one in which any bullish momentum can only go so far before it encounters reality.

. . . .

But all is not bad news. Albeit in its earliest stages—and it may take a few years—we really are on the road to recovery. Thanks to **Uranus**, when the going gets rough, we know how to reinvent ourselves. Uranus will always tell us where the next big craze will be, thus giving us the inside track on hot stocks. On March 11, Uranus enters the first and fastest sign, Aries, where he will stay for the next eight years. Aries has to do with anything motorized. Perhaps it will reverse the fortunes of our ailing auto industry, or breakthrough inventions in electronics may give new life to the automobile. Aries is also a military sign. We will probably see major changes in the way in which we go to war. The last time Uranus was in Aries, the cavalry was rendered obsolete. We may see battle shift from the ground to communications. We are dependent on the computer for everything, from banking to driving. Many believe that "cyber-warfare" may be the wave of the future. If our computerized networks were to take a major hit, the effects could be devastating. Look for high-tech security to be heftily rewarded. And if asked, feel free to tell; Uranus in Aries may finally allow gay service members to serve openly in our military forces.

Uranus in Aries is also about to revolutionize the lighting industry. That old incandescent bulb is going the way of the gas light. In fact, inefficient incandescent bulbs will begin being phased out in 2012. No, it is not time to invest in compact fluorescents; they still pose significant environmental hazards, giving off poisonous mercury vapors when broken. Thus, it's only a matter of time before compact fluorescents will also be replaced. The real wave of the future is the light-emitting diode, better known as the LED. These tiny bulbs use less energy than both incandescent and fluorescent bulbs. Not only that, they last much longer. The problem right now is that they are still a bit expensive. Many companies throughout the world are working to make them more economical, and these could be good buys going forward.

Incumbents of government, beware! Uranus in hot-headed Aries demands the change we thought we'd get back in 2008. Had our leaders read the fine print, instead of touting change and "yes we can," they would have been more honest to say we couldn't change, even if we wanted to. This is because way back on March 1, 1999, the United States signed on to the World Trade Organization's Financial Services Agreement (FSA). This little agreement had big implications. In a nutshell, we were forced to prop up worthless banks. When we signed on the dotted line, our leaders agreed that we would not set limits on the size, corporate form, or other characteristics of companies doing business with the WTO! You might be familiar with the phrase "too big to fail," and this is when it was born. We also committed to deregulate our financial markets. In doing so, we foolishly agreed to impose no regulations on the financial sector! In other words, we are now forced to bail out the giant behemoths, even foreign ones!

Uranus' purpose is to rid us of things we no longer need. Considering the amount of money thrown down that black hole, haven't we spent enough time enriching the very culprits who gambled away our hard-earned money? Perhaps it's time to take a second look at our "free trade" policies.

Neptune is the planet of dreams. Whatever sector is represented by the sign he is in will at first be cast in a rosy glow. It will seem to be so heavenly, we want to be a part of it, but that is the problem. Heaven is up there; we live down here. Neptune is just the opposite of Uranus, in that whatever sector the dreamy planet touches goes cold. For example, while in Capricorn, big business bought up all the independent news outlets, radio stations, and television networks, crushing independent thought by monopolizing the media with their corporate message. Once Neptune entered computing Aquarius, new technology spawned by the Internet wore down publishing empires, sending the newspaper the way of the horse and buggy. Will network television be next? Neptune is also the most religious of planets. It will make us willing to sacrifice for our beliefs. Religious fanatics have thrived under this placement. As we start the new year, some of these terrorists may be at the end of their rope.

In the meantime, chocoholics and drinkers, get ready for sticker shock. Brazil, the leading producer of sugarcane, has decided to devote a higher percentage of its arable soil toward biofuels, leaving a worldwide sugar deficit in its wake. If this trend continues, we may see a rise in the price of alcohol, baked goods, candies, and all things sweet. The wise farmer might consider beets, which are a good northern alternative to sugarcane, and one of the healthiest foods for the diet conscious.

Pluto is here to transform whatever sector it touches. Depending upon the millennium, it takes Pluto 240 years to complete one cycle around the Sun. Since Pluto has only made it through six of the twelve signs since its discovery, we still have much to learn about its influence on markets. It sets the stage for extremely long-term trends. It is a bearish planet, and will transform any sector it touches. Right now it is in the early stages of transforming the banking industry. The bumps of the past few years have plagued many businesses, as the easy money-lending practices of the past dried up. Pluto takes on a Darwinian aspect when in Capricorn. In other words, only the strong survive. Competition is stiffer than it has ever been in our lifetimes. Businesses and personnel will need to work harder and longer hours to get ahead. Pluto puts us through the mill because we are carrying too much useless baggage.

. . . .

Those who will come out ahead this year will be the flexible. It won't help to give people a discount for goods and services in view of the present circumstances. In business, the victor in deals will be the most tenacious and the most ruthless. Hard as it is, in this time of massive shortfalls, wise management would do well to take the long view and invest in research and development. This is a climate where those who dig get ahead, especially in July when Jupiter will trine Pluto. Look for mining stock to do well at this time. Pluto is the planet of triage, forcing us to change our way of being. In business it twists the arm of both labor and management so that they may reform wasteful practices. Some of us may have to face that it's time to throw in the towel. Just remember, when one door closes, another always opens. Needless to say, when the constituents are squeezed, it is never an easy time for the administration.

The Financial Quarters

First Quarter, Winter Solstice 2010 to Spring Equinox 2011

This Christmas season promises to be one that will be engraved in the hearts and minds of people everywhere. Our shipping and travel industry could see some action just before the new year.

Holiday air travel may take on a macabre atmosphere, as restrictions and delays become the name of the game. Plan your travel wisely. The meeting of the two titans of the solar system, Jupiter and Uranus, may put a jolt in the markets, bringing seismic changes not just to the market but elsewhere. Those living in earthquake country, be prepared!

We open the year with a sense of relief. Shoppers seem to be starting to part with their cash again. Holiday shopping was better than anticipated. Look for stocks to rally on that news. All this exuberance masks reality. Paper profits are just that: paper. There is no recovery if people remain jobless. Any true return to growth has to be tied to employment. We are not yet seeing this, and so skeptics of this deficit-riddled "recovery" stock up on stable gold.

Don't be surprised if that cheap stuff from China isn't quite as cheap any longer. China may raise the value of the yuan. There are rumors that it may go up as much as 5 percent. This means that, in effect, prices are going up. Other foreign powers may be having financial problems of their own, changing our relationship with them. We need to do our homework. Big changes are coming up, and we want to be ready.

Second Quarter: Spring Equinox to Summer Solstice

The old saying that the only things you can count on are death and taxes has never been truer. Global tensions are mounting. Unfortunately our dependence upon the goodwill of others has weakened us. Americans are now import junkies, dependent upon the goods of foreign powers that have their own interests at heart. Frustration with the status quo is mounting. We are disappointed in our leaders, who seem too paralyzed to do much of anything, except make conciliatory gestures. Main Street is tired of yet another so-called jobless recovery. With no fewer than five planets in Aries, that old adage "haste makes waste" is doubly true. Expect prices to rise. Can inflation be far behind? Consider

2010 © Sergey Filkin. Image from BigStockPhoto.com

shifting some profits into gold while tensions peak. Look for government contractors, military, and metals to do well in this atmosphere.

In late March and early April, do not sign on the dotted line. Make sure you avoid signing any important contracts from the last week of March until April 23, while Mercury's backward jaunt casts its shadow. We don't want to be left with anything that will come back to haunt us when Mercury goes direct.

Third Quarter: Summer Solstice to Fall Equinox

Can inflation be far off? Well, actually no. Valuations may have gone too high, and stocks are starting to stall. It may be time to take a very unsentimental inventory of your holdings. Consider dumping nonperformers. Markets may be peaking for now. As volume dwindles, it may be time to reallocate to blue chips and other places of stability. It's always a bull market somewhere, but the U.S. may be feeling the pinch. The much maligned dollar is ready to make an about-face. Look for the dollar to increase in value against the other major currencies. After all, cash really is king as worried investors flee to safety in an increasingly unfriendly equities market. Terrorist threats could make for an uncomfortable Fourth of July holiday. In general, this quarter is one of readjustment and reallocation. Real-estate vultures are rewarded during this quarter, as there are some hopes that real estate might have bottomed out. This is a great time to hunt down good companies that may be getting beaten up, and then wait for the right time to act. Believe it or not, that roller coaster ride we have been on is easing up. Don't sign on the dotted line, though; August contracts will come back to bite us you-know-where. Avoid committing to any new project that you will need to affix your signature to between August 2 and 26. Mercury's retrograde motion will trick you into thinking you are buying something that you are not. Your word must be your bond, so do not agree to any promises that you cannot keep.

Fourth Quarter: Fall Equinox to Winter Solstice

Once the earnings season is in full swing, instead of biting our nails, perhaps we can take a sigh of relief with a little bit of positive news about employment. Gold and metals thrive in the beginning of the season, but we will have to watch them carefully as more confidence comes to the marketplace. It is still early, but there seem to be positive indications on the horizon. While it's still too early to call it a full-fledged boom, the beginnings of a recovery may be ahead. Look for good figures from the bellwethers of the business sector, the tech stocks. However, with better numbers, we could be see a bit of a standoff from labor in October, when an exhausted workforce may try to get more money out of management. Gold may retreat in November. Christmas shoppers are being less careful than they have been in recent years. Basically, if you have managed to keep your wits about you while those around you lost their head, pat yourself on the back. However, it's not time to rest on your laurels. We are still in a sideways market, spelling gains in one place with losses in another. Until something is done to bring back jobs to our shores, our financial fate will continue to shift with the wind.

About the Author

Dorothy J. Kovach is a traditional astrologer who utilizes both Eastern and Western methods in her work. Best known for using the traditional methods of William Lilly, she called the market downturn in 2000 to the month, five years in advance. More recently, she warned her readers to get off the markets by the beginning of 2008. She also called both the drop in oil and the fall of the euro, to a rather skeptical audience, back in April of 2008. If you would like to have a more specific idea of what the markets are going to bring, sign up for her newsletter at www.worldastrology.net or write her at Dorothy@worldastrology.net.

2010 © Peter Kirschner. Image from BigStockPhoto.com

New and Full Moon Forecasts

By Sally Cragin

When I was expecting my daughter, a family member jokingly suggested we name her Luna, as a tribute to my astrological profession. Yes, my family knows I pay attention to the Moon, and I actually did explore some multicultural "Moon" name options. As I'm half Armenian, I considered *Lucine*, which means "Moon" and is pretty, but isn't quite right.

The more I researched, the more I found that various cultures make sharp distinctions between the phases of the Moon when naming children. Hindi girls born at the Full Moon would be named Purnima, or Poornima. Arab girls could be Badriyyah,

241

Thai girls, Pen-Chan. The New Moon also had particular baby names associated with it. Migini or Taigi was used by Native Americans of the Omaha tribe to mean "returning Moon," while Turks used Tulay.

Of course, there are general Moon names, like Pensri, which is Thai for "beauty and goodness of the Moon," or Candra, an Indonesian name from a myth about the princess Candra Kirana of Kediri who was incarnated by Dewi Ratih, the goddess of love (yes, every mythology has one!). Candra is pretty and means "glowing like the Moon." Even aspects of lunar phenomena are alluded to: Hala is Arabic for "Moon halo," and Rishima is a Hindi name for "moonbeam."

So even though we didn't name our daughter Monday (which is named after the Moon—she was born Sunday afternoon), it was interesting to see so many variants. Lunar awareness is cross-cultural and extends across millennia, and no matter how modern and up-to-date you think you are, taking the Moon into account when making decisions, taking action, organizing your plans, or even naming a child has plenty of precedents.

How to begin? Check your calendar right now as you read this article. Is the Moon new? Waxing? Waning? Full? The desire to get organized can be a waxing Moon impulse; the desire to reorganize is a waning Moon activity.

Waxing? Waning? How do we know? The days leading up to the Full Moon are the waxing phase (Moon is getting bigger) and the days after the Full Moon are the waning phase (Moon is getting smaller). About two weeks after the Full Moon you'll notice the Moon is no longer present in the sky. This is the New Moon phase, which initiates another lunar cycle.

Eric Carle's children's book *Papa, Please Get the Moon For Me* concerns a little girl, Monica, who wishes to play with the Moon. And when her father brings it to her (this involves a very long ladder), the Moon gradually gets smaller and smaller until it is only a sliver. And then it grows big again.

To update this story for teenage and adult readers, some understanding of lunar phases will definitely get you the Moon. And even though you can't hold it in your hand, you can use its light for guidance.

New Moon: Subtlety Rules

In the book Numbers in the Old Testament of the Bible, the New Moon was the time to make burnt offerings. But not of just any old sacrifice—this was a specific combination of objects including lamb with grain mixed with a precise amount of flour mixed with oil. A bull, ram, and lamb each were sacrificed, and in case that wasn't enough, a male goat was also offered to the Lord as a "sin offering."

Yes, the New Moon is all about starting over and bringing everything back to zero. Projects or relationships can end (or begin) during this time, and it's easier to have an enlightened perspective because the confusion that can occur during the Full Moon is absent.

There is also a tentativeness to the New Moon, so if you are uncertain about proceeding, give yourself a day or two. Perhaps wait until you see the waxing crescent (which is shaped like a D rather than a C), when the first quarter is well underway. People born during the Full Moon often feel aimless or low in energy during the New Moon; people born during the New Moon feel more "at home" within themselves and more productive during the New Moon. During this phase, you shouldn't experience a lot of pressure (from others or from yourself). This is a great time to experiment with cooking, with crafts, with gardening, with journeys, and with relationships.

Quarters: First and Last

O Lady Moon, your horns point toward the east: Shine, be increased;
O Lady Moon, your horns point toward the west: Wane, be at rest.

If you memorize that elegant couplet by pre-Raphaelite sister and poet Christina Rossetti, you'll always know what phase the Moon is in. The Moon takes 29.5 days to go through the full cycle, thus when we only see "half" of the Moon we call it a "quarter," because it's a quarter of the way through its cycle.

The waxing Moon is one of the most beautiful sights in the sky, and its appearance heralds the start of feast times, celebrations, rituals, and religious events. Numerous cultures use the appearance of the New Moon (that thinnest of crescents, shaped like the right side of a capital D) to begin or end a ritual. In Islam, Ramadan is the most holy and precious month in the faith. It's a movable holiday, according to our solar-based calendar. If you use the Islamic lunar calendar, it stays on the same day every year, and begins at sunset the day before the sighting of the New Moon.

Note: The actual "sighting" versus "astronomical calculation" is still a point of debate, and various Muslim countries begin their religious holidays at different times, depending on where the Moon is from a geographical perspective. Yes, this is confusing, and when I went Web surfing to find some background using the keywords Islam, holiday, and lunar, up popped a number of plaintive queries along the line of "Can anyone tell me when Ramadan begins?" In an industrialized world, such reliance on natural phenomena seems charming, even quirky. Remember: you don't always "see" the New Moon, due to cloud cover, pollution, or lack of visibility because you live someplace filled with tall buildings that are always alight.

No matter what your religious beliefs may be, I'd always advise you to use the New Moon as your personal starting point for projects, relationships, decisions, financial transitions and transactions, planting, nurturing, and buying.

As the Moon is growing (more white on the right, as the shadow on the left diminishes), you may feel a sense of anticipation as the Full Moon approaches. Quarter Moons can be turning points—or not. Such are the vicissitudes of the Moon. But take note of the first quarter Moon regardless, because you have about ten days from that point to the Full Moon phase to go completely, absolutely, stark-raving crazy about a course of action.

Full Moon: Everything's Obvious

"Is it possible on nights there's a Full Moon we could shut the lights off?"
–City Council President Jody Joseph, not entirely joking, during budget hearings with Department of Public Works supervisors, June 2007, Fitchburg, Massachusetts

The Full Moon can make you feel like you can do anything, but also unable to focus on any one thing. The Full Moon (Luna) gives us *lunacy* and *lunatics*. The Full Moon can indeed find us turning into lunatics.

The New and Full Moon forecasts that follow provide specific signposts for each phase, with an emphasis on signs that are more affected (positively or adversely) depending on the time of year. Full Moons are the ones that get people stirred up and make them think, "Hmmm, maybe there is something to astrology after all!"

Activities for the Full Moon include outside nighttime games or excursions, parties, and other public events. During this phase, the spotlight is on and the Sun and Moon are aligned with Earth. Decisions made during this time could be impetuous and short-sighted, although if you've been planning a course of action for some weeks, the Full Moon could push any ambivalence to one side. You'll find yourself hurtling full-tilt, pell-mell into something exciting. I've heard from clients and friends that the first warm Full Moon in the spring—once the snow has passed and the ground softens up—finds everyone in an erotic mood. Flirtation happens among the most unlikely personalities, and even the wallflowers want to be in the middle of the dance floor.

If you find you're impatient or need some peace and quiet during this phase, you may have been born during the New

Moon—you instinctively find the time of the Full Moon confusing or dramatic. When I talk to new clients, I always point out what phase the Moon was in when they were born. Invariably, clients born during the Full Moon (when the Sun and Moon are in opposite signs) always crave more stimulation and have a greater capacity for socializing than do people born during the New Moon.

But don't get me wrong: use the Full Moon the way you'd use a cup of espresso or a brisk walk. You can be very sharp mentally, as long as you can exert some control over the variety of your thoughts and notions. It's also a time when generosity and sharing come more readily. A hairdresser once wrote me to say that her tips were noticeably more generous during the Full Moon; conversely, they radically dropped off during the New Moon.

Robert Louis Stevenson made drolly accurate observations about the Full Moon in *A Child's Garden of Verses*, when he wrote:

> *The Moon has a face like the clock in the hall;*
> *She shines on thieves on the garden wall,*
> *On streets and fields and harbour quays,*
> *And birdies asleep in the forks of the trees.*
> *The squalling cat and the squeaking mouse,*
> *The howling dog by the door of the house,*
> *The bat that lies in bed at noon,*
> *All love to be out by the light of the Moon.*

Why do we like to be "out" on the Full Moon? Why are some Full Moons more potent than others? The Full Moon is the one phase that draws descriptive titles from the world's cultures. For example, the Algonquin tribes of the New England area decided the Full Moons in winter, from about November through February, were the Beaver Moon, the Long Night's Moon (the Moon closest to the Winter Solstice), the Wolf Moon, and the Snow (or Hunger) Moon. That last Full Moon makes you pause. In a pre-industrial world, the last weeks of cold weather would be the most difficult to get through without a cache of food. The Full Moon that follows the Hunger Moon is the Worm or Sap Moon. If you make it to that point, you had a chance of living until the Fish Moon, the Corn Planting Moon, and the Strawberry Moon (April through June, respectively).

Navigating the Lunar Phases, Sign by Sign

The calendar of New and Full Moon dates that follows provides some specific assistance for the signs, depending on the Full Moon, but here is also a sign-by-sign narrative for the coming year as well.

Aries: You're ruled by Mars, so the Moon's influence can make you have feelings when you'd rather take action. The Full Moons in harmony with your Sun sign will be in February, June, and October. The Full Moon will be in conflict with your Sun sign in January, April, and July.

Taurus: Venus is your ruling planet, so the Moon acting in concert with that pretty star will bring out your aesthetic talents and your friend-making ability. Nurturing should come easily to you when the Full Moon is in sync with your Sun sign in March, July, and November. The Full Moon is not your friend in May, August, or February.

Gemini: Mercury gets you up and running, and this tiny planet of communication and short messages can lighten up the Moon's more emotional influence on your chart. You'll be at odds with the Full Moon's touchy-feely message during the Full Moons of March, June, and September. The Full Moons of April, August, and December will find you functioning efficiently (even maniacally).

Cancer: The Moon rules you, and my experience with your sign is that you feel everything during every Full Moon. But the Moons that could really unnerve you occur in April, July, and

October. A sense of being at one with the universe could be the saving grace for you in January, March, May, September, and November.

Leo: The Sun is your ruling planet, and the Sun and Moon are the alpha and omega of world religions. Full Moons that deter you from your goals come in May, August, and November. Full Moons that bring out your ability to have fun and get things done come in February, June, and October.

Virgo: Mercury rules your sign, and a Mercurial influence on a Full Moon cranks up your analytical ability. Do others think you're a fussbudget? They probably will during the Full Moons of June, September, and December. You'll seem more on top of things during the Full Moons of March, July, and November.

Libra: Venus is your shining star, and the Full Moon's influence will affect your taste for pleasant experiences and interactions. But your instincts may not be at their best during the Full Moons of January, July, and October. Trust your instincts during the Full Moons of April, August, and December.

Scorpio: Pluto rules your sign, and Pluto and the Moon don't have a very harmonious relationship, even at the best of times! Nevertheless, your probing sensibility will be awakened by the Full Moon. Just be skeptical of your own responses, desires, appetites, and actions during the Full Moons in February, August, and November. You'll make smarter choices during the January, May, and September Full Moons.

Sagittarius: Jupiter is your ruling planet, and when the Full Moon comes along, all your jovial impulses are awakened. These can include friend-making, gift-giving, exploring other cultures, or going hog-wild at the buffet table. Times when you may over-indulge are the Full Moons of March, September, and December. Full Moons that are your friend come in February, June, and October.

Capricorn: Saturn runs your sign, and Saturn and the Moon also have an adverse relationship with one another. Saturn says "time's up," and the Moon asks for still more time. Limits are where Saturn likes to live, while the Moon likes to feel things out. You'll probably feel conflicted during Full Moons of January, April, and October. But all is not lost: take action during the Full Moons of March, July, and November.

Aquarius: Uranus is your ruling planet, and the Moon and Uranus together can make for an electrically charged good time—plus eccentric personal relationships. The Full Moon will definitely put you off-kilter during February, May, and November. Fortunately, the Full Moons that occur in April, August, and December are excellent times for creativity.

Pisces: Neptune rules your sign, and when that dreamy, far-flung planet collaborates with the Moon, you could find all your appetites (especially for escapism) at full tilt. The Full Moon will make mischief with your Sun sign in March, June, and December. Take time during the Full Moon in January, May, and September to get in touch with your feelings and frustrations.

New and Full Moon Forecasts for 2011

New Moon in Capricorn, January 4

Mars in Capricorn amplifies this New Moon, so male/female relations could be passionate, yet not particularly communicative. You know you're feeling something, you're just not sure what! If you haven't reviewed your finances for a while, or have let some debts pile up purely through inaction, this New Moon is super for getting all that data together and looking at it with an eye toward simplifying your life.

Full Moon in Cancer, January 19

Since Mars just finished its journey in Capricorn and Mercury has just begun, this Full Moon brings us an energy that opposes any conservative impulses. Getting to the bottom of emotional situations is the point of this Full Moon, and feelings of insecurity are likely, particularly if you let your thoughts linger on how things used to be. Romantic impulses will come naturally to some, including water signs Cancer, Scorpio, and Pisces.

New Moon in Aquarius, February 3

Make time for brainstorming, as this New Moon wants novelty in your life. This means that relationships or projects that have gotten stale will hold no interest, so it's not the best time to be thoughtful around those who need more attention. Aquarius, Libra, Gemini, Aries, and Sagittarius should explore activities that ignite their creativity and imagination.

Full Moon in Leo, February 18

With Mars opposing the Moon, male/female relations could be tense, particularly for Taurus and Scorpio. If your expectations are that another could or should make a big effort on your behalf, you may be disappointed. This Full Moon is all about public image, big parties, and finding the humor in tense situations.

New Moon in Pisces, March 4

Since Pisces is the last sign in the zodiac, it brings a lot of intense but not-easily-analyzed psychic and subconscious activity, particularly for Pisces, Scorpio, Cancer, and even for practical Capricorn and Taurus. If your thoughts are wandering and it's hard to focus on completing a project, give yourself some leeway, and figure you'll take care of business by the first quarter Moon on March 12. This is an excellent phase for brewing, canning, working with preserves, or having radical dentistry or podiatry work done.

Full Moon in Virgo, March 19

Order prevails, so save your spring-cleaning urges for this Full Moon. You'll see dirt, dust, and grime and will attack it with a vengeance. Solo cleaning is advised, because your impulse toward other human beings is not particularly sensitive. Reorganizing is another satisfying activity, as is cooking. This goes double for Taurus, Capricorn, Scorpio, and Cancer—triple for Virgo.

New Moon in Aries, April 3

Self-reliance is the theme, which means that those who can't make a move without approval will be anxious. This is the most natural New Moon of the year for initiating projects, and momentum will be easy to find. But it's better to start than to finish, better to cut short than prolong. Those who understand this philosophy most thoroughly include Aries, Sagittarius, Leo, Aquarius, and Gemini.

Full Moon in Libra, April 18

It's another Mars/Moon opposition (see February 18), so correspondence and communication between the genders will be compromised. Women will be in that "I'm only trying to find common ground" zone, while men will be impatient if women need time to think, process, explore, or examine a relationship. The good side of this is that those of you with an inclination for partnership (and Gemini, Libra, Aquarius, Leo, and Sagittarius) will be well-nourished.

New Moon in Taurus, May 3

Earth sign Moons, no matter the phase, will prompt a spirit of acquisitiveness and "I must HAVE that!" So, if you've finished your spring cleaning, treat yourself to something elegant and antique, or fresh from a garden. Taurus, Capricorn, Virgo, Cancer, and Pisces should trust their instincts (and their taste), and can offer useful advice to friends and loved ones. Just remember that Taurus Moons are about bluntness, also!

Full Moon in Scorpio, May 17

Even one more Moon/Mars opposition can't derail the sensual potential of this Full Moon. Water signs, Virgo, and Capricorn are in a mood for intimacy. Folklore advises brewing beer during this lunar phase, and with Scorpio's penchant for controlled escapism, taking a break from reality could be refreshing.

New Moon in Gemini, June 1

An excellent day for collecting information or getting a medical diagnosis. Still smoke? It's a fine day to quit—Gemini rules the lungs. Doing things two by two or making purchases in pairs is a good use of resources, and smart decisions will be made by Gemini, Libra, Aquarius, Capricorn, and Taurus (who are benefiting from Mars moving through their Sun sign, enhancing decisiveness).

Full Moon in Sagittarius, June 15

If you have not made travel plans, make them during this lunar phase. Trips overseas or to exotic cultures will appeal to all, and those of you in the travel field should expect an uptick of business. (If not, it's a great time for soliciting customers.) Sagittarius, Leo, Aries, Libra, and Aquarius are in friend-making mode, and

they'll have the best ideas for fun. It's easy to be hyper-stimulated, and so some folks (Gemini, Virgo, and Pisces) could be accident-prone.

New Moon in Cancer, July 1

An excellent Moon for getting (or receiving) therapy, or taking time out to "molt." (Just remember, a real molt involves a period of solitude while your new shell hardens.) Folklore advises you to undertake domestic activities: baking bread and cakes, brewing or making preserves, or

2010 © Pavel Losevsky. Image from BigStockPhoto.com

improving your home by making it more secure and/or cozy. Cancer, Scorpio, Pisces, Virgo, and Taurus are highly attractive right now, and if they want to be of service, let them.

Full Moon in Capricorn, July 15

The usual craziness that goes with a Full Moon is tempered, in that if people want attention, they'll figure out a way to make it last. Improving your reputation should be a goal, particularly for Capricorn, Virgo, Taurus, Pisces, and Scorpio. Since most fiscal years end on June 30, this Full Moon means you get to see how functional your finances can be if times are tough. Fortunately, setting limits comes easily to all right now.

New Moon in Leo, July 30

Improving appearances or getting sufficient attention is a worthy activity for Leo, Gemini, Aries, and Libra. This New Moon runs counter to Leo's need for recognition, so if folks who usually have no problem speaking up suddenly become very shy, it's a passing phase. Sagittarius may think they're being funny or light, but others could misinterpret (Mars is not your friend until September).

Full Moon in Aquarius, August 13

An excellent Moon for new ideas, wild plans, rewiring a room or workplace, and generally having more "light" in your life, whether it's actual light bulbs, or someone who has a fresh outlook. Folklore advises you to excavate a space and/or pour cement during this lunar phase. Keeping with Aquarius' theme of electricity, it may be time to clear away broken appliances and upgrade.

New Moon in Virgo, August 29

Just as last March's Full Moon in Virgo was excellent for spring cleaning, this New Moon will sharpen your eyes and instincts for simplifying or analyzing what you need versus what you have. Monday New Moons are good times for planning meetings. This isn't an obvious time for romance, but some earth and water signs may be in the mood. Since Virgo is fastidious and precise, make an effort to be well-groomed if you're looking for love.

Full Moon in Pisces, September 12

A "Saturday night special" is what we get with this Full Moon, and the three Es (escapism, ease, and eccentricity) will bring great pleasure to water signs, Taurus, and Capricorn. Folklore says to make sauerkraut, but if you consider that the Sun is lined up with Virgo and Mars lined up with the Moon, you'll find opposites attract right now. Summer's not officially over, and many will feel torn between wanting to have fun and needing to get serious about work. If the weather is good, this Full Moon is glorious for romance.

New Moon in Libra, September 27

Even-handedness comes easily to Libra, Gemini, Aquarius, Leo, and Sagittarius, and if you need to make a decision this week, late in the day or Wednesday is your time to step up. Aries may be agitated and not easily soothed right now, and this Full Moon favors couples or partnerships. You may find you're looking at someone you never regarded before as a possible "other half." Even if nothing's at stake, half a banana split is better than a whole one, right?

Full Moon in Aries, October 12

The Full Moon and Mars are in harmony (finally!), but there's combustibility in the world. Aries, Leo, Sagittarius, and Gemini can be highly persuasive, even if they lose interest in a project almost instantaneously. Aries Moons help us live with less, move quickly through life, and avoid lingering regrets. Those who will function best during this Full Moon are those who can take a childlike delight in delays and changes of plan.

New Moon in Scorpio, October 26

It's a great day for hearing a secret! Some signs (Taurus, Leo, Aquarius) may need to spill one; other signs (Cancer, Scorpio,

Pisces) are having remarkable insights. If you work in finance or in a purchasing realm, this is an excellent lunar phase for seeing how easy it is to reduce consumption (that's also a metaphor). Folklore advises dentistry on this date, and since Scorpio also rules surgery, those of you who work with knives will be extra dexterous.

Full Moon in Taurus, November 10

Hard work pays off and despite an awkward angle with Mars (making Aquarius and Scorpio testy), beauty treatments for yourself or your home are worth pursuing. Romantic urges can make some signs highly distractible (especially those Capricorn/Leo pairs). Enjoying musical performances, particularly vocals, will enhance this Full Moon for all.

New Moon in Sagittarius, November 25

This New Moon is another fine day to plan a long trip or explore the advantages of furthering your education. The same old-same old won't do when it comes to food or cultural experiences, and some signs (Pisces and Gemini) will be irritable thanks to an awkward angle between the Moon and Mars. If you have had automobile difficulty, the day after Thanksgiving is a fine time to drive a family member's new gas-conserving vehicle to see if you like it.

Full Moon in Gemini, December 10

With Venus and Mars in earth signs, an unlikely cosmic event occurs: earth signs open up and share, share, share. Gemini Moons bring out a chatty congeniality. If you're planning a holiday party this month, this is the day for it. Gemini, Libra, and Aquarius are eager to "move on to the next thing" but should make time to spend with siblings or peers. Writers are favored during this transit, and even the most private types will consider starting a blog.

New Moon in Cancer, December 24

Home and hearth is the focus of this New Moon, with an emphasis on domestic arts and baking—Santa is expecting homemade cookies on the hearth this year! Cancer, Pisces, and Scorpio are in a sentimental mood, but Libra and Aries could be doing a lot of last-minute shopping. Virgo and Taurus are enjoying a boost of energy from Mars, which helps them organize everything.

About the Author

Sally Cragin, as Symboline Dai, writes "Moon Signs" for the Boston Phoenix *newspaper chain. She is the author of* The Astrological Elements, *from Llewellyn. Sally is available for private consultations and can be reached at www.moonsigns.net/*

2011
Moon Sign Book
Articles

2010 © Kevin Britland. Image from BigStockPhoto.com

2010 © Laura Stone. Image from BigStockPhoto.com

Growing Community Gardens

By Dallas Jennifer Cobb

At the grocery store, it is common to see fruits and vegetables imported from Mexico, Chile, and even as far away as China. But after learning more about global warming and the disastrous effects of long-distance travel and consumption of fossil fuels, many people are acutely aware of the distance food travels before it comes to their plate.

For the average consumer, our access to locally grown fruits and vegetables is as limited as our access to land on which to grow them. For people living in apartments, condos, and townhouses in the city, there is no access. But even for folks who own a house with a yard or live in a suburban or rural setting where there is easier access to land, their dependency on imported foods has separated them from its production. For many, the skills of gardening have been all but forgotten.

But a growing movement aims to revolutionize both access to fresh food and the land on which to produce it by providing growing plots and instruction in the fine art of food production. Community gardening, the practice of people collectively growing food on (usually) public land, is providing solutions to the lack of access to land, allowing people to "farm" publicly held spaces. Growing solutions to the problems of food scarcity, environmental pollution, reliance on foreign food markets, and myriad other social ills, community gardening has many benefits.

A History of Community Gardening

The community gardening movement is not a new one. Community gardens have been around as long as there have been communities, and gardens have thrived in cities throughout the world. Archeological digs have even unearthed evidence of shared gardens in most major historic cities.

Existing archival information documents the existence of community gardens and allotment gardens as far back as the 1700s. In America, such gardens have their roots in historic Bethabara Park in Winston-Salem, the site of the first Moravian settlement in North Carolina and the oldest community garden in the country (that we know of), dating back to 1758.*

In the inner city areas of North America, these gardens have been commonplace since the 1890s. Aimed at helping to feed the poor, beautify neighborhoods, and bring people together for community development, community gardens have sprung up in vacant lots, on school grounds, around food banks and community centers, and in public parkland.

During World War II, many people supported the Allied war effort through the practice of maintaining a victory garden. The garden enabled families to feed themselves while growing a little

---

*City of Winston-Salem, North Carolina, "Colonial Agriculture", http://www
.cityofws.org/Home/Departments/RecreationAndParks/BethabaraPark/
HistoricArea/Articles/ColonialAgriculture (accessed August 4, 2009).

extra produce to feed the troops or others in need. "Plant a Victory Garden: Help Win the War!" was the message that prompted patriotic citizens to cultivate backyards, empty lots, and rooftops into fertile areas. These gardens supplied the Allied troops with food when the Axis forces were suffering shortages and their troops were starving. By devoting to the war effort a precious resource that was grown and gathered in many households, victory gardens helped to win the war.

What is a Community Garden, Exactly?

A community garden is any space gardened by an organized (or perhaps slightly disorganized) group of people who might not otherwise have anything more in common than living in the same general community. No longer limited to a piece of land, many people create gardens in planters, buckets, and pots. A community can be located rurally, in a city, or in the suburbs, and is as diverse as the people living in it. Participants can come from all walks of life, varied religions, ages, nationalities, ethnicities, languages, and social customs. They are united by the practice of gardening in the same space.

While most community gardens produce fruits and vegetables, such a garden can produce herbs, seeds, nuts, berries, and flowers. The growing is not limited to tangibles, either. A community garden also grows intangible goods, such as a sense of community, social connection, and personal empowerment.

Not just a movement aimed at feeding the poor or hungry, community gardening has often resulted in response to social and economic change.* It is a way for people to feel more secure during insecure times. Producing food security and economic

---

*Sean Cosgrove, "Community Gardening in Major Canadian Cities: Toronto, Montreal and Vancouver Compared," Toronto Food Policy Council, http://www .cityfarmer.org/canadaCC.html has a great table comparing the different kinds of gardens developed in the United States and Canada, their names, and what they developed in response to.

opportunity, community gardens also produce social safety nets during times of socioeconomic upheaval.

Greening urban areas, breaking down social isolation, and integrating newcomers are some of the far-reaching benefits of community gardens.

Allotment Gardening

In Britain, the term "allotment gardening" is used in place of "community gardening." The implication is that people gain access to an allotment of land. Individual plots are allotted to people, who plant their own gardens. Such allotments are often rented or leased, and involve an exchange of money, but allotments are also made available to those who cannot afford to pay.

Because of the dense population of the island country, allotment gardening preserves people's access to land on which to grow food; in some allotments, participants even keep bees or raise poultry. Like community gardening, allotment gardening protects green space from urban development. Many such allotments are located adjacent to dense urban development, enabling area residents who dwell in flats, apartments, and row houses access to land on which to grow food.

In England and Wales, the right to allotment gardening is protected by law. Laws in the two countries contain a written requirement for district councils (like a municipality or county) to provide allotments for their citizens. Anyone interested, and over the age of eighteen, can request the council to provide space for an allotment garden. The right to this access to land is protected by the laws of the community and is another meaning of the term "allotment gardening."

The Benefits of Community Gardens

The benefits of community gardening are most studied by community health advocates, who believe that community health is improved by myriad conditions. Community gardening with its long list of benefits has been studied extensively.* The research shows that these gardens act as a catalyst for neighborhood development, encouraging social bonds and communication across a spectrum of residents. Cross-cultural and intergenerational contact increases social sensitivity and decreases social isolation. Social health is improved through interaction, increased self-reliance, the acquisition of new skills, and the opportunity for recreation, education, and collaboration.

Community gardens improve participants' quality of life, providing them with fresh nutritious food at little or no cost—participants primarily invest time and energy. Gardens provide food security for people facing poverty or economic downturn, reduce reliance on imported goods, and reduce family food budgets. Economic development is stimulated by spin off businesses resulting from the gardens—the sale of fresh produce, or the sale of products made from garden produce, such as jams, pickles, and herbal ointments. So the gardens not only save participants money on household food budgets, but they can also provide income opportunities.

There are positive environmental benefits resulting from community gardening. Food is produced locally, resulting in resource conservation. Oil and gas are not used to transport this food around the world. Derelict lots are beautified, soil enriched, and neighborhoods transformed. Green space is conserved, directly improving air quality through oxygen generation, the creation of shade, and reduction of the urban heat effect.

When ugly, abandoned lots are reclaimed and made over into community gardens, neighborhoods often experiences a decrease in crime as a result of an increase in the number of people on the

*For a wonderful overview of the research, see Sarah Wakefield, Fiona Yeudall, Carolin Taron, Jennifer Reynolds, and Ana Skinner, "Growing Urban Health: Community Gardening in South-East Toronto," *Health Promotion International* 2007 22(2):92–101; http://heapro.oxfordjournals.org/cgi/content/abstract/22/2/92 (accessed August 6, 2009).

street, improved access to public space, and an appearance of care and beauty that pervades the gardens. When residents inhabit the outdoor public spaces, they are more connected to the "street" or "sidewalk life" of their neighborhood.

One other benefit of community gardening is community. This is not just the social relationships that stem from working gardens side by side, but the sharing of seeds, tools, compost, and techniques. The community garden is a place of human cross-pollination, fertilizing wonderful new things like sharing, collaboration, and communal celebration, cooking, and eating.

People Love Community Gardens

People who get involved in community gardens amass stories about their experience. And there's no wonder—not only are they a great way to grow food, improve health, make positive environmental change, and meet your neighbors, but they also serve as attractive outdoor spaces in which communities gather.

With an increased sense of ownership of public land, community garden participants often feel more connected to and responsible for their community. Participants get to know area shop keepers, they collaborate with local businesses and groups, and some even become more civic-minded, gathering garbage off the street in an attempt to keep the area beautiful. Community gardens can be a place for an individual to connect, feel a sense of belonging, develop relationships and roots in their home area, and increase their feelings of security and happiness.

Community garden spaces can be used as outdoor meeting centers, a place where participants can host gatherings, parties, celebrations, and events that might not have been possible in small living spaces.

Community gardens provide innovative ways of living sustainably within a city, building ecologically viable and socially just food systems, and fostering a deep sense of neighborhood connection. Beyond these obvious social and economic benefits, community gardens are great places to learn about gardening, sharing local knowledge, tradition, and even seeds. Community gardens are spaces in which people come together as a group with a common purpose.

It's no wonder participants love their community gardens!

Food Security

The Food and Agriculture Organization (FAO) of the United Nations states, "Food security exists when all people, at all times, have physical and economic access to sufficient, safe, and nutritious food that meets their dietary needs and food preferences for an active and healthy life." This statement was first drafted at the World Food Summit in 1996.*

The Centre for Studies in Food Security at Ryerson University in Toronto, Ontario, goes into further detail, stating that Food Security is determined using the following five components:

- **Availability**—There is sufficient food for all people at all times.
- **Accessibility**—There is physical and economic access to food for all at all times.
- **Adequacy**—There is access to food that is nutritious and safe, and produced in environmentally sustainable ways.
- **Acceptability**—There is access to culturally acceptable food, which is produced and obtained in ways that do not compromise people's dignity, self-respect or human rights
- **Agency**—There are policies and processes that enable the achievement of food security.**

---

*Food and Agricultural Organization of the United Nations, "Food Security" Policy Brief, ftp://ftp.fao.org/es/ESA/policybriefs/pb_02.pdf (accessed August 6, 2009).

**Ryerson University, "Food Security Defined," Centre for Studies in Food Security, http://ryerson.ca/foodsecurity/ (accessed August 5, 2009).

For most of us, food security means being able to feed ourselves and our families good food. By providing access to land on which to grow good food, community gardening contributes significantly to food security by enabling us to produce food for ourselves.

A secondary aspect of food security is the security of knowing exactly what went into the production of the food we are eating. By growing our own food, we can make choices about organic gardening that clearly affect the quality of our food, such as limiting its exposure to pesticides and manufactured chemicals. Community gardening organizers often teach simple yet effective natural gardening techniques like companion planting, composting, integrated pest management, and the growing of heirloom seeds. These techniques enable people to grow food suited for their region and climate without the use of harmful chemicals.

And this kind of food security impacts soil security. Organic growing techniques focus on soil health and do not rely on the addition of chemicals, which eventually break down the natural quality of the soil, depleting it of its fertility.

Community Empowerment

Many studies have been done that document the correlation between community development and community gardens. Historically, community gardens often developed in response to defined social or economic change. But community gardens are not just a response to social change; they also produce social change, enabling communities to develop social bonds, identity, economic opportunities, and security.

In North America, there are a number of organizations that have sprung up around community gardening, taking the growing of food to another level by developing businesses that bring real money and power to the community.

Utilizing urban spaces, nonprofit organizations have developed fish farms, hydroponics production, greenhouses, and farms that are collectively organized and operated. Many of these organizations have resulted in community supported agriculture (CSA) projects—a process of involving a community in the farming, even if they don't want to get their hands dirty. A CSA member can pay a set amount of money to the organization which entitles them to an amount of fresh food on a regular basis. If a person can't afford to pay the money, some CSAs allow them to work in exchange for food, or they may choose to combine work and money as their payment. Not limited to just vegetables and fruits, there are CSAs offering meat, poultry, and fish products as well. The money collected early in the CSA season is used to purchase seeds, hatchlings, piglets, lambs, and calves, which are then tended all season long and result in the harvest of produce, eggs, beef, pork, and lamb for the members.

Community Organizing

Interested in joining or starting a community garden in your area? You can either try to organize one yourself, connect with an organization that supports community gardening, or join an established community garden or network. In the resource section below, you will find links for resources throughout North America that will help you to connect to groups in your area, and even some free downloads with pointers on how to organize and set up a community garden.

Regardless of your location, your access to land, or your social or economic situation, you too can grow your own food in your neighborhood and enjoy all the benefits of community gardening. Why not get involved, growing food, friends, and community?

Grow Fresh Food in Tiny Spaces

Not sure where to start or what to grow? Why not opt for some of the easiest of crops? You can grow lettuce, spinach, and a variety of other leafy greens in trays placed in your southern-facing windows in even the smallest of apartments.

If you have access to a planter, why not try a tomato plant in the center of the pot, surrounded by chives and basil? One medium-sized pot can yield lots of tomatoes and herbs.

Potatoes are also really easy to grow in planters. A space-effective technique for growing a large volume of potatoes involves using a barrel with good drainage. A big old wooden barrel is the best, but a modern plastic garbage can could be modified with holes in the bottom for drainage. Place 8 inches of soil in the bottom of the barrel, and place your seed potatoes in, covering them with soil. As the potatoes sprout, forming the green tendrils of the plant, continue to fill the barrel with soil, covering the stalk of the plant, leaving the tips exposed. As these tendrils continue to grow, continue to fill the barrel with soil and good compost. When the barrel is almost filled, with soil 6 inches from the rim, let the plants continue to grow. Potatoes will form on the stalk, vertically, and a decent-sized barrel can produce up to 100 pounds of potatoes in very little space.

Start small, plant what you like to eat, and watch what sort of miracles you will grow.

Recommended Web Sites

The American Community Gardening Association has a wonderful Web site. Visit them at www.communitygarden.org/ for resources, information, and a community garden locator that will help you find a community garden near you.

At http://communitygarden.org/learn/best-practices-10-tips-series.php you can find free printable tip sheets covering all the basics of community garden planning, startup, and operation. Harvest the free wisdom grown in community gardens, available for the printing or downloading. Enjoy!

I love the Burlington Community gardens Web page. It contains tons of information and resources, all absolutely free. Visit http://www.burlingtongardens.org/gardenorganizer.html where you will find everything from checklists for organizing to garden guidelines and designs. There is also a long list of Web sites for community gardening programs in other states.

For additional links to organizations in North America that participate in the American Community Gardening Association, please visit http://www.communitygarden.org/connect/links .php#Gardens

For Further Reading

Boston Urban Gardeners. *A Handbook of Community Gardening*. New York: Charles Scribner's Sons, 1982.

Halverson, Beret, and Jim Flint. *Patchwork: Stories of Gardens and Community*. Claremont, CA: Community Works Press, 2005

Kiefer, Joseph, and Martin Kemple. *Digging Deeper: Integrating Gardens Into Schools and Communities: A Comprehensive Guide*. Montpelier, VT: Food Works, Common Roots Press, 1998.

Lawson, Laura J. *City Bountiful: A Century of Community Gardening in America*. Berkeley: University of California Press, 2005.

National Gardening Association. *Schoolyard Mosaics: Designing Gardens and Habitats*. South Burlington, VT: National Gardening Association, 2002.

About the Author

Dallas Jennifer Cobb cultivates gratitude, prosperity, and peace. Believing that "life is what you make it," she has made a magical life in a waterfront village on the shores of the great Lake Ontario. Forever scheming novel ways to pay the bills, she currently teaches Pilates, works in a library, and writes to finance long hours spent following her heart's desire: time with family, in nature, and on the water. Contact her at jennifer.cobb@live.com.

2010 © Vadym Graifer. Image from BigStockPhoto.com

Weather Watching

By Laurel Reufner

As I sit here writing this, in early August 2009, Weather.com and Yahoo.com are predicting a high today of 94—probably one of the hottest days we've had during what's turned out to be a rather cool summer. Our helpful meteorologists are also predicting the humidity will hit 84 percent, making it a soggy, hot day in southeast Ohio. Oh, and we're going to see fairly clear skies all day. To be honest, I already suspected the high humidity thanks to the heavy fog last night. The reddened sunset forecast a fairly clear day. The high temperature is about the only thing I couldn't predict from paying attention to my surroundings, although that heavy fog should have been a clue—it takes a hot day to hold that much moisture in the air. Either way, it is August, and it was hot and humid yesterday. Ergo, it's going to be even more hot and humid today.

While we have some very sophisticated technology to help predict what Mother Nature is going to do next, the lure of old weather proverbs remains. This brings us to the question of the day: do those old bits of lore really work? The answer depends on which bit of lore we're talking about, as well as where you are in the world. Some of the weather lore that follows is pretty accurate, letting you forecast local weather even better than the professionals. For each bit of the following lore, I've tried to explain why it does or doesn't work.

Please keep in mind while reading that most weather phenomena we'll talk about occurs between 30 and 60 degrees longitude in both the Northern and Southern Hemispheres. Weather patterns are pretty predictable and slowly changing in the equatorial areas, as well as around the poles.

> *Red sky at night, sailor's delight.*
> *Red sky at morning, sailor take warning.*

This is possibly the most recognized bit of weather lore out there. There are variations in the UK, Denmark, and Italy. It's referenced in the Bible (Matthew 16), and Shakespeare even uses it once or twice. There's good reason for this, since the "red sky at night" proverb tends to hold true. It has to do with air pressure. Higher air pressure means the air weighs more, pushing contaminants in the air closer to the ground. These particles scatter the shorter wavelengths of light, leaving only the longer, redder ones to color the evening sky.

Furthermore, air needs cooler temperatures for water vapor to condense. Higher pressure means the air is closer to the ground, where it's warmer. If the humidity is high enough, you can still have condensation as things cool off a bit at night, but it usually takes the form of fog or dew, leaving too little water in the air to make rain. So, a red sky in the evening almost always means there will be no rain that night.

The second part of the proverb about a red sky at morning isn't as sure a weather predictor as a red sky in the evening, but it still holds true more often than not. Just as the red sky in the evening indicates lots of solid particles in the air, a red sky at dawn occurs for the same reason: lots of particles in the air. The higher pressure front has likely passed and a low has perhaps moved in to take its place. A low-pressure front usually brings rain with it, hence the "warning."

Let's take a moment to look at how a pressure front forms and much of this will hopefully make a little more sense. Hotter air weighs less than colder air because the air particles are more excited and are farther apart. (Remember high school science classes?) Since it is less dense, it rises, where the thinner atmosphere lets it cool off. Cooler air becomes more dense, because the gases aren't as excited, and it sinks back toward the Earth. This slow cyclical process of rising warm air and falling cool air is known as a convection current.

The warmest part of Earth's atmosphere is here at the surface, but our planet has an uneven surface. This surface roughness is what causes the air to heat unevenly, leading to the high and low pressure differentials that form these convection currents. These giant masses of warming and cooling air create our weather. Wind, air pressure, and cloud formation can all be attributed to these pressure areas.

A lot of weather lore, rhyming or not, has to do with sensing changes in air pressure. Allergies tend to be worse just before a heavy rain because all allergens are held closer to the ground. Although not everyone is sensitive enough to detect it, some folks with bad joints will sense the change in air pressure as well. And those of us with sensitive sinuses can really suffer when a storm front comes through, thanks to intense, painful headaches.

> *When the rooster goes crowing to bed,*
> *he will rise with a watery head.*

Animals are sensitive to pressure changes as well. Many birds settle in and roost since they have a difficult time getting food in lower pressure weather. Flies seem to be just awful before a rain as well, clustering around windows and doors as though they were trying to get in from the coming wet. Horses and cows seem more agitated, swishing their tails around more than usual to swat away the flies and other bugs that like to bite them.

> *When the wind is out of the east,*
> *'Tis neither good for man or beast.*

Pack your umbrella on days when the wind blows out of the east, as that's usually a good sign we'll see rain before the end of the day. Weather systems generally travel west to east, so a system moving east to west is usually a sign of stormy weather. (The opposite is true for those in the Southern Hemisphere—wind from the west is a harbinger of wet weather.) Winds from this direction often bring low-pressure fronts, which generally give us are bad weather.

> *It ain't the heat, it's the humidity.*

A co-worker of my mother's was fond of saying this. At least in southeastern Ohio, it's not really the heat that's oppressive; it's the amount of water vapor in the air, making us feel like we'd be happier as fish with gills every time we take a breath. Actually, as far as weather is concerned, heat and humidity go hand in hand. When the evening news weather forecaster tells us we have 68 percent humidity, she's actually telling us the *relative* humidity, which is how much moisture the air can hold at its current temperature before it is completely saturated. Once the relative humidity hits 100 percent, a phenomenon called "dew point," it rains. However, the relative humidity is dependent upon the air's temperature. Warmer air can hold more moisture before it has to squeeze some out, which is one of the reasons a hot summer day can be so miserable. The air on a hot day can hold a lot of water before it can be considered "full."

As the air cools, either because night is setting or the air is rising up in the atmosphere, it holds less moisture. Particularly in the summer, excess moisture is often lost as dew or fog when the air cools. This is especially true when there's cloud cover helping to hold in the day's warmth. If it is a clear night, rain is often the welcome result of the cooling air.

> *I know ladies by the score*
> *Whose hair foretells the storm;*
> *Long before it begins to pour*
> *Their curls take a drooping form.*

You can't have rain without humidity, and a spell of high humidity makes for the ultimate bad hair day. As the humidity rises, your hair will actually get longer, curly hair gets frizzy and droopy, and straight hair may gain some curl. Frizzy hair by itself doesn't necessarily foretell rain, but the higher the humidity, the more likely it is to rain. Also, the higher the humidity, the more likely it is to storm as one weather front violently breaks onto another.

Other signs of increased humidity include chairs that squeak when you sit down and salt that clumps and sticks in the shaker. Both have absorbed excess moisture out of the air. (Note that this won't happen if your home is air conditioned, as an air conditioner takes excess moisture from the air.) Sometimes this excess takes the form of fog or dew, which means we probably won't have any rain.

> *If smoke hovers near the ground, it is likely to rain.*

In order for water vapor to form raindrops, they need to condense around something solid, like dust or smoke particles. Smoke particles can absorb a good bit of moisture, making them too heavy to disperse easily. When smoke heads straight up, there's little moisture around to latch onto the smoke particles, so it's probably going to be a clear day.

When the night has a fever, it cries in the morning.

According to Cowboy Bob's Weather Lore Web site, if there is a temperature rise between 9:00 pm and midnight, a warm front full of rain has probably moved into the area. I'm not sure how accurate this is overall, but it does sometimes indicate that a storm front has moved in. If the front lasts long enough, the ensuing rain can bring a welcome relief from the discomfort of both the high humidity and temperature. Otherwise it just makes things more miserable the next day by adding to the humidity.

Mackerel skies and mares' tails
Make high ships carry low sails.

Mackerel skies (or mackerel scales) and mares' tails refer to the appearance of cirrocumulus and cirrus clouds, both of which often precede a low-pressure front. Cirroculumus clouds are high spotty clouds, and cirrus clouds are high and wispy. Common lore predicts that when you see these clouds, you'll have rain sometime in the next couple of days. Of course, there is also always the possibility that the bad weather will pass you by. Weather lore works best, like professional forecasts, on the short term. (See Cowboy Bob's Weather Lore for more in-depth information.)

When clouds look like black smoke,
A wise man will put on his cloak.

Big, fluffy, cotton candy clouds don't produce rain, but tall, dark, fortress-like clouds signal rain. The cumulonimbus clouds aren't dark because they are bigger but because they're full of raindrops. Of course, you may need to look for other weather signs before you decide if those raindrops are meant for your head or someone else's, as the cloud's path is not entirely predictable.

When the wind is in the east, 'tis neither good for man nor beast.
When the wind is in the north, the skillful fisher goes not forth.
When the wind is in the west, then 'tis the very best.
When the wind is in the south, it blows the bait in fishes' mouth.

I am not even going to pretend I like fishing, but this rhyme is also good for understanding weather and wind direction. Winds from the east usually indicate the arrival of a low-pressure front and bad weather, which we've already established. (In the Northern Hemisphere, our weather systems usually travel from west to east.) Actually, the only good wind direction here is when the wind is from the west, because it would indicate that any potentially bad weather has already blown over. Winds from any other direction usually indicate some sort of weather change, usually for the worse.

When the ditch and pond affect the nose,
Look out for rain and stormy blows.

It's not just the smells from ditch and pond that are released when a low-pressure front moves in, but we probably notice the nastier smells more easily since they are, well, more offensive. All smells are stronger in a low-pressure system. My guess would be this is because the air isn't as densely packed with air molecules, so there's lots of room for other stuff, stink included. This is probably also the reason there are more allergens in the air before a rain.

Trout jump high
When a rain is nigh.

As the SkyWatch Web site points out, lower air pressure probably releases gases from decaying plant matter in the water, which turns loose small microorganisms living in that plant matter. The phenomenon then works its way up the food chain to where larger fish are breaking the surface water while feeding on the smaller fish. I'm not sure how much of a rain predictor this particular

2010 © Witold Krasowski. Image from BigStockPhoto.com

one is, as a person out fishing for trout has hopefully already checked the weather, and therefore avoids being out on the water when rain is blowing in! This rhyme may serve to back up the predictions of some of the other bits of lore.

Seasonal Predictions

While the previous bits of wisdom are great for figuring out what the weather is going to do short term, what about the long-range weather lore? Most of those reading this will have heard of at least the predictions of February 2, or what we call Groundhog Day in the United States. Honestly, there's little merit to such predictions based on what the weather is like on one particular day of the year.

The thickness of an onion skin is more of a reflection on the type of summer just past than it is of the coming winter. The same can also be said for how many nuts the squirrels are storing away for their winter's hoard—although my stepfather would always notice and comment if he noticed fewer nuts being gathered while he was out hunting in the woods.

My mother reminded me of the saying about hornets' nests: the higher they build their nests, the worse the winter weather that's on its way. I'm not sure why they build their nests higher or lower in any given year, but I'm pretty sure it doesn't necessarily indicate a bad winter all by itself.

As a child, my favorite bit of weather prediction was the woolly worm, or the woolly bear caterpillar. They were one of the few worms or caterpillars I wasn't afraid to pick up, and the fact that they could foretell the winter just added to my delight. The bigger the black bands on the caterpillar as compared to the brown bands, the harsher the winter will be. As I've gotten older, though, I've noticed big discrepancies in how big those weather-predicting bands of color are. My mother will argue with me on this one, as will quite a few other folks out there. Perhaps I'm taking my weather forecasting sample from too large an area. Who knows? It's still a fun bit of lore to teach your children, who will be delighted at how tightly the little guys curl up into a defensive ball when picked up.

These next, and last, two bits of lore also come from my mother. I had completely forgotten the correlation between a hard winter and how the animals ate toward the end of summer and into the fall. Some would argue that it was purely coincidence, but our pony obviously knew something about the coming weather. Princess liked to eat no matter what, don't get me wrong, but she would really pack on some extra weight just before a harsher winter (the mid-1970s come to mind) and her coat just kept getting thicker and shaggier. She's the only animal other than dogs and chickens that we had consistently throughout my childhood, so my experience is limited to just her behavior, but I've also heard farmers say the same thing about their cattle and horses. The part that baffles scientists and lands this bit of lore in the "probably myth" column, though, is how an animal could possibly know what the coming winter would be like. Perhaps it's part of some cycle that they can detect. Perhaps we humans used to be able to notice the same subtle hints ourselves, but time and an increasing reliance on science has removed us from still being able to detect such nuances in nature.

Finally, here comes a last bit of lore from my mother. I've no idea how valid it actually is, but it could serve as an indicator of a wet spring. Be that as it may . . .

If the river floods and leaves behind ice, it'll come back for it later.

(Meaning there will be another flood in warmer weather.)

For Further Reading

Allaby, Michael. *How the Weather Works: 100 Ways Parents and Kids Can Share the Secrets of the Atmosphere.* Pleasantville, NY: Reader's Digest, 1995.

Lemen, Bob. "Cowboy Bob's Weather Lore." http://www.lemen.com/ WeatherLore1.html (accessed April 14, 2010).

Tate, Ken, and Janice Tate. *Good Old Days: Country Wisdom.* Berne, IN: House of White Birches, 2001.

Walker, Nick. "Weather Proverbs: True or False?" http://www.wxdude .com/proverb.html (accessed April 14, 2010).

Wilson, Jerry. "SkyWatch: Signs of the Weather." http://www.wilstar .com/skywatch.htm (accessed April 14, 2010).

About the Author

Laurel Reufner's mother can verify that she grew up a "wild child" in farming country. She's been a Pagan for nearly twenty years now and really enjoys writing about topics that grab her attention. Laurel currently calls southeast Ohio home, where she lives with her wonderful husband and two wild children of her own. This article was inspired by a book her father loaned her a few months before he passed away. He'd have found it an interesting read. You can find her blog at trylsmeanderings.blogspot.com.

2010 © Tim Fischer. Image from BigStockPhoto.com

Aquatic Gardening by Moon Sign

By Janice Sharkey

Life began in water. We need it first before food. Water is an essential ingredient in any garden, not just to sustain plants but as one of the best ways to attract wildlife. It doesn't matter if you only have a tiny backyard for a garden, creating a water garden from a small container can be beneficial and beautiful as you watch all manner of wildlife come to call.

Sites and Shapes

Take a little time to think exactly where and what size your pond should be. Maybe it should be seen from the kitchen window if you have young children. Or maybe it would have more impact tucked away in a surprise corner of the garden. It's best not locate a pond near overhanging trees whose leaves will be a chore to remove from the water in the autumn. Remember that wildlife thrives in sunshine and so ponds do better with a reasonable amount of sunshine.

The shape of your pond will reflect just how you want the water garden to be. It doesn't have to be oval or rural looking. It could be rather formal and so be shaped by straight rectangular lines, which often work well in modern gardens and where ponds are located near the house or courtyard. Raised formal water gardens can be ideal where excavation is really difficult or because you need extra safety against children falling in. And that extra layer around the edge can double as a makeshift seat. The more natural pond is better located farther away from the house, set in a more natural open space. Even if you don't have acres of garden, there is no real minimum pond size, as long as it looks in proportion to its surrounding environment.

Pond Life

Think about how the contours, shape, and layers of depth of your pond will determine what can survive in the water. There are six growing areas within a typical water garden that act like mini ecosystems, allowing different types of plants and wildlife to flourish. There are water lilies; those plants that have their roots submerged, with their leaves floating on the water; some are just floaters with dangling roots; marginals are clearly above the surface; others are oxygenators, entirely submerged; and bog plants like to be around the poolside, in moist soil.

Amphibians and insects colonize the shallowest ponds, so a depth of 12–18 inches should be OK. Allow beachlike shallows to make access easier for frogs. Having a 12×12-inch-deep shelf for marginals provides attractive spawning spots for frogs. Fish love to eat frogspawn and other small creatures, so wildlife ponds are really better off without fish. You'll find water boatmen and dragonflies in and around your pond within hours, along with other flying insects like damselflies and water beetles. Frogs, newts, and toads often live in gardens even without ponds, so it won't be long before they too appear around your pond. Put some undisturbed wood from garden waste nearby to provide a useful place for them to hole up over winter.

Building Your Pond

Now that you have decided the best place for your pond, mark the shape with a hose or pegs. It's helpful to hammer in pegs to the required water depth around the edges, then dig out the deepest part of the pond, putting in shelves where necessary. As you dig, remove sharp stones, then cover the hole with damp, soft sand or with a felt underlay before laying a flexible butyl rubber liner on top. The next step is to weigh down the edges with bricks, then fill the pond with water, forming the liner as you go. To hide unsightly edges and protect the liner from damage around the top, lay feature stones or brick or turf to hide the top edge of the lining. If you laid stone or brick into mortar, you will need to wait until this is cured before adding the water to its full depth. Otherwise, plants can be added right away!

Six Aquatic Plant Groups

Nymphaea: Otherwise known as the water lily, *Nymphaea* is only one genus, but it contains many hardy species and varieties in nearly every color. It is not harmed by cold weather unless frozen and is ideal for keeping the water clear and cool in summer. Depending upon the variety, the recommended planting depth is between 3.5 inches and 3 feet. There is such a variety of types to suit every size of pond, from vigorous ones such as N. *colossea*, which will grow in lakes, to dwarf varieties such as N. *pygmaea helvola*, which is one of the smallest to survive in a modest pond.

Deep-water surfacing plants: These plants are useful for keeping the water clear and cool and their flowers can rise above the surface. They like being in a shallower depth, about 1 foot. These plants can usually take partial shade even with a fountain of water splashing around them.

Floaters: As the name suggests, these plants float on the water's surface with their roots submerged, leaves and stems free-floating on or just under the surface, and flowers above the surface. These plants give surface cover where the big showy plants, such as water lilies, are rare or absent. Only a few floaters are actually ornamental. You just drop the plants into the water and they find a way to survive. During winter, floaters sink to the bottom of the pond and survive as buds or seeds.

Marginals: These plants like their roots submerged, with leaves and flowers clearly above the surface. They are ornamental and sit on the boundary between the water and the pond edge, providing a good display in the growing season. The usual planting depth is 0–6 inches. The best way to grow them is in baskets that sit on the shallows of the pond.

Oxygenators: You'll hardly notice these plants, as they are hidden under the water doing the vital job of absorbing minerals and carbon dioxide, which helps inhibit algae. As the name implies, oxygenators also generate oxygen. They keep the water clear and provide food and a spawning area for critters. Oxygenators come in a bunch of cuttings held together at the base by a lead strip. The best way to plant them is to put them into heavy soil in a shallow basket and cover the top with gravel before placing the basket at the pond bottom. You'll need one bunch per 3 square feet of pond.

Bog plants: These are plants that love moisture and need damp, humus-rich soil that is never allowed to dry out. However, it's very important that these moisture lovers do not sit in water-logged soil. The ideal place for them is at the side of the pond.

The Ideal Mix of Plants for a Small Pond

Opt for a contrast of textures within a selection of types of water plants. The best mix is usually one deep-water plant, a few marginals, and an oxygenating plant to stop the water from going stagnant. Try the diversity of the flat leaf of a water lily, the grassy form of a mini bulrush, and the jaggy leaves of arrowhead. A good substitute for a water lily is water hawthorn. Be prepared to thin out the oxygenator once a year. Most importantly, use an aquatic soil that is clay-based and heavy so it holds more nutrients.

Plant under a water sign but subdivide under a dry sign, such as Leo or Sagittarius. Cutting back growth works best during the decrease of the Moon in its third quarter and in Scorpio.

Aquatic Plants by the Zodiac

Aries: Water hawthorn is a deep-water plant that can take partial shade. Its curious white spikes float on the water and smell of vanilla. Another Aries plant is the cardinal flower, which is a marginal that has wonderful fiery flowers in summer.

Taurus: The pond lily is a cousin of the water lily; its flowers are smaller but it goes with the advantage of surviving light shade and a stronger water current. Bog primrose is considered to be the queen of the bog plants and comes in many colors. Giant cowslip has a spiral of florets giving out a splash of color.

Gemini: Golden buttons is a marginal and has wonderful yellow pom-pom flowers. Its foliage is aromatic, and it's an annual that self-seeds and will produce seedlings next spring. One of the most popular marginals is marsh marigold. The basic and most popular species is the kingcup. In April the bright yellow, waxy flowers adorn water gardens and river banks. A bog plant that comes under Mercury (and thus Gemini) is royal fern. It is a very impressive hardy fern, reaching 4 to 6 feet high. Its tall, lime green fronds change to bronze during the fall.

Cancer: Grasses come under the Moon and Cancer. Sedges are generally considered a marginal plant, but these grassy perennials are generally happier growing in wet soil rather than within the pond. When grown as a marginal, plant to about 1.5 inches. Sedges such as 'Bowles Golden' give interest to the pond with movement and color. Another marginal under Cancer is cotton grass. It likes to be at the edge of the pond in shallow water or in a bog garden. From June to August, silky cottonwool-like seed heads appear above thin stems.

Leo: Astilbe is one of the most common bog plants, mainly due to its recognizable plumes of white, red, and pink during summer. Another red-tinged bog plant under this fire sign is boneset. This plant needs a large pond, as its stems grow 2–4 feet tall and bear a canopy cluster of reddish-purple flowers.

Virgo: A marginal ruled by Mercury and Virgo is marsh St. John's wort. It's a useful carpet plant to grow between taller plants. One plant that's easy to grow and guaranteed to give abundant blooms from May until August is water forget-me-not. It only reaches about 4 inches high and will grow in partial shade.

Libra: Venus rules lilies, and what could be more beautiful than the marginal white arum lily? Its glossy, arrow-shaped leaves reach 2 feet with blooms that come in white with a yellow poker-shaped spadix that has a large white spathe. This plant can survive winters in most areas, provided the crown is 6 inches below the water surface. Daylily is an ideal bog plant with its long flowering season and tolerance for sun or partial shade. Modern hybrids are available in lovely rich yellows and reds.

Scorpio: Water violet comes under Pluto and Scorpio, as it needs still and soft water. It's an oxygenator with bright green foliage below the surface and whorls of pale lavender flowers. Bog gardens are linked with Scorpio, carrying the traits of wet earth and shade. *Ligularia*, with its large leaves that cover the ground and smother weeds, loves boggy soil. The summer blooms are yellow or orange.

Sagittarius: The Jupiter-ruled plant arrowhead has leaves sharply shaped like arrows. Three types are grown as marginals: *Sagittaria japonica* with white, three-petaled flowers and yellow centers; 'Flore Pleno,' the most popular *Sagittaria*, with a mass of white petals that look like the stock flower; and *S. Sagittifolia* has white flowers with have dark red centers and can be quite invasive. Sagittarius also rules floaters like water hyacinth, a beautiful floater in outdoor ponds that can be invasive in waterways. A classic marginal is yellow flag iris with yellow florets.

Capricorn: It's fitting that the bog plant goat's beard is ruled by the old goat Capricorn. During June and July, the tall stems are crowned with large fluffy flower heads. It needs plenty of room at the side of a pond.

Aquarius: Being an air sign, it's fitting that fairy moss should come under Aquarius. This is the most widely available of all the floaters, and the one to look out for is *Azolla caroliniana*. It has tiny fernlike fronds with dense matting of pale green leaves that spread quickly. Only plant this floater in a small enough pond for you to remove excess growth by netting. You can over winter some of the fern in a jar filled with water and soil, then reintroduce the plant to the pond in the spring.

Pisces: The water lily is the queen of pond plants. There are many varieties, but all seem to flourish in full sun. Colors range from yellow to deep pink, but white is a favorite choice. They range from small, such as 'Paul Hariot' (dwarf) to vigorous, such as 'Gladstoniana.' Each size has a different planting depth and each variety is full of surprises. Water lily blooms usually open from late morning to late afternoon and last about four days.

. . . .

Creating a wildlife water sanctuary needn't cost you much. Even installing a small solar pump is economical and helps keep the water sweet. So go on, build a pond that reflects your needs and watch a world of wildlife within your own garden.

About the Author
Janice Sharkey is a compulsive gardener. Having formerly been a garden designer, she now concentrates on her own garden. Janice writes articles and fiction.

2010 © Lijuan Guo. Image from BigStockPhoto.com

Shade Gardening

By Misty Kuceris

Walking through the woods is a delightful experience as you follow paths and listen to the sounds of birds and other creatures in nature. At times you see them in the trees or flitting by you. At other times you know they're somewhere close by because their sounds reach at you like a hand caressing your face. You marvel at the various plants surrounding the trees, perhaps even spotting a jack-in-the-pulpit peeking back at you. You feel exhilarated as the shade casts its protection from the heat of the day and invasion of the Sun. This place is magical not only because it brings you joy but also because this is your place—your private shade garden.

For years people have sought to remove trees and shrubs in order to let the sunlight into their yards and grow their manicured lawns with sterile green blades and few sounds from birds and other creatures. They've espoused the formality of the English garden with rows of sun-loving plants neatly compartmentalized around their home. Now people want to be close to nature. They want to feel alive, to perhaps hear the fairies and wood nymphs hiding in their yard. In being closer to nature, we realize that the landscape we live in is a place to be embraced, warm and nurturing like Gaea (Mother Earth), the Moon, and Ceres.

Planting in the shade may feel overwhelming as you consider the types of plants that will thrive in that area, but the benefits are worth it. You'll create a space that is in harmony with your environment. You'll attract more birds and other creatures to your yard because you are providing them with a protected environment. You'll use less water since shade retains more moisture. You won't have to cut down trees that provide much-needed clean air. You'll use less fertilizer since much of the soil has more micronutrients. And, once established, shade plants actually need less care than those found in a sunny garden.

Shade gardening gives you so many possibilities, from a quiet, serene Zen-type garden to an unstructured woodland pathway. There are so many gradations of shade that you have opportunities to create a space that not only varies the color of flowers but also the tints and textures of the plant's foliage. To have a shade garden, it's important to know what type of shade you have in your yard.

Types of Shade

Shade varies from the very light to the very dark. Basically, there are four types of shade:

Dappled shade: This is shade created by patterns of light that flicker through trees and their branches. While there is no direct sunlight in dappled shade, it is the lightest form of shade. The pattern of shade shifts and moves as the Sun travels across the sky. In spring, before deciduous trees leaf out, there is actually some direct sunlight that makes it through the branches. As the trees reawaken in spring, the leaves start forming and the growth changes the pattern of the area of light.

Open shade: This shade is created by the northern exposure in your yard. Again, there is no direct sunlight, but the light can be very bright. Often the shade is created by buildings and walls that reflect any light found in the area.

Part shade or partial shade: This is an area that receives sunlight during part of the day and shade during the rest of the day. If sunlight is seen in the morning part of the day, the heat in that area of your yard is less scorching and the area is considered partial shade. If, however, the sunlight penetrates the yard in the afternoon, fragile plants have difficulty in this area and you may actually have a sunny location, not a shade location. When the Sun shines in the afternoon, it is hotter and can cause drought stress.

Deep shade: This is the darkest of all the shade. It might be created by evergreen trees, where the canopy is so tight that it doesn't let in any light. It might be created by buildings, walls, or an elevated deck. Deep shade is usually found in north-facing yards. Occasionally you see a strip of light coming through.

Planning Your Shade Garden

No matter what type of garden you want in your yard, planning the garden is always the first step. Whenever you want to create a new garden, it's best to wait one solar cycle (one year) before doing any design or planting. This gives you the opportunity to understand the life force of your land. You want to see how the Sun creates patterns throughout the year in different parts of your space. You want to feel how the wind currents circulate and create little micro-environments. Based on the shading and wind currents, you may have warmer regions on your property than is typical for your zone. Or, you may have colder regions on your property than is typical for your zone. It even helps to look at your space during the times of the Full Moon so that you can see how the evening light gives your yard life.

Keep a diary of your observations. If you are an artistic individual, you may even find yourself creating drawings that show the shade patterns and wind currents.

Once you are aware of your land, decide on your project. Chose one area where you want to start. Some people like to start in the front yard because they want curb appeal. Others like to start on the side or backyard because they feel there is greater room for experimentation. In truth, there is no wrong place to start creating your shade garden.

Now that you've determined the space, look at what is in that space. Is the shade created because of trees? Or is that shade created by buildings, walls, or other structures? Would you call that area dappled, open, partial, or deep shade?

In areas where shade is created by trees, you have several important considerations. First, you need to determine what type of trees you have. Are they deciduous or evergreen? A deciduous tree loses its leaves during the winter months and therefore provides more sunlight during both winter and early spring months. An evergreen tree is usually a conifer of some sort, although there are some leafy trees that are evergreen. These are trees that don't lose their leaves or needles during the winter months; they stay green throughout the season and provide wonderful protection for birds, especially during the winter months.

The other reason you need to know the type of trees you have is because you need to understand the root structure of the trees. Maple trees have very shallow roots. They actually need to come near the surface in order for the tree to breathe and survive. So planting shrubs will be very difficult in areas with maple trees. Oak trees, on the other hand, have very deep root structures. Planting shrubs under oak trees is not difficult. There are also trees, such as the black walnut, which emit toxins and can create difficulty for nearby trees and shrubs.

Evergreen trees, such as yews and spruce, have a shallow root system. They really don't like to compete with other shrubs. Meanwhile the needles of pine trees are very acidic, so it's important that anything you plant near these trees likes to have acidic (around 5.7 pH) soil. Hydrangeas, which can be planted in either acidic or alkaline soil, turn a deep blue to violet when planted near pine trees.

If your shade is created by buildings, walls, or other structures, it'll be easier to plant shrubs, flowers, and ferns because there are no roots competing for the same soil. However, you'll need to consider the radiant heat these structures might create during the winter months. Also, the color of the structures is important. White radiates more light and heat than darker colors.

It's always a good idea to sketch a design before you begin plantings. The winter months are really the best for sketching these designs and a Moon increasing in light (waxing) always provides creative energy. The Full Moon is the time to reevaluate your design, and the decreasing (waning) Moon is the best time to make revisions and changes. If you don't feel creative, there are many books available that have some design ideas already planned out.

It's a good idea to keep a list of shade plants as you think about your design. You may even want to get pictures of them so you can remember the various colors and textures. Most shade gardens are actually dappled shade or partial shade. Open shade is not always mentioned in gardening books, but consider that you can plant either dappled shade or partial shade plants in that location. A couple of nice options for these gardens are the annual

2010 © Stacey McRae. Image from BigStockPhoto.com

flowering tobacco, which attracts butterflies and hummingbirds, and the perennial bleeding heart, which produces beautiful pink flowers shaped like hearts. Both of these plants die back in the winter, so you might want to also consider some evergreens such as the shrub laurel, or ground cover such as wintercreeper.

Deep shade is really your woodland garden. You might want to put some hardscape features in this area, such as a bench for sitting and meditating, especially on those Full Moon nights. Or, you may want to create a stone pathway that leads you by the various plants. Still, there are many options for a deep shade garden, such as the annual wax begonia or the perennial cast iron plant, which has beautiful foliage and evergreen leaves. If you want to plant, a shrub in a deep shade garden, consider the gold dust plant also known as Japanese aucuba, another evergreen that loves being in the shade. The female plant will get berries if there's a male around. And don't forget the ferns—there are many types of ferns that will work in any shade garden.

Creating Your Shade Garden

When you're ready to plant your shade garden, you'll have to take into consideration some of the drawbacks.

- As you dig into the soil, you'll probably find more roots from trees than you expected. If that's the case, you may need to make a slight change in your plans. But there are still many other plants that will work in these situations, such as ground covers with shallow roots.

- Until the plants are established, you'll have to water regularly. Trees are very selfish when it comes to water and nutrients. Since they have the largest root structure, they absorb water and nutrients first. Once the plants are established, you'll find that the garden is very low maintenance.

- The number of flowered plants available for a shade garden is limited since many flowering plants need sunlight. However, there are spring ephemerals that come out before deciduous trees develop their leaves, as well as many ferns that can bring exotic interest to your shade garden.

- Plants grow more slowly in shade. It may take anywhere from three to five years before your shade garden fully develops. You may want to plant your flowers, ground cover, and ferns closer together than you normally would for a sunny garden to avoid gaps while the plants grow in.

Now that you know some of the drawbacks, get ready to prepare your garden. If you're planting trees or shrubs, try to plant when the Moon is in a water or earth sign and, if possible, forming a good aspect to Jupiter. Perennials and annuals are best planted when the Moon is in a water or earth sign and, if possible, forming a good aspect to Mercury. Whenever possible, try to plant when the Moon is increasing (waxing) in light.

After you've prepared the soil, place your shrubs and plants in the location that you think will look the best. Don't plant them yet. Step back and take a look. Do you like what you see? If so, grab your shovel or hand tool and start digging. Most shrubs need to be planted about 1 inch higher in the ground than in the pot or burlap they came in. Hydrangeas, perennials, and annuals need to be planted at the same level that they were in when you took them out of the pot. Water the ground thoroughly. Now you're on your way to a beautiful shade garden!

Shade Gardening In the City

There are many shade plants that do well in containers, either in pots on the floor or in hanging baskets. If you live in the city and have a balcony, you can still create your shade garden. Just take time to design your space and find the plants that do well in both shade and pots. Think in odd numbers when you decide how many pots to have. Also, put the tallest plants near the walls and the shortest plants next to them. While you may not attract all the birds and creatures that an outdoor garden will, this shade garden will give you a wonderful place to relax after a long day.

For Further Reading

Appleton, Bonnie Lee, and Lois Trigg Chaplin. *The New York/Mid-Atlantic Gardener's Book of Lists*. Lanham, MD: Taylor Trade Publishing, 2001.

Burrell, C. Colston. *Native Alternatives to Invasive Plants*. Brooklyn, NY: Brooklyn Botanic Garden, 2006.

Ferguson, Barbara, Deni W. Stein, and James Stockton. *Ortho's Complete Guide to Successful Gardening*. San Francisco: Chevron Chemical Company, 1983.

Hodgson, Larry. *Making The Most Of Shade: How to Plan, Plant, and Grow a Fabulous Garden That Lightens Up the Shadows*. Emmaus, PA: Rodale, 2005.

294   *Shade Gardening*

———. *Perennials for Every Purpose: Choose the Plants You Need for Your Conditions, Your Garden, and Your Taste.* Emmaus, PA: Rodale, 2000.

Phillips, Ellen, and C. Colston Burrell. *Rodale's Illustrated Encyclopedia of Perennials.* Emmaus, PA: Rodale, Inc., 2004.

Trout, Darrell. *Country Garden Planner.* Des Moines, IA: Country Homes Books, 1998.

Online Sources

University of Illinois Extension. "Groundcovers as Lawn Alternatives in Shade." http://urbanext.illinois.edu/lawntalk/groundcovers_as_lawn_alternatives.cfm (accessed August 7, 2009).

Dana, Michael N., and B. Rosie Lerner. "Landscape Plants for Shady Areas." Purdue University Cooperative Extension Service. www.hort.purdue.edu/ext/pubs/HO_222.pdf (accessed June 23, 2009).

Kaiser, Kristen Geer. "Shade Gardening in the Houston Area: Annuals and Perennials for Color." Texas Cooperative Extension: The Texas A&M University System. www.harris-tx.tamu.edu/hort/pubs/pubs/shadegardening.pdf (accessed August 7, 2009).

Moncrieff, Beverly. "Plants in the Right Place for Sierra Foothills, Zone 7." University of California. www.ceplacemevada.ucdavis.edu (accessed June 23, 2009).

Nuss, N. Robert, Scott Guiser, and Jim Sellmer. "Shade Tolerant Trees, Shrubs, and Groundcovers." Pennsylvania State University. www.consumerhorticulture.psu.edu/?q=node/50 (accessed June 23, 2009).

Weber, Hope. "Herbaceous Ornamentals for Shade." Ohio State University: Horticulture and Crop Science. http://ohioline.osu.edu/hyg-fact/1000/1243.html (accessed August 7, 2009).

About the Author

Misty Kuceris is a horticultural specialist and astrologer working with individuals advising them in plant and lawn care. She is a Master Gardener volunteer specializing in the diagnosis of plant diseases and insect identification. Misty views nature as one of the best forms of meditation and one of the best means for feeling the life flow of energy. She can be reached at misty@EnhanceOneself.com.

2010 © Kathy Libby. Image from BigStockPhoto.com

Fabulous Fungi

by Penny Kelly

Mushrooms have always been a bit creepy to me . . . ugly to look at, strange to touch, unappealing on every level. Like many people, if I thought of fungi at all, I thought of the mushrooms on my pizza or in my salad. Yet appearance is not everything, especially where fungi are concerned.

Fungi have a history that is unfathomably ancient, yet it is their present form and function that is downright amazing. Once considered to be part of the plant kingdom, today they are in a kingdom of their own. They are actually more closely related to animals than to plants, the difference being that fungi digest their food externally by secreting a few acids onto the food source and then absorbing it, whereas animals eat by surrounding the food and then digesting it internally.

Fungi can be single- or multicelled organisms whose cell walls are made of chitin, a substance similar to the outer structure of beetles and other insects. They live mainly in soil and reproduce by creating spores. On planet Earth, fungi outnumber plants six to one. There are between one and two million species of fungi that do an astounding array of tasks, everything from building soils and recycling forests to producing antibiotics and feeding us. Each kind of fungi builds its own type of mycelial membrane and secretes unique enzymes and acids.

Of all the possible perspectives you could hold about fungi, none is more inspiring than Paul Stamets' view that mycelia form interlacing neural networks throughout the soil, and that these networks function just like the Internet to infuse habitats with information-sharing capacities.

"These membranes are aware, react to change, and collectively have the long-term health of the host environment in mind," Stamets writes. "The mycelium stays in constant molecular communication with its environment, devising diverse enzymatic and chemical responses to complex challenges."*

Not only does the mycelial network function like the Internet, its architectural structure is also reminiscent of the Web. Single cells arrange themselves end-to-end in long branching threads with thousands of small intersections. If you lined up the mycelial cells contained in 1 cubic inch of soil in a chain, the chain would be 8 miles long! One could imagine that with every footstep out-

---

*Paul Stamets, *Mycellium Running* (Berkeley, CA: Ten Speed Press, 2005). Stamets is a *mycologist,* someone who studies fungi, and except where noted, the information in this article is drawn from his inspiring book.

side the house, millions and billions of mycelial cells are reporting our activities, where we are going, what effects we are having on the landscape, and perhaps even intuiting our moods based on how we move about.

Among the tasks that fungi perform, one of the most important is that of recycling the nutrients in an ecosystem. Fungi can kill an entire forest. Yet when they bring down those trees, they make them into better, richer, deeper topsoil and then switch gears to partner with all new trees, putting up a new forest that is more appropriate to the changes that have taken place in climate, geography, or environment.

In an unusual experiment designed to test the intelligence of fungi as a living organism, Toshuyiki Nakagaki put some tasty oat flakes in a maze and inoculated the maze with a mold fungus. The fungus made a beeline for the oats, skipping all the possible wrong turns. It arrived unerringly at the oats, always taking the shortest, most direct route possible.

Stamets suggests that we might one day consider partnering with this intelligence to make fungi an ally. Mycelia might be able to track the movement of animals, monitor nutrient levels, dispose of toxins, and accelerate repair of damaged ecosystems. Toward this end, one group of researchers managed to get mycelia to incorporate gold into its structure, and the mycelia were then able to transmit electrical signals. Another group developed a biological computer chip that was "home to bacteria that glow when in the presence of PCBs and heavy metal toxins."

This highlights the ability of mycelia and other forms of fungi to recognize the vast library of living information within Mother Nature and still respond locally in ways that support and nurture life. We have just begun to explore these possibilities in the form of mycorestoration.

Says Stamets, "On land, all life springs from the soil. Soil is ecological currency. If we overspend it or deplete it, the environment goes bankrupt. . . . Habitats, like people, have immune systems which become weakened due to stress, disease, or exhaustion. Mycorestoration is the use of fungi to repair or restore the weakened immune systems of environments."

Mycorestoration could benefit us in four primary ways:

- mycofiltration
- mycoforestry
- mycopesticides
- mycoremediation

Mycofiltration is the use of mycelium membranes to filter and clean water. Every mushroom creates its own kind of mycelium membrane, which looks something like woven cheesecloth when seen under an electron-scanning microscope. The difference between the filtering abilities of cheesecloth and the mycelium membrane is that the mycelium is alive and doesn't just trap bacteria, viruses, and parasitic protozoa—it emits enzymes and acids that kill and digest them. One strain of fungus, *Plasmodium falciparum*, is 100 percent effective in destroying the parasite that accompanies malaria. Other strains of fungus emit pesticides. What if we used these two naturally occurring fungi together to eliminate the problem of malaria altogether?

Selected forms of mycelium membranes could be used around farms to clean up *E. coli*, coliform bacteria, *Staphylococcus aureus*, and *Streptococcus* problems. The filtering mats in which mycelium grows are easily constructed by layering sawdust, wood chips, old corn cobs, and straw. Building mycofilters in habitats where run-off enters large bodies of water has been shown to reduce coliform bacteria a hundredfold. Mycofilters could also be used around factories, especially if we used species of fungi that thrive on certain toxins.

Mycoforestry is the use of appropriate fungi to renew and stabilize land where trees have been clear-cut or damaged in a forest fire or other type of natural disaster. When trees are cut down and new ones planted, the new seedlings deplete major nutrients in the soil as they grow to harvestable size. Each successive replanting produces smaller trees with less tonnage, until logging finally becomes unprofitable.

Stamets contends that "trees are NOT America's renewable resource." An industrial system that cuts down an entire forest in one season without regard for the fact that it took ten thousand years to produce enough soil and nutrients to grow those trees cannot claim that it is using a renewable resource, because the forest cannot be restored in our lifetime. Worse, the practice of raking up brush and burning it adds insult to injury because it releases tons of carbon dioxide into the atmosphere while destroying the layer in which new mycelia and their accompanying bacteria could begin a new forest.

He recommends that, after the trunks have been removed, loggers turn everything left into wood chips and spread those chips across the floor of the former forest. If those wood chips are then inoculated with specific fungi, a mycelial membrane will form within months. This membrane will hold water, prevent silt from washing downstream into creeks and lakes, and nurture the birth of a whole new plant community. New trees planted by logging companies would grow bigger root systems, creating healthier, more stable trees in second- and third-growth forests.

Mycopesticides have spectacular possibilities for dealing with troublesome insects because the fungi that are fatal to say, fire ants, termites, carpenter ants, and flies do not harm other insects, nor do they compromise the health of plants, mammals, fish, or bees. Since only about 5 percent of insects are destructive to human endeavors, we could develop mycopesticides that target only the troublemakers without suffering side effects such as destroying groundwater or poisoning ourselves and other living things.

Of all the uses of fabulous fungi, perhaps the most dazzling is that of mycoremediation. This is using fungi to clean up toxic

2010 © Dmitry Vorobiev. Image from BigStockPhoto.com

waste sites. Mycoremediation works first by denaturing toxins such as petroleum products, and second by absorbing heavy metals. The mycelia of the oyster mushroom have demonstrated that they can digest petrochemicals with zest, disposing of 97 percent of them within eight weeks! They work by degrading the long-chain hydrocarbons, breaking them down into simpler compounds and then using these as nutrients to continue their own mushroom growth!

One project in a maintenance yard at the Washington State Department of Transportation transformed soil that had been contaminated with diesel and oil for more than thirty years. Before the project, nothing would grow in the soil, and tests showed that it was saturated with various fuels. Afterward, the hydrocarbons in the soil had been reduced from 20,000 ppm to less than 200, and the soil had been returned from the realms of the dead to a living condition with growing plants.

Another problem successfully handled by fungi and their intelligent mycelium membranes was that of neutralizing persistent neurotoxins such as DDT, dioxins, PCBs, and the chemicals used in chemical warfare, such as the nerve agent sarin. Stamets and a team of researchers at Batelle Pacific Northwest Laboratories "taught" strains of mushrooms to digest these toxins as food.

Other fungi thrive on radiation and serve as bio-accumulators of it, which could make the cleanup of a nuclear site much easier. Instead of trying to scrape up tons of soil and haul it away at a cost that approaches $1,400 per ton of soil, we could put down woodchips, inoculate them with the appropriate mushroom spawn, and allow the mushrooms to pick up the radiation—all at a cost of around $50 per ton, a much cheaper, simpler process, and one that works in harmony with Mother Nature.

Although the field of mycology is a relatively young science, it is clear that fungi have truly unique capacities to heal and balance ecosystems and to nurture Mother Nature, as well as humans. Fungi are already necessary, well-recognized, symbiotic partners in the world of plants. It is likely only a very short time until fungi are widely recognized as necessary partners in the human drama of planetary restoration that continues to unfold as we move into a sustainable future.

About the Author

Penny Kelly is the owner of Lily Hill Farm and Learning Center in southwest Michigan. For thirty years she has been studying, researching, teaching, consulting, and writing about consciousness, perception, and intelligence. She is also a Naturopathic physician who gardens organically and teaches courses in organic gardening that are designed to increase sustainable living and food security in Kalamazoo, Michigan. Penny is the author of five print books, the lead author of fourteen e-books on self-development, and runs two small publishing companies. She lives and writes in Lawton, Michigan. For more information, visit her website at www.pennykelly.com.

2010 © Shelby Armbruster. Image from BigStockPhoto.com

Eat Your Weeds!

by Calantirniel

While the rewards of organic gardening are evident, keeping the weeds at bay can be more challenging. But what if we knew we could use the weeds, and so gave them some leeway? You don't even have to plant them, and you would harvest them anyway—it's a process known as pulling weeds! This article will address thirteen common and safe weeds found throughout most of the temperate regions of the world, including most of Europe (from which nearly all of these plants originate), the United States, and even some areas of Australia and New Zealand.

To familiarize yourself with some of these plants, try a Google image search on the Internet with the Latin name rather than the common name. If you have a different species in your area, try searching the genus term alone. Rather than one picture, as in plant identification books, the Internet can provide hundreds of examples, close-up as well as entire plant, and even many grouped together (usually infestations, especially if the plant has made it onto the local noxious weed list). Make sure you use weeds that are chemical-free for your food and medicine. It's always safest to consume only weeds that have grown on your own property, so you are sure no one has been blasting them with pesticides to try getting rid of them. This information is also not meant to replace the advice of a qualified medical professional, so you should consult a doctor for any illnesses before beginning a healing weed treatment.

How to Eat Weeds

Dried Herb: When choosing herbs to dry for making tea and infusions, make sure they are at their peak and are not too moist. You can place the weeds upside down and hang them away from sunlight, or if you have a wicker basket, they often dry nicely in one of those—just keep it in a dry place out of sunlight (for humid areas, near the heat or air conditioning helps). Any bugs and dirt will fall away in the drying process.

When the weeds are thoroughly dry, place in a glass jar (again, out of the sunlight) and use 1 teaspoon of crushed herbs per 8-ounce cup of tea. Pour boiling water over the herbs, remove from heat source, and steep for 10 to 15 minutes (20 minutes for roots and barks).

Vinegar: Place as much of the fresh herb into a glass jar as you can and pour raw apple cider vinegar up to the top. Seal and allow to sit (even in the fridge) for 6 to 8 weeks, shaking the contents periodically. Filter out the plant material with layered cheesecloth or an unbleached coffee filter, and keep the vinegar in the fridge.

This is as much food as it is medicine, and vinegar is particularly good for accessing the plant's minerals into a more usable form. The ideal dose of weedy vinegar is 1 to 3 tablespoons per day, as a greens or salad dressing or even straight, chased with water or tea. Using weedy vinegars is especially important if you drink lots of mineral-draining fluids like coffee, nonherbal tea, sodas, and so on.

Tincture: Collect fresh plant material and fill a glass jar. Pour either vodka or brandy (40 to 50 percent alcohol) to the top. Seal and allow to sit for 6 to 8 weeks, shaking the jar every now and then to assist the further extraction of medicinal properties. Filter plant material out with layered cheesecloth or an unbleached coffee filter, and keep in a dark, dry place.

These tinctures are not foods, but are wonderful medicines. They store nearly indefinitely and you can use when needed for six days a week, taking a break the seventh day. Dosage can be 15 to 30 drops two or three times a day, or more if needed, and can be taken until the condition improves or dissipates, which could take many months.

Oil: Collect fresh plant material and allow it to wilt slightly (to remove excess water content) before packing in a glass jar. Pour cold-pressed olive oil, grapeseed oil, apricot kernel oil, or other nonprocessed vegetable-based oil to the top. Seal and allow to sit out of sunlight for 6 to 8 weeks, shaking periodically. Filter with unbleached coffee filter—this takes longer than the vinegar or tincture and can be messier. Oils are best used for external applications.

Liniment: Combine one part filtered weed oil and one part filtered tincture. Adjust the proportions as you like for best effect. Shake well before applying to affected areas. Liniments are for external use only.

Weeds on the Menu

Chickweed (*Stellaria media*)

Ruled by the Moon, this tasty emollient weed can even grow under the snow and has great longevity, being one of the first weeds to sprout and lasting well into autumn. Its delicate leaves and small white flowers are indicative of its mild, moist taste; it dresses up salads wonderfully. Medicinally, its external application is soothing and wonderful for inflammations, itchy skin (poison ivy and such), and burns. With internal use, it is said to break up fatty tissue, making it good for weight loss. This "breaking up" quality is being further investigated for helping to eliminate tumors and fibroids.

Cleavers/Bedstraw/Sweet Woodruff (*Galium aparine, G. boreale, G. odoratum*)

Ruled by Saturn, this sweet-tasting relative of the coffee family sticks to nearly everything, so use it medicinally as a tincture. This tincture (recommended with brandy) is one of the best medicines for a sluggish lymphatic system, a problem nearly everyone has at one time or another. It is also said to shrink ovarian cysts and help in tonsillitis. Remember to use with lots of spring water.

Dandelion (*Taraxacum officinale*)

Ruled by Jupiter, this is a plant you likely already know well. The entire plant is usable as an excellent nutritious food and as wonderful spring tonic and blood-purifying medicine. The leaves are a tasty addition to salads in the early spring and the fall, and the flowers, when dried, make a wonderful tea. The leaves also make an excellent potherb; you can cook it similarly to spinach. Any time of year, you can place any part of the dandelion in raw apple cider vinegar. Use the vinegar on your foods to increase your nutrition (especially minerals) and help your entire digestive system, especially your liver (roots) and kidneys (greens). The roots—if cut up small, cleaned, dried, and then ground and roasted—are a divine coffee substitute; whereas coffee is not good for the liver, dandelion is.

Filaree/Storksbill (*Erodium cicutarium*)

This delicate pink-flowered plant tastes good in salads. Medicinally, it is said to be astringent and help to stop bleeding, though the midwife herb shepherd's purse (*Capsella bursa-pastoris*) or yarrow (*Achilles millefolium*) may work better, if you have access to it. (However, yarrow is too bitter for salads.)

Goldenrod (*Solidago canadensis*)

Ruled by Venus, the "Liberty Tea" plant was used by the colonists instead of British tea in the Boston Tea Party era, and colonists likely saw better health for their efforts. While many people believe they are allergic to the "dill-ish"-tasting goldenrod, it is likely they are instead allergic to a weed that blooms at the same time, ragweed. In fact, goldenrod can be the cure for these allergies, as nature often places its cures next to the problems. As well as clearing up lingering flu/congestion symptoms, goldenrod vinegar is excellent for the kidneys and helps those who feel like they lack stamina. This wonderfully versatile plant is also excellent for wounds and muscles soreness when applied externally; you can make an oil out of its flowers, leaves, stems, and/or roots. Apply the oil or liniment to affected areas.

Henbit (*Lamium amplexicaule*)

Related to the mint family (though not aromatic like other mints) the mild-tasting upper parts of the henbit plant are wonderful in salads for their taste and color when in deep-pink bloom. My daughter swears this is a fairy flower, and she is probably right!

Lambs' Quarters (*Chenopodium album*)

This plant is in the same family as quinoa, and the leaves are a near-perfect substitute for spinach, though a touch bitter (it even shares the oxalic acid problem, so people with gout may not wish to eat lambs' quarters raw; cooking does alleviate the acid and taste issues). In the autumn when the seeds come on, harvest the seeds by pulling the plant and placing it upside down in a paper bag, allowing the seeds to fall into the bag. Sprinkle these in soups to add texture, protein, and flavor.

Mallow/Cheeseweed (*Malva neglecta*)

As a salty mucilage, the mild pretty scalloped leaves and pretty pink flowers of mallow can be used in salads, though they are a tad bit hairy. When dried, these make a lovely mild tea and are actually an ingredient in Dr. Miller's Holy Thistle tea. If the fruits develop, they are said to impart a cheeselike taste when boiled in water, and the roots will thicken soup broth, making it useful for vegetarians. The roots are emollient and have the same healing qualities as marsh mallow (*Althea officinalis*) and hollyhock (*A. rosea*). A tincture is soothing to the kidneys and an inflamed urinary tract. Externally, it can be used as a liniment on stiff joints and to reduce pus caused by an infection or other inflammation.

Nettle (*Urtica dioica*)

When weeding/harvesting stinging nettle, please use leather work gloves and wear clothing that can be washed in hot water and dried in the dryer, as heat deactivates the stinging hairs. Ruled by feisty Mars, this tonic plant packs a powerful healing punch on many levels and is very worth the trouble of gathering. The sting alone is sometimes desired by those who have arthritis pain, as the sting helps the pain temporarily fade, and there are no side effects. Nettle has some of the best rounded nutrition available in the plant world and can be dried for tea, cooked in soups, placed in vinegar, or tinctured for wide-ranging medicinal applications. It is said to be a menopausal woman's best friend, likely due to

2010 © Tyler Olson. Image from BigStockPhoto.com

the nutrition and hormone-balancing qualities of the plant. It is an excellent blood builder, kidney cleanser, adrenals booster, and even helps with hair regrowth and thickness. It is a must-have for those with allergies, and the seeds are said to have concentrated healing powers.

Plantain (*Plantago major, P. lanceolata*)

Ruled by Venus, plantain has very interesting qualities. It is a plant everyone should identify, since it is so useful in emergency applications, such as drawing poisons from bites, rashes, and wounds (snake/dog/spider/insect bite, bee sting, poison ivy/oak rash, rusty nail puncture, or such). The dried plant won't have much medicinal property, so use it fresh or in tincture, and always have some on hand. Apply the wilted (or chewed) leaves right to the wound, or a cotton ball or cloth soaked in tincture directly to the wound, and feel its pulling action. Internally, plantain is an excellent digestive cleanser, particularly for the colon. The swiss chard–tasting fresh leaves can be eaten, made as tea, or a tincture can be used. In the case of severe bites (rattlesnake or brown recluse spider), the patient can use plantain internally and externally and it is recommended they also take an entire bottle of *Echinacea* tincture as quickly as they can—this will help isolate the poisons for the body to get rid of them—in addition to obtaining proper medical treatment. Copious amounts of yarrow tea can also help by bringing on a healing, "moist" fever, and though this will work well, check with a doctor for any follow-up care needed.

Red Clover (*Trifolium pratense*)

Ruled by Mercury, red clover is best known for its tonic, blood thinning/cleansing, and gland-balancing qualities. It is also one of the main cancer-fighting herbs. It is less known for but effective in promoting brain health and mental function. Dry the flowers for a very delicious tea, or tincture them in brandy or vodka. Remember, if cleansing the blood, make sure that a colon, liver, and kidney program was implemented first, so toxins in the blood have a place to leave.

Salsify (*Tragopogon dubius, T. porrifolius*)

Looking like giant dandelion heads when in seed, the western salsify (yellow flower) is not as versatile as the eastern variety (purple flower). The purple variety is actually called oyster root because the root is considered an oyster-tasting vegetable. The root of the yellow variety is dry, pithy, and bitter—not palatable in the least. However, many people don't know how delicious the greens of this plant are, and it is usually quite plentiful when in season (salsify usually comes after the dandelions in the summer). Where the dandelion greens are bitter, the greens of salsify are wonderful and mild. Because their leaves are narrow (almost like grass), it may take a while to harvest, but they taste good and are worth the effort for salads and for adding to cooked vegetables.

Self-Heal/Heal-All (*Prunella vulgaris*)

I saved this lovely Venus-ruled, purple-flowered member of the mint family for last, but it is surely not least. This emollient-yet-astringent plant had versatile and popular medicinal use before the modern era, and I believe it is worthy of revival. It can be added to salads for culinary use, as well as used medicinally, especially externally (for example, the plant juice alleviates nettle stings). Like goldenrod, an oil or liniment can be made of the upper parts of the blooming plant. This oil is useful for burns, wounds, stings, rashes, and irritated skin. Alternatively, you can juice the plant and add a small amount of vodka to preserve (75 percent self-heal juice, 25 percent vodka). Internally, as a tea or vodka/brandy tincture, it is excellent for tonsillitis and nearly all kidney and digestive disorders, including ulcers (combine with chickweed, cleavers, and/or plantain for further effectiveness) and is even believed to combat tumors.

. . . .

Next growing season, take some time to study the weeds in your garden and around your home before chucking them away to discover which varieties you might have. Alternately, devote one Moon cycle of the year to each of these thirteen beneficial and tasty "weeds."

For Further Reading

Tilford, Gregory L. *Edible and Medicinal Plants of the West.* Missoula, MT: Mountain Press Publishing Company, 1997.

———. *From Earth to Herbalist: An Earth-Conscious Guide to Medicinal Plants.* Missoula, MT: Mountain Press Publishing Company, 1998.

Wood, Matthew. *The Earthwise Herbal: A Complete Guide to Old World Medicinal Plants.* Berkeley, CA: North Atlantic Books, 2008.

About the Author

Calantirniel has been published in over a dozen Llewellyn annuals and has practiced many forms of natural spirituality since the early 1990s. She is a professional astrologer, tarot card reader, dowser, flower essence creator and practitioner, Usui Reiki Master, and became a ULC Reverend and a certified Master Herbalist in 2007. She has an organic garden, crochets professionally, and is co-creating Tië eldaliéva, *the Elven Path, a spiritual practice based upon the Elves' viewpoint in Professor J. R. R. Tolkien's Middle-Earth stories, particularly* The Silmarillion. *Please visit www.myspace.com/aartiana for more information.*

2010 © L. David. Image from BigStockPhoto.com

Grow Your Own Salad Bar

By Maggie Anderson

Would you like to grow your own vegetables but feel you don't have a green thumb? Leave your worries to the scarecrows and begin your gardening career with a simple salad bar garden. Few things can go wrong with this project, so start small and build on your success next season.

Many beginning gardeners believe that gardening requires extraordinary skills, but this is a myth: seeds want to grow, which puts nature on your side. Some plants do need extra attention, but given adequate amounts of soil, water, air, and sunshine, you're likely to experience good results with a salad bar garden. It's small, simple, and a great first gardening project.

Below are a few tips for growing lettuce, tomatoes, cucumbers, onions, and radishes. Once you've grown these five veggies and discover how great fresh, homegrown food tastes, you'll be ready to expand your garden next year.

For optimal growth, most vegetables need sunlight for eight hours or more a day, so identify those bright spots in your yard, patio, or balcony. The closer your salad bar garden is to your kitchen door, the better. If planting early in the spring, consider how much sunlight you might have when all the leaves come out on nearby trees and the rays come in from different angles.

You can plant directly in the ground after your ground temperature is 55 degrees F. Measure off a sunny 3×3-foot square and outline the boundaries with lines of white flour before digging. If grass is growing there, cover it with weighted plastic bags or a tarp for several weeks, then cut the dead grass out, shaking loose dirt back into the garden. With a shovel or garden spade, dig to a depth of 1½ feet. If the soil is heavy with clay, cover it with one to two inches each of sand and compost. Dig the materials in and rake until fairly smooth. If you have rabbits nearby, plant first, then surround your garden plot with rabbit fencing.

You can also plant your salad bar garden in a raised bed. The 3×3-foot size is a standard in garden supply catalogs, and kits for raised beds are available at big box hardware stores in the spring. After stripping grass from the designated spot, turn over a small layer of dirt, install the raised bed according to directions, then fill almost to the top with an even mix of soil, clean sand, and compost. The raised bed will provide some rabbit protection, except for the really big or bold ones! For these critters, you will also need a rabbit fence around the top.

If your sunny space is on a balcony, concrete patio, or driveway, you'll need an assortment of containers to hold the soil mix. Almost any vessel will do, including large baskets with plastic liners, big flower pots, ice chests, plastic storage bins, and wheelbarrows. Please do not use plastic buckets that have held paint or other toxic materials. Five-gallon food-grade buckets are fine, though, especially for root crops like onions and beets. (I buy recycled five-gallon buckets from my supermarket bakery department for $1: they originally contained frosting!) Wooden containers set directly on the ground can draw termites but are fine to set on concrete if you first line them with plastic.

Let your gardening mantra be "seeds want to grow." It's their cosmic job, so don't be afraid to challenge them with new environments. I've grown lovely bunches of parsley in old boots and basil in discarded teakettles, huge batches of chard in a wooden crate lined with 3-mil plastic, and very fine lettuce in 4-inch deep cat litter boxes (new, not used). Your container choices are limited only by your creativity and imaginative recycling.

Some varieties of lettuce can bolt and go to seed in intensely hot weather. As you prepare your garden bed, consider how to provide partial shade during the hottest months of the summer. You can cover lettuce with shade netting held above the plants with sticks or hoops of ½-inch PVC pipe. Large containers on wheels can be moved to a spot with more shade when necessary. You can also purchase three different mixes of lettuce for planting in spring, summer, and autumn. The special summer selection does not bolt easily and will continue to flourish under intense sunlight.

Your onions, radishes, and cucumbers will need containers of some depth, and the tomato container should be the deepest of all. Lettuce containers can be as shallow as 4 inches, but up to 8 inches deep is better. You will need to poke, punch, or pound holes in the bottom of every container, then add enough rocks to cover the bottom for good drainage, fill with the soil mix mentioned above, and plant.

Next, purchase your seed packets and plant sets! Lettuce is the mainstay of your salad bar garden so look for a lettuce or mesclun mix. These include green and red leaf lettuce and sometimes small head lettuce too. Seed catalogs often offer spring, summer, and winter lettuce mixes that are geared for seasonal temperatures and have the most variety. Baby greens are popular now. They are cut from leaf lettuce plants when only 3 inches tall or smaller. Most leaf lettuces are "cut and come again" varieties and can be given "haircuts" up to three times.

Plan to sow lettuce seed once a month throughout the growing season, preferably during a New Moon. Plant half of your in-ground garden or several of your largest containers with lettuce seed. Gently tap them in with the overturned prongs of a light-weight rake. As your baby plants appear, thin them according to directions on the seed package. If you have other containers filled with a soil mix, poke those babies in any free growing space, or transplant them in between your rows of flowers.

Every great salad must have a few tomatoes in it. Cherry and grape varieties are easy to grow, but the new hybrid grape variet-ies seem unusually prolific. Buy and plant one tomato plant on the north side of your bed or in a large tub, five-gallon bucket, or half of a wooden barrel. If you have a reliable way to hang one of the new hanging tomato systems, these are perfect for anyone with limited space. (However, the hanging system requires almost daily watering in hot weather.) Tomatoes in the ground and in containers both need the support of a tomato cage for all those luscious ripe tomatoes. Press a cage into the soil around your plant and, as the tomato grows, gently move the stems to rest on the wires.

Also buy a seed packet of a bush variety of cucumber. Plant one "hill" or mound of six to eight seeds around the hill in a cor-ner of your in-ground garden or in one or two large containers. Thin to two or three strong plants when distinct leaves become visible.

Your in-ground garden will still have room for onions and radishes, so buy a bag of white onion sets. Plant a double row, spacing onions 2 inches apart. Pull up and slice to add to your salads when they develop long green tops. Next, choose one seed pack of your favorite radishes and sow them next to the onions, following packet directions.

When you have finished planting your salad bar garden, water seeds and plants with the gentle sprinkler head of your hose, giving it all a good soaking. Keep the ground moist around your seeds until they germinate.

About the Author

Maggie Anderson is a traditional astrologer and unconventional gardener living in Marion, Iowa. Her earthy Virgo goal is to grow a sustainable organic garden that is largely permaculture. If it weren't for moles, rabbits, and Japanese beetles, she'd be making more progress.

2010 © Tatiana Belova. Image from BigStockPhoto.com

Flower Essence Moon Magic

By Fern Feto Spring

Flora was the Roman goddess of blossoming flowers, love, and fertility. On her feast day, the ancient Romans celebrated the abundance of life and the flourishing generosity of nature. Though the Floralia festival has faded into the shadows of history, it is still possible for us to draw on the historic gifts that Flora offered. Flower essences draw on the wisdom of nature to support and calm emotional, spiritual, and sometimes physical challenges. Created by soaking the blossoms of a flower in spring water and bottling the extract with alcohol or another natural preservative, the origin of flower essences is simple and straightforward, yet able to address a variety of complex issues.

Though flower essences can be taken at any time, they can be particularly powerful when incorporated with the cycles of the

Moon. Beginning a flower essence routine in conjunction with a Moon sign or phase can maximize the benefits of the essence and increase the flow of natural energy available for healing.

The New Moon is an excellent time to start taking essences that are related to initiation, change, and creating new habits or patterns. Cayenne, california wild rose, and borage are good New Moon flowers to work with during this early lunar phase. Essences taken at this time help to support rejuvenation, blossoming, and new life.

Full Moon flower essences are those that support the qualities of awareness, clarity, and understanding. This is the phase to begin a course of essences such as fuschia or scarlet monkeyflower that will help you shed light on behavior that is troubling or hard to understand. This is also a time of manifestation and so essences like blackberry, sunflower, and larch can help facilitate the birth of new projects into the world.

Dark Moon essences such as walnut and yerba santa are designed to help you let go of and release issues and situations that are holding you back. Honeysuckle is also a great essence for helping you to shed feelings of nostalgia and creating the space for you to move forward into the present day.

To bring an even finer level of enhancement to healing with flower essences, you can incorporate the astrological sign of the Moon into your essence selection. Decide on an essence that feels the most relevant to you and then consult pages 136–158 to find when the Moon is traveling through the sign that supports that particular essence. Listed below are detailed descriptions of the essences and the astrological signs that correspond with them.

Tips for Taking Essences

Take the essences two to four times a day for at least three weeks; longer is recommended. You can mix a dropper of essence into a larger water bottle and sip on this bottle throughout the day.

Essences can also be applied topically by adding them to lotion, baths, or a spray bottle. Frequency and length of application is more effective than taking large quantities of the essence. Essences are available at a number of natural foods markets and online. Essences described in this article are derived from the Flower Essence Services and Bach Flower Essence collections.

> **Aries** Moon essences either help you to develop qualities of bravery, courage, and initiative; or to conquer impatience, competitiveness, and hostility.

Cayenne: This essence is a great catalyst for change, encouraging new energy and breakthroughs. If you are suffering from procrastination or inertia, this essence will jump-start your will and move you forward.

Impatiens: Calms impatience and the desire to rush through life. Helps you to slow down and move with the natural flow of energy. Particularly helpful when experiencing road rage, standing in line, and during other slow-moving or boring experiences.

> **Taurus** Moon essences encourage security, stability, and a sense of being connected to Earth and the physical body.

Corn: Helps the physical body to feel connected and grounded on the earthly plane and provides an "anchor" for those who feel disoriented. This essence is particularly helpful for nature lovers who must live or spend time in urban environments.

Star Thistle: Promotes generosity and security and alleviates a fear of lack or not having enough in life. This essence is useful for those who withhold their time, energy, or resources from others for fear that they will lose it all.

> **Gemini** Moon essences help to focus and integrate information and encourage healthy maturity and responsibility in life.

Fairy Lantern: For those who have "Peter Pan" syndrome or are afraid to grow up and mature. They may be stuck in a youthful stage of life and feel an overwhelming sense of stagnation or lack of progress in relation to goals and dreams.

Madia: This essence helps to foster clarity and focus in the mental realm. It's particularly useful for studying or in situations of over-stimulation or information overload.

> **Cancer** Moon essences provide nurturing and emotional support. They lessen nostalgia and help you to be fully in the present.

Mariposa Lily: This essence supports a warm, nurturing, and maternal energy and helps to heal issues related to mothers and mothering. Mariposa lily promotes bonding and emotional connection in individuals and families.

Honeysuckle: Brings the spirit into current time and alleviates feelings of nostalgia or longing that may prevent the soul from moving forward. This essence is useful for big moves or life changes, when the past is being left behind and a whole new reality is emerging.

> **Leo** Moon essences encourage a healthy and balanced ego and also promote playfulness and lightheartedness.

Sunflower: Creates a balanced ego and an awareness of one's own gifts, strengths, and talents. Helps to promote confidence and self-esteem. This essence also helps to heal issues related to fathers and fathering.

2009 © Jeanne DeCarolis. Image from BigStockPhoto.com

Zinnia: Promotes a carefree and playful energy, helping one to open up and have fun with life. Good for times when life appears to be serious, boring, or without humor. Zinnia can help to lighten energy and attitudes so that there is more openness.

Virgo Moon essences help to promote self-esteem, boundaries, and perspective; they also calm worry and anxiety.

Centaury: If you have a hard time saying no to others or find yourself taking on work or projects in order to be helpful, this is the essence for you. Promotes boundaries, strengthens the will, and promotes an awareness of one's own needs and desires.

Filaree: This essence eases mental strain and worry and provides a larger perspective on life. When you find yourself spending too much time thinking about the details of daily life and not enough time meditating on your overall life purpose, filaree provides a gentle reminder to broaden your viewpoint.

Libra Moon essences facilitate decision making, inner and outer balance, and a sense of confidence in one's own inner wisdom.

Cerato: Facilitates a greater awareness of your own inner wisdom and guidance. Cerato is helpful when you may have gotten so much advice from others that you've become confused about what to do next.

Scleranthus: When you have a decision to make and keep going in circles, this essence can help to clarify the decision-making process and support a clear sense of direction or inner knowing.

Scorpio Moon essences support compassion, trust, and an ability to integrate depth and intense emotions with grace.

Scarlet Monkeyflower: When going down deep into scary emotions and issues seems impossible, this essence helps to facilitate and guide your progress. Scarlet monkeyflower helps to develop an honest and clear connection with the more "hidden" parts of the self.

Holly: For feelings of jealousy or paranoia in intimate relationships. This essence helps you to open your heart and develop a sense of trust and expansiveness in relation to others.

> **Sagittarius** Moon essences help to clarify life purpose and vision; they also support balanced expression of ideals and philosophies.

Wild Oats: If you are searching for your life direction or a sense of purpose and feel pulled in a number of different directions, wild oats helps to clarify and focus your attention. This essence is particularly helpful for those who have just graduated from a school or training program and aren't sure what to do next.

Vervain: Helps to develop more balanced leadership qualities for those who have a tremendous amount of passion or enthusiasm to lead but may alienate others with their intense energy.

> **Capricorn** Moon essences encourage a sustained approach to responsibility and provide support during hardships.

Elm: If you feel trapped in a drudgery of responsibility and overwhelmed with your tasks, elm can help to balance your energy. This essence is good for those who feel they are shouldering the complete burden of care for loved ones.

Penstemon: Helps with persevering during challenging times and discovering a sense of inner strength and resolve. This essence develops an ability to sustain and survive in difficult circumstances.

> **Aquarius** Moon essences alleviate feelings of alienation from others and promote community bonds and a sense of "place."

Shooting Star: For those who feel like aliens from another planet, shooting star helps to develop a sense of connection to the earthly plane and assists in promoting an embodied experience of life.

322 Flower Essence Moon Magic

Sweet Pea: Strengthens roots and a sense of community for those who have a hard time settling down or who are compelled to wander. Sweet pea encourages and strengthens a sense of connection and an ability to nest and remain in one place.

჻

Pisces Moon essences help to strengthen boundaries and build confidence and a focused presence in the world.

Clematis: Encourages the ability to be incarnate in the physical plane and manifest talents, gifts, and skills in the world.

Pink Yarrow: If the urge to merge is so strong that you sometimes forget where you end and others begin, pink yarrow can help you to develop a greater awareness of the difference between your energy field and someone else's. This essence promotes boundaries and a greater sense of personal awareness.

For Further Reading

Kaminski, Patricia, and Richard Katz. *Flower Essence Repertory*. Nevada City, CA: Flower Essence Society, 2004.

About the Author

Fern Feto Spring, M.A., has been an astrologer and flower essence practitioner since 1990. Fern is the coauthor of Simply Sacred: Everyday Relationship Magic *and has written for the Mountain Astrologer, Tarot.com, and Astrocenter.com. She also writes regularly for Sasstrology.com. Fern teaches classes and sees private clients in the San Francisco Bay area and nationally. She gardens avidly, if a bit wildly, at her flower-filled family home in Fairfax, California, where she lives with her dog and her partner.*

2010 © Denisa Haveldova. Image from BigStockPhoto.com

Moonmatch.com

By Pam Ciampi

Relationships begin in the blink of an eye. When two people meet and sparks begin to fly, the attraction is usually credited to appearances. Most people are unaware that the real driving force behind relationships is something hidden deep inside each individual. If you'd like to take a quick peek into the hidden force that drives your relationships, take a look at your natal Moon.

Your natal Moon holds the hidden key to your core needs, the unconscious longings that drive you into (and out of) relationships. These core needs lie deep beneath the surface of what you *think* you want. They are shaped out of your earliest memories and carry all the experiences of how you grew up. Whether positive or negative, these memories make up the place that you call home. Your core needs are not changeable or negotiable and they signal your "default settings" in times of stress. By matching natal Moon signs, you can discover not only your basic relationship needs but also how other Moon signs affect you. You will also learn what you can do about a match that's not made in heaven.

The first step is finding your natal Moon sign. Everyone knows their birthday (Sun sign) but to find your Moon sign, you will need your birth date and time. Type "my Moon sign" into a search engine to find numerous free sites that will calculate this for you.

Here's a letter from the MoonMatch.com* mailbox that explains how to use your Moon signs to find out if your relationship is a good match.

> Dear Moonmatch.com,
> My partner is a wonderful person and I want to be in a committed relationship, but deep down I feel like I am not getting what I really need. Is there anything in our chart comparison that can tell me why I feel like this?
> —Concerned in CT
>
> Dear Concerned,
> Yes, the first thing you can do is to check your natal Moon signs to see if they are compatible! Your natal Moon sign reveals how you go about meeting your basic security needs. Think of your natal Moon as your own personal "default setting"—the place you revert to when you things start to get crazy and you go on auto pilot. If your Moon is not in harmony with your partner's Moon, you are running on different operating systems, which is like asking a PC to be a Mac! Each of your systems has the right stuff, but they aren't compatible. While it is possible to run a Mac on a PC or vice versa, you must install an additional program—there may be a lot of extra work involved. I hope it's a match!
> —Moonmatch.com

*Moonmatch.com is a fictional website that exists only in the imagination of the author.

2010 © Stephen Coburn. Image from BigStockPhoto.com

Moon Sign Compatibility

Moon sign comparisons can be applied to any one-on-one emotional relationship: fathers/sons, mothers/daughters, husbands/wives, or siblings.

Once you know the natal Moon signs, refer to the table to find out whether that sign is in the element of fire, earth, air, or water.

Fire Signs: Aries, Leo, and Sagittarius

Earth Signs: Taurus, Virgo, and Capricorn

Air Signs: Gemini, Libra, and Aquarius

Water Signs: Cancer, Scorpio, and Pisces

Most Compatible

If both Moon signs are the same element, the relationship will be compatible because you share a core operating system. You may discover that you have one or more of the following: similar backgrounds, jobs in the same field, shared religious beliefs, similar levels of education, and most importantly, compatible ways of problem solving.

Fire Moons crave adventure and excitement, are hot-blooded and passionate but also forgiving, and tend to laugh things off.

Earth Moons are serious and grounded and put security first, appearances a close second, and risk-taking trails by a mile.

Air Moons solve their problems through talking. Air Moons value communication, theories, and social skills. They get bored easily and need lots of space to avoid feeling confined.

Water Moons are intense and emotional. They prefer feeling the vibes to talking and tend to hold on to the past.

Very Compatible

If both Moons are in similar elements (fire/air, earth/water), your core needs will be complementary.

Fire Moons feel instantly appreciated and energized by talkative air Moons, and air Moons get a charge when a fire Moon wants to run with their ideas.

Water Moons feel safe and protected when paired with a sensuous and a capable earth Moon, while earth Moons love the emotional infusion of water Moons, which inspires them to get up and go.

Not Compatible

If your natal Moons are not compatible, the relationship could be challenging at best and unfulfilling at worst. Incompatibility reflects different backgrounds, dissimilar family issues, and a different set of coping skills. Incompatibility is not a total dealbreaker but the relationship will require a certain level of maturity and detachment in order to work.

The sparks can really fly with fire/water Moons. The fire Moon just wants to have fun and feels like the water Moon is always crying about something and throwing a wet blanket on the party. The water Moon feels like the fire Moon is shallow and insensitive and never listens.

When air/earth Moons get together, the air Moon wants to talk endlessly but not about anything practical. Earth Moons crave security and take everything slow; air Moons are fast and spontaneous.

Fire/earth combinations are not generally compatible. The fire Moon feels like the earth Moon is mired in boring details and is holding him back. The earth Moon responds that the fire Moon has trouble focusing and refuses to make a commitment.

Air/water Moons have problems because an air Moon has a core need for space and lightness and action in the social realm, and a water Moon prefers emotional face time. Water Moons feel that air Moons are superficial, and air Moons think water Moons are too intense.

. . . .

A model for a solution to incompatibility came in the unlikely form of a computer program called Parallels that turns a Mac into a PC or vice versa by creating separate platforms on your computer's operating system. See how this concept is applied to two incompatible Moons in another letter from the MoonMatch .com mailbox:

> Dear Moonmatch.com,
> My brother and I are planning a 600-mile bike/camping trip this summer. Although we are close we have always been very different. I just found out that his Moon is in Capricorn and my Moon is in Leo. Is there a way we can spend 24/7 together for two weeks without wanting to kill one another?
> —Cyclist from Cincinnati

> Dear Cyclist,
> A Leo Moon is a fire Moon and a Capricorn Moon is an earth Moon. Since fire and earth are not compatible elements, let's

take a look at your individual needs and see if there is a way to get around the incompatibility.

As a Leo Moon, your core need is that this bike trip is FUN. You want to have a grand adventure and be able to tell your friends about it when you get back. Because your need for pleasure trumps practicality, you may prefer to get a late start, stop frequently, and kick back. Your brother's Capricorn Moon need is completely different. Like the goat, he has a need for climbing the mountain and achieving the goal. A Capricorn Moon can make anything—even a vacation—feel like work. Getting the job done is number one and stopping or playing doesn't even make their to-do list. Since setting the daily goals for speed and mileage will make a Capricorn Moon happiest, early starts and long, hard days are not a choice but a practical necessity.

If you can both take a step back and see that one "operating system" is not inherently better than another, you can both have a good time! If the Leo Moon can turn down the fun meter and make an effort to get into high gear once in a while and the Capricorn Moon can lose his work ethic and stop to smell the roses, there is every chance that at the end of the road, you will both be able to say, "It was a great trip!"
—Moonmatch.com

The natal Moon is the key to what you really want, not what you think you want. Comparing Moon signs is a quick way to see if your core needs match up (or not). If they are compatible, congratulations! If not, remember that it's not necessarily a deal breaker. If you are invested in making the relationship work, you can always accept your differences and work on figuring out ways to modify (not change) both your needs to create a separate peace where both "operating systems" can coexist in harmony.

About the Author

Pam Ciampi is a professional astrologer in San Diego, California. She and her husband both have their natal Moons in fire signs. She can be reached through www.pciampi-astrology.com.

2010 © Georgios Kollidas. Image from BigStockPhoto.com

Eclipses and Relationships

By Carole Schwalm

Many relationships start out fast-paced and in high frequency. Then, sad to say, the only way to go is down. The worst-case scenario is that romances turn off altogether. Relationships at their best should lead to commitment, step by step.

Eclipses are moments of enlightenment, one to another; they string together like beads, step by step. When you get in sync with the cosmic flow, you do the right thing at the right time, in the right place, and—most importantly—with the right person.

Can you date the same way? Yes, you can. You can resonate with the cosmic rhythm almost immediately after your 2011 New Year's Eve date. If you didn't have a date and want one next year, you really should tune in!

This year's eclipse pattern and point of dating resonation involves the ancient and medieval elements of fire, earth, air, and water. Fire—Aries, Leo, and Sagittarius; earth—Taurus, Virgo, and Capricorn; air—Gemini, Libra, and Aquarius; water—Cancer, Scorpio, and Pisces.

Let's pause and look at the different ways the signs approach the dating process.

First, the perspective is easy if you think of the natural elements. For example, fire thaws frozen water. Earth and water make something solid and strong like adobe brick. Fire and air combine to create transferable heat. Fire and water make steam like a steam engine. Water puts out fire. Air sends fire out of control.

Translated to people's natal signs, fire and air are freedom-oriented compared to the closeness-focused earth and water signs. To fire and air, earth and water can seem like a cold, damp hand that might not get any warmer or dryer or softer. To earth and water, fire and air signs not only do not know how to love, they are never around when you need them.

There are calm and comfortable times within your element and with a compatible element. You can see how much easier the procedure is if earth and water unite and fire and air get together. However, people don't always follow those lines because opposites attract. This natural attraction occurs because the missing element completes you, no matter how much you fight that idea.

January 4, Capricorn: Partial Solar Eclipse

The phrase "I hate to rush things" epitomizes distinct rules of the game starting with this earthy eclipse. It is a subdued aura, not one of unrealistic hopes. The influence lasts for months, in which, with patience, you find gold. This eclipse is literally a low-frequency beginning.

This is the most romantic time for earthy Sun signs. You are in your element. You feel confident. Even though it may be cold outside, warmth rises inside. Water signs are almost as fortunate under this eclipse energy. Now, water signs can form unique bonds with earth signs. You may find yourselves naturally drawn together.

Earth and water, you have learned things about yourselves. Yours should now be wise voices of experience. You are better partners because of the 2010 eclipse pattern. The 2011 Capricorn and Cancer eclipses are the last of a pattern that also occurred nineteen years ago and will not reoccur for another nineteen years. You are cosmically motivated to take a chance on love. Naturally commitment-oriented, if you meet someone now, a July wedding could be in your future.

At this eclipse's light and in the months to follow, earth and water signs feel they have found The One. But fire and air don't necessarily want the pressure of being The One.

Synchronously, this earthy eclipse represents opportunity for slow enlightenment. From January to June 1, reintroduce the line "What's your sign?" into conversations and translate it to its element.

June 1, Gemini: Partial Solar Eclipse

This eclipse comes months after the first eclipse. Air signs are in their element and experience a romantic time. Take advantage of it. Don't feel that you must hurry anything along. Your major romantic decisions will be made in 2012 during the last of this pattern.

With this eclipse, the escape clause is in effect. Earth and water people who got together during the January eclipse are closer to being drawn toward something serious, if they aren't there already. Fire and air signs are ready to run away from involvement. They may have stuck around this long, but now they yearn to find out what else is out there. There is a short span of time between this eclipse and the next. Expect temporary encounters for the most part.

The challenge for air signs during this eclipse period is to watch that you don't say too much. If you call often, the other person—especially earth and water signs—will think you are interested, when you really just want to talk to someone. The more you try to pull away, even in the next two weeks, the more someone wants to hold on to you.

Fire signs should take advantage of that tried-and-true approach called playing hard to get. In fact, it always works. The less available you are, the more interesting you become, especially to air signs. The more you aren't there, the more time people have to think about you.

Earth and water signs can take advantage of the enhanced communication during this eclipse. They may be at the point when they start to contemplate commitment decisions—especially earth signs. Neither element will be comfortable with elusiveness (take note, fire folks).

June 15, Sagittarius: Total Lunar Eclipse

It is now June, when fire signs are in their element. Always ready to take a good gamble, popular fire signs should take advantage during this total lunar eclipse.

Air and fire signs are attuned to the idea that earth/water rules are meant to be broken. Earth signs are uncomfortable now because they like to stick with what they start.

Fire and air signs are linked in dynamic and exciting communications, drawn to each other like moths to a flame. Sometimes it is only a temporary dance. A few relationships may last, however.

Earth and water signs get close and one step closer to saying "I love you," in more frequent moments of passion. Your words are backed by thoughts of the wonder of commitment or marriage.

Earth and water should be alert to commitment-phobes. Your steel-trap memory reminds you of the promises people do not keep. Get ready for the next step; air and fire are ready to run away. Your eclipse enlightenment is to accept the idea that some people will pass through your life and then disappear.

July 1, Cancer: Partial Solar Eclipse

July is a time when water signs are in their element. Earth and water natives are prone to commit when this eclipse activates feelings and the need to express them. This is a benchmark time for relationships that began in January.

Water and earth conjure images of the beach and hot, steamy summer novels. The next person who sails in or walks across the sand could be a soul mate, even though that person might only be there to soak up the sea air and bask in the fiery sunshine.

Fire and air signs are antsy under this eclipse. Water and earth beings must understand that perspective when you feel like saying "I miss you," even when you've only been apart a few hours.

Fire and air really don't want to be missed and must be kind, understanding, and thoughtful to water and earth beings in this light. You like them, but they like you more. It is too easy to take what people give so lovingly and forget to return it. Your elements need to realize that earth and water fear losing partners even though you are just dating.

To avoid being taken for granted, water and earth should now step back and let the relationship breathe.

November 25, Sagittarius: Partial Solar Eclipse

Time is fleeting. The year comes to an end soon, and we see an accenting of the fiery element in this eclipse before the last airy eclipse. Again, a few short days separate the two. The heat is on.

2010 © Gennady Kravetsky. Image from BigStockPhoto.com

It's speed dating, an extravaganza that involves table hopping, always on the lookout for something better. This acts as the ultimate excuse for not doing anything. Notice how much the deeply romantic mood has faded since July.

Fire signs enjoy attention and popularity. Air signs get a secondary boost. It is easy to meet people and could well be a time to make friends and not lovers. This is also a beneficial approach for water and earth signs. Earth signs may struggle with the spontaneity of this approach, but you must try to keep one step ahead. Bear in mind that air and fire need to keep it simple because "tender" is too complicated for them. Believe that people mean nothing more than they say, especially when the word *space* is involved.

Water and fire create steam. Do not mistake lust for love over the next few weeks. Earth and fire are in a similar situation, and energy blazes between them like a wildfire. With the perspective of safety first, earth and water should be drawn together. Let fire and air ignite together—they can handle it.

Under this eclipse, there could be a second chance at an encounter you had in mid-June. It could have the same ending or a third chance next year.

December 10, Gemini: Total Lunar Eclipse

Air is in its element in the last, total lunar eclipse. Fire knows how to handle this energy as well. Communication is an aphrodisiac. It is time to be social and meet many people, not just a potential one and only. Air and fire touch the surface. "Let's be friends. Oh and by the way, I may only be interested until I find out all I think there is to know about you. My memory is fuzzy about what you said. I barely remember what I said." It's sizzle and pop and comparison shopping until the first eclipses of the next year.

In nature, the snow (water) blankets and covers the earth almost warmly. No words are necessary. Earth and water signs do not want talk, nor do they want to think anyone is just passing through. They understand this together, and earth and water snuggle their way through the season.

The Dating Game

We each vibrate with our own special energy, and we each approach the dating game in our own way. Dating is a roller coaster ride of passion and pitfalls. It fascinates and dazzles with heart-stopping twists and turns. But if you survive the ups and downs of love, you can find a treasure waiting for you at the end of the ride.

About the Author
Carole Schwalm lives in Santa Fe, New Mexico. She has contributed self-help articles and horoscopes for many people through America Online and other Web sites. She currently provides a variety of astrological work for Astrocenter.com.

2010 © Neil Speers. Image from BigStockPhoto.com

Cooking by the Moon

By Susan Pesznecker

Do you ever beseech, dance under, or howl at the Moon? Many of us acknowledge that the Moon influences much of our life here on Earth. But how many of us think to extend these workings into our kitchens? Think about it: the kitchen is, after all, heart and hearth of one's home and nothing less than a culinary laboratory. Carefully chosen ingredients and cooking processes can dovetail with lunar phase and energy to create a deliciously empowered, Moon-centered result.

Cooking by the Lunar Phases

For more than two hundred years, the *Old Farmer's Almanac* has told us how to garden, farm, and carry out other activities in accordance with the Moon phase. In general, seeds that grow into plants and bear fruit above ground—beans, tomatoes, berries, etc.—should be planted and harvested during the waxing phase when the Moon's energies pull upward, encouraging expansion, germination, and vertical growth. Seeds that produce fruit below ground—potatoes, onions, carrots, etc.—are best planted and harvested on a waning Moon, when ebbing lunar energies benefit a plant's root system.

We can apply the same rationale to cooking. Waxing lunar energies correspond well with baking, in which yeasts, powders, butter, and hot oils swell baked products, filling them with potential and making them larger. Anything fried or cooked quickly over a grill or campfire is subject to the Moon's waxing, upwelling energies as well. Cooking with flowers or with fresh fruits and vegetables—those harvested above ground—is another splendid way to honor the Moon's growing phase.

In contrast, the waning period is a great time for stews, soups, braising, and roasting, where a mélange of materials are melded together and cooked down, simmered or braised over time to merge flavors and create something new and complex. Gelatins, custards, puddings, and anything that congeals or gels are another example of cooking with waning lunar energies, with the Moon's pulling down symbolized in the way the ingredients come together and "set." Simmered, steeped, or mulled beverages and syrups are also appropriate, as is working with veggies dug out of the ground.

You might want to consider the specific Full Moon name when planning your culinary adventures. Cooking a hearty harvest feast during the September and October Corn or Harvest Moons links you to seasonal cycles of prosperity. Working with berries, eggs, and new greens during June's Strawberry Moon echoes the fresh energies of springtime, while simmering up a pot of soup or stew during the Snow Moons of January and February brings home the essence of winter.

Cooking with Lunar Symbols

When one thinks of the Moon, familiar symbols pop into mind: the round disk, the bright white or solid dark face, the craters, and the phased crescents. For an extra lunar "oomph," work this symbolism into your cooking. For example, consider the images created by these foods:

- bagels, spread with snowy white cream cheese
- balls of fresh mozzarella
- beets, sliced into circles
- bleu cheese (perfect for "blue Moon" rituals)
- cauliflower
- chocolate, dark and white
- citrus fruits, esp. lemons
- coconuts
- cold cuts and meats, sliced
- cucumbers
- currants
- meatballs
- melons cut in rounds or crescents, or scooped into balls
- milk, milkshakes, eggnogs
- olives
- pancakes
- pasta rounds
- peas
- pomegranates (sacred to the dark Moon)
- provolone cheese in round slices
- pumpkins (round squashes)
- scallops
- shortbread cookies or biscuits baked in either round or crescent shapes
- soy products
- stuffed mushroom caps
- swiss cheese (pocked with lunar craters!)
- white cheddar
- white onions, onion rings
- whole hardboiled eggs

Working with Lunar Correspondences

Colors can be used to great effect in your lunar cooking. Focus on white and silver for Full Moon energies and black and dark jewel-tone colors for New Moon celebrations.

Keep a supply of Moon-charged waters to add to your recipes. To charge, allow spring water to sit out under the Full Moon overnight.

Greeks celebrate the festival of Anthesterion—a
nysus—at the January/February Full Moon. Th
Take part in Anthesterion by holding yo
Festoon the wine vessels with herbs, vin
Full Moon–style appetizers, served
March 31 marks the Roman
Luna's temple on Aventine H
ing and dancing. The w
Luna's grand parties.
of your own, feasti

Cooking
Full Mo

The festival is observed through the making and eating of Moon cakes—thick, round pastries filled with lotus paste and imprinted with Chinese characters representing longevity or harmony. Carry out your own version by baking round pastries in which you carve appropriate symbols or runes.

Aboriginal South Americans honor the earth goddess Mama Paca on the first Full Moon after the autumnal equinox. Rituals are carried out to bless the Earth and the harvest. A feast honors newly harvested foodstuffs and cleans out those remaining in last year's larder.

Divali (Diwali) is an Indian feast held on the October/November New Moon. The five-day celebration recognizes light, particularly that light that shines within. Candles, bonfires, fireworks, and the sharing of sweet treats accompany the festivities.

tribute to Dio-
focus is on wine.
own wine-tasting!
s, and blossoms and add
round platters.

east of Luna. In ancient Rome,
ll marked the site of orgiastic feast-
rd *lunatic* may refer to the craziness of
oin her celebrations by throwing a blowout
ng well and dancing under the night skies.

p Your Own Lunar Meal

n Feast: Set the scene with a white tablecloth and table-
hang white lights and paper lanterns around the table. Pour
ite wine, then begin with an appetizer of large mushroom caps
stuffed with bread crumbs, sweet butter, and minced onions.
Follow with a salad of fresh greens, tossed with edible blossoms
(violets are especially good), cucumber slices, pine nuts, and
sliced fresh mozzarella. For the main dish, grill your favorite meat
or protein and accompany with a whole steamed cauliflower
(adorned with grated white cheddar and fresh parsley) and a
round loaf of fresh-baked bread. For dessert, serve round short-
cakes topped with in-season berries and spooned crescents of
whipped heavy cream. Or, bake a pie! If possible, serve the meal
under the Full Moon—your guests will be dazzled.

New Moon Feast: Create a tablescape of dark colors; festoon
the area with deep blue or purple lights and black candles. Pour
a dark red wine and begin with an antipasti plate of dark olives,
roasted peppers, and sliced cold cuts, with pomegranate seeds
scattered over the top. Serve a creamed leek and onion soup
course, then follow with a pot roast, slow-cooked with potatoes,
turnips, carrots, and rutabagas. For an extra treat, add a casserole
of rich spoon bread. For dessert, serve molten chocolate cakes

topped with raspberry syrup—or turn things around with an upside-down cake. Finish with a pot of jasmine tea. Ask your guests to dress in dark clothing and turn the lights down low.

For Further Reading

Conway, D. J. *Moon Magick.* St. Paul, MN: Llewellyn, 1997.

Drew, A. J. A *Wiccan Formulary and Herbal.* Franklin Lakes, NJ: New Page, 2005.

Farmer's Almanac. "Farmer's Almanac Gardening Calendar." http://www.farmersalmanac.com/home_garden/gardening.

About the Author

Susan "Moonwriter" Pesznecker has practiced Earth-based spirituality for three decades; she currently teaches Nature Studies and Herbology in the online Grey School of Wizardry (www .greyschool.com). In mundania, she is a registered nurse, holds a masters degree in nonfiction writing, and teaches college composition, creative writing, and English. Sue has published several nonfiction essays and the books Crafting Magick with Pen and Ink *(Llewellyn, 2009) and* Gargoyles *(New Page, 2007); her work has also appeared in the Llewellyn annuals and calendars. She lives in beautiful northwest Oregon, a perfect, temperate setting for her works with herbal and natural magicks. In her spare time, Sue writes, enjoys organic gardening, explores the outdoors with her wonder poodle, and works magick under the Moon.*

2010 © Jacqueline Perez. Image from BigStockPhoto.com

The Hundred-Mile Diet: Reflections on Eating Locally

By Harmony Usher

I smiled at the sucking sound the borrowed rubber boots made as I worked my way across the muddy barnyard, following a cheerful woman clad in a yellow plaid jacket carrying an empty egg carton. A flock of white hens pecked along the wall of a bright red barn. It was 7:00 on Saturday morning, and I was grocery shopping.

This was my initiation into a three-month experiment initiated by my sixteen-year-old daughter, who was doing a school project about "The Hundred-Mile Diet." Sometimes called "the slow food movement" or simply "eating locally," it involves eating food grown or raised close to home. I was familiar with the idea because it was popular among my friends, but aside from frequenting the farm stands on the roads to and from our home, I had never consciously tried to adopt it. I had certainly never grocery shopped in a stranger's barnyard, clad in their oversized rubber barn boots!

"These are some of the happiest hens in the county," the woman said, with obvious pride. "Their eggs taste best in the fall when they get a lot of pears from the tree in the yard there." She described how she and her husband insulated the hen house to keep the flock warm even on the coldest winter nights. "A warm hen is a happy hen," she said, smiling.

I hadn't asked to be shown the hen house, but when I knocked on the mud room door (as per instructions on their Web site) the woman assumed this was part of what I needed to know to buy her eggs, and she promptly swung on her barn jacket, passed me boots, and told me to follow her. She was right, of course; knowing she had happy hens became part of what I needed to know.

I visited six other farms in the area that day, coming home with organic beef, smoked pickerel, locally grown spelt (a type of wheat) and buckwheat flours, ground lamb, spring greens, goat cheese, and hydroponically grown red and yellow peppers. Although it took me six hours to shop for the week, I soon realized that it wasn't just food I'd picked up that day.

Why Eat Locally?

Reasons for eating locally are as varied as the people who choose this lifestyle. In rural areas, many folks eat locally because this is how their families have eaten for generations. It's simply part of a farming tradition. They don't cite philosophical reasons for this choice; it simply makes sense.

Others make the choice to eat locally for ecological reasons, citing statistics showing that eating locally makes less of a footprint on the Earth by using fewer fossil fuels to produce and distribute food.

Nutritional benefits from eating food that is less processed, picked at the point of ripeness, and consumed soon after it is harvested is another factor. Some, like myself, stumble onto this path almost accidentally but find themselves forever changed in the most unlikely ways.

Pure Pleasure

Although all the above reasons for eating locally make sense to me, I continue to eat locally well beyond my daughter's three-month school project for other reasons altogether.

Grocery shopping had always been a chore for me. It was a necessary evil, something I did as quickly as possible and gave little thought to, aside from making a list. Shopping locally was more of a journey than a chore. It began with Internet research of farms in our area selling their own products. We were fortunate, as our local business community has a site devoted to compiling a comprehensive list of local farmers, complete with product information and contact numbers. I made calls to check the availability of particular products and the next day set off with a cooler in tow, knowing I would be gone a good part of the morning. Each stop was unique and educational. With every naïve question, I learned a little about the animals and crops I was buying and a lot about the people who raised them. As different as each farmer was, there was something that linked them all together. They were all real people spending real time and emotional energy growing and raising food to share with our family.

My pleasure didn't end on "grocery day." The first time my two children and I ate a meal composed of only locally grown and produced food (scrambled eggs with farm fresh butter, locally raised organic pork sausage, hydroponically grown tomatoes, and fresh steamed fiddleheads) we raved about it for days. We had never eaten anything so delectable. To be able to talk about each farmer and each farm simply added to conversation around the breakfast table. We noticed (although we still question whether we imagine this or not) that we feel more "satisfied" with less food. We also discovered we were less willing to waste food, perhaps because we valued it more, knowing exactly who had created it.

Increased creativity was another surprise benefit. Because you tend to have larger amounts of fewer types of foods at one time, you put energy into devising a variety of ways to enjoy seasonal food. For example, when rhubarb was in season (and little else had appeared at the market yet!) we made rhubarb custard, rhubarb and spelt muffins, stewed rhubarb, and rhubarb sauce for pancakes. So, although initially it seemed we had less choice, the desire for variety sparked some very creative cooking!

Getting Started

Two pieces of advice for beginners: Start your journey in spring or summer when fresh produce is readily available, and don't expect to transform your family's eating habits overnight! I strongly suggest allowing a month or so for a gradual change. If you are like me, you have quite a bit of food stocked in your cupboards and there is no sense in it going to waste. During this time, make only one commitment: Do not set foot in a grocery store. Just gradually eat what you have in your cupboards and begin adding local foods from the market and farmers as you need it.

This one commitment will invite other changes to occur without effort. You will run out of staples one or two at a time, and this will set you on a path to find local products to replace them. Or, as we discovered, it will lead you to wonder why you were ever so dependent on a product to start with (we found that we didn't miss peanut butter, despite years of consuming a large jar every two weeks!). You will grow accustomed to seeing less food in your refrigerator and become more excited anticipating the preparation of each meal. Since we shopped twice a week at the market, we were much more aware of what food was in the house and much less likely to waste it.

We ran out of dairy products first, sugar second, and flour third. Replacing these three products alone was enough to fundamentally change our food habits. Our search for dairy products led us to a local producer of a myriad of artisanal goat cheeses; our loss of white and brown sugar led us to the incredible diversity of maple syrup and honey (which are abundant in our area); and the disappearance of flour led us to spelt, which we all discovered tasted fantastic and was much more satisfying than the overprocessed white variety of flour.

So that we didn't feel deprived in any way, we allowed for eating food given as gifts or offered at another's home. We continued to eat out occasionally as well, and when there were no local food options on the menu, we allowed exceptions. Essentially, our journey began as a change in our shopping patterns and habits, which was manageable and fun.

Food Finding

Eating locally introduced us to what we now playfully call "The Secret Society." I knew our local market ran on Tuesdays, Thursdays, and Saturdays in the town-hall square, but beyond that, I had no idea where I would find local food. So, I began at the market. I felt sheepish (pardon the pun) asking basic questions like, "Is there anyone here who sells lamb?" There was clearly a whole new community at work in the stalls overflowing with produce and buzzing with activity. People chatted over spring greens and stalks of freshly cut rhubarb; each vendor had a clear idea of what was being produced by others in the area and were happy to refer. On the second week of our experiment, I sent the kids (ages sixteen and thirteen) down to the market on their bicycles with backpacks, panniers, and $50 and told them to carefully consider what they wanted to eat all week. They chatted about this experience of shopping for a long time!

Aside from weekly markets, many areas now have local food

communities that advertise in local papers, through business organizations, and on the Internet. Our community's tourism bureau is making use of growing interest in local eating to attract like-minded people to the area. Local health food stores can also be a wonderful resource for those seeking local food, sometimes having food co-ops where one can buy a share in the season's harvest or simply order a box of fresh produce a week for the season (CSA: community supported agriculture). In our area, we are fortunate to have a farmer who even delivers the box!

We also decided to put in a small vegetable garden after a hiatus of a number of years. This has offered us fresh greens, parsley, cilantro, peas, beans, and tomatillos. We have harvested our carrots and our first sweet cucumber, and anxiously wait for the tomatoes to redden. On the advice of a local farmer, I planted heritage tomato varieties and have never seen such monstrous plants with such a large quantity of fruit hanging from the branches!

One of the things I have enjoyed most about a change to local eating is not having to go into grocery stores! I hadn't realized how devoid of emotion and appreciation the experience of shopping had become until I began to anticipate, with great pleasure, my weekly or biweekly visit to my new farm friends.

Seasonality

One of the most basic differences between eating locally and eating from a grocery store is the change from planning what you are going to eat, to eating what nature has planned for you. Every trip to the market is a seasonal surprise. We began our local eating at the beginning of May, after using April to research where local food could be found. As time passed, we watched our pantry shelves empty. Our first trips to the market yielded primarily seasonal greens, fiddleheads, asparagus, eggs, and meat. Soon, the market stalls were overflowing with more food choices than we could eat in a week! And the selection keeps changing. Who has time to miss strawberries when you're swimming in apples; or cucumbers, when you're exploring every potato recipe in the book?

Putting Away

Dealing with Mother Nature's bounty led us on another journey altogether. "Putting away" or preserving in preparation for the winter is not something I'd ever considered, having access to almost any food year-round at the grocery store. In truth, I need to work on it. I've discovered that if you turn away from your garden, even for a couple days, large amounts of food can overgrow and lose appeal. I learned this by going away for a few days in early June and returning home to two quarts of woody beans.

Getting in touch with nature's rhythms, and learning to allow time for harvesting and putting away (whether by freezing, can-

2009 © Elena Ray. Image from BigStockPhoto.com

ning, or pickling) is obviously a learned art, and something that will take time to understand. For the time being, I will be gentle on myself as I learn the old ways and allow myself to work on one thing at a time. Mother Nature has her own schedule, and I am learning to respect it. Along the way, if I find myself discouraged, I will simply think about that first day, and the joy of discovering that I still lived in a world where there were happy hens.

About the Author

Harmony Usher is a freelance writer, researcher, and social worker in small-town Ontario. She shares her world with two creative, dynamic teenagers and is blessed to celebrate life, love, and the phases of the Moon with a fantastic circle of like-spirited women.

2010 © Rodney Lynn. Image from BigStockPhoto.com

Making a Little Italy: Visions of Local Economic Renewal

by Penny Kelly

Good ideas often have muddled beginnings. This idea started with my daughter. She was talking about going to Italy to get married, which started me thinking about going to the Mediterranean "boot" for vacation. Years before, I had watched a movie set in Italy. The movie was OK, but what I couldn't forget was the landscape—a fabulous coastline, rolling hills covered with vineyards and drenched in sunshine. It reminded me of the landscape of my home area of West Michigan.

West Michigan is the home of the fruit belt—a wide strip of land that runs along the Lake Michigan coastline in lower Michigan. Thanks to the regulating and moisturizing effect of Lake

Michigan, we grow almost as many fruits and vegetables in our brief growing season as some parts of California. And we have two factors that make this bioregion shine: one is water; the other is the extraordinary temperature range, thus giving plants superior taste, texture, and nutrition. From the Big Sur–like coastline and cherry tree orchards in the north to the huge sand dunes and rolling vineyards of the south, the area is stunning and unique.

"Gee," I thought, "this area looks a lot like Italy. Why doesn't it feel like I imagine Italy would feel?" The answer to that question was obvious: Michigan was struggling, economically and spiritually. Things had been difficult for at least ten years. A family left Michigan every twelve minutes. Those who stayed looked tense, and lots of people were out of work.

Nevertheless, the more I thought about it, the more it seemed we had everything that Italy had . . . except the old-world consciousness. We had the superb Lake Michigan coastline; the award-winning wines; the vineyards, orchards, and gardens; the Victorian-style bed-and-breakfast hideaways; and an active artists' colony. If we could shift the consciousness in our region, we might be able to create a little Italy right here in West Michigan. People might come here for a sun-drenched vacation, great food, and nights tucked into Victorian beds instead of ancient castles. I could close my eyes and with a little effort, I was there . . .

Across the region, small towns dotted the rolling landscape where people followed a natural calendar and clock. The angst of joblessness disappeared, replaced by hundreds—no, thousands—of small businesses, the "get a job" mentality replaced by the realization that there was plenty of work to be done. People got together, decided what had to be done and how to coordinate the work, then went through the day doing it. Without the stress-driven schedules that came with "jobs," a more natural lifestyle evolved. Families gathered, some blood-related and some not, to help one another fix a roof, harvest a crop, or share stories. The idea of going to a job had been replaced by the more mature attitude of service to the family or the community, and once a task had been decided upon, whatever money was needed always appeared.

In my little Italy, gardens sprouted everywhere and old, traditional recipes handed down by grandmothers were passed around to all. Small, family-run food processing companies appeared everywhere, and cooking—a lost art—became a passion. There were new food artisans in every town. I could smell unique and unusual breads, spicy salsas, and satisfying granolas. There were fabulous sausages, cheeky cheeses, sparkling wines, and a wide variety of basic vegetables and fruits in fresh arrangements with tasty dips and dressings on the side. A local food system had sprung up, and each town and city had taken responsibility for feeding itself, creating great diversity in diets, while lots of extra fruits and veggies were frozen or canned for winter use.

In my vision, the big chain stores faded into the background, and an active community of local artisans and craftsmen began producing everything from socks, rugs, and purses to furniture, artwork, and tableware, each putting their unique creative stamp on what they produced and sold.

In an effort to mitigate the ups and downs of the dollar, a local currency had sprung up. It allowed things to move throughout our region and provided enough stability to maintain basic wealth in terms of home, food, clothing, transportation, and communication.

The region was home to many healers and healing spas, as well as spiritual teachers. A wide assortment of natural therapies was available, and spiritual activities took place year-round, all of which nurtured the well-being of the visitors who came here. Music was everywhere, laughter was in the air, and the good food that flowed from the gardens had a profound effect on the well-being of the visitors who came for a vacation in my little Italy.

It was a unique cultural experience, as attractive as going across the ocean to visit Italy itself. Our guests returned again and again, coming from all over North America to spend a little time here. When they went home, they took memories of people who had time for breakfast, *a place where relationships healed, romance flourished, and a spirit of peace pervaded the land.*

When I returned to the present, the essence of little Italy stayed with me. Casually, I began to talk about the idea and was surprised at the enthusiastic response it garnered. When a friend who had lived in the real Italy said, "You're talking about a powerful way to regenerate your local economy," I was speechless. That perspective hadn't even occurred to me!

When the idea would not go away, yet no one else seemed motivated to get it rolling, I started it myself. I had no experience and no clue as to how to make anything like this happen. However, people continued to respond with fortuitous tips and leads.

Today, amazing things are afoot! The West Michigan Sustainable Business Forum is hosting a summit conference on sustainable business this fall. The goal is to map, connect, and support businesses interested in sustainable practices, including those that will help them to sustain themselves!

Another group has taken up the challenge of exploring and creating a local food system for our bioregion.

A third group is working on starting a complementary currency system, and there's a growing sense of possibility and excitement in the area as people catch the West Michigan consciousness of self-sufficiency, sustainability, renewable products, and organics. In truth, it's a healing shift in consciousness, one of renewed and renewable energy. I can't wait to see where it all leads.

As it turns out, to shift the consciousness of an entire region, you just need a vision that is big enough for others to get involved in. You need a group wish, a dream, a vision of how it might look, sound, and feel. Share that with others, and voilà! People have something to organize their minds around. And then everything starts to feel different. It's almost like being in Italy!

About the Author

For Penny Kelly's full bio, see page 301.

2010 © Sergey Goruppa. Image from BigStockPhoto.com

Marriage by the Moon

by April Elliott Kent

A friend and her husband, married for many years, have a running gag that pokes gentle fun at their affable relationship. One of them will say something like, "Of course, we're only happy together because you are so sweet/wonderful/patient/ etc." To which the other fawningly replies, "Oh no, it's you, it's you." Then they giggle at their charade of exaggerated sweetness (though the twinkles in their eyes imply that they aren't exaggerating by much).

Not surprisingly, they were married on a day when the Moon was in Libra, the sign of harmony, diplomacy, and flattery. Individually, both are driven and highly independent; yet somehow, the character of their marriage is tranquil and accommodating. Their marriage is definitely greater—and quite different—than the sum of its parts!

I'm sure you've heard of your natal chart, based on the date, time, and location of your birth. But did you realize that your marriage has a birth chart, too? To a trained astrological eye, the horoscope for your wedding—specifically, the chart for the moment you exchanged vows—is a schematic of your union and all its unique strengths, weaknesses, blessings, and challenges.

Each planet's placement on that date offers a glimpse into your marriage. The Sun's placement hints at your marriage's purpose (see my book *Star Guide to Weddings* for all the juicy details!); Venus describes your style of expressing affection and reaching compromise; Saturn weighs in on the role of structure, rules, and obligations in your marriage; and so on.

The Moon's sign on your wedding day symbolizes the soul of your marriage: the home you make together, the tempo and rhythm of your daily domestic lives. What comforts you as a couple and nourishes your relationship?

Walk into a place and you immediately sense the rhythm of the people who spend time there. Is it a steady, quiet cadence, or a stimulating, syncopated one? Do you feel at peace there, or challenged? As the Moon moves along in its monthly turn through the zodiac, it takes on the colors and perspectives of each sign in turn—some peaceful, some assertive, some sensitive, some acerbic. The Moon's sign on the day of your wedding illustrates your marriage's daily pleasures, comforts, and rhythm: where you live as a couple.

How to Find Your Marriage Moon Sign

The Moon moves through the zodiac quickly, and unlike the Sun, is not always conveniently placed in the same sign on the same date every year! If you're getting married in 2011, refer to the tables on pages 136–158 of this book to find the Moon's sign on your wedding day. If you were wed in another year, ask an astrologer to calculate your wedding chart using the date, time of your vows (estimate if necessary), and location of your ceremony. Or, you can use a free online system such as Astro.com to calculate the chart yourself.

The Moon's Modality

The twelve signs of the zodiac are commonly classified into three modalities, or fundamental approaches to life. Cardinal signs initiate action and set goals. Fixed signs sustain and maintain the status quo. Mutable signs are flexible, adaptable, and comfortable with change. The modality of your marriage's Moon sign describes the way you move through the world as a couple, your daily tempo.

The Moon in any cardinal sign (Aries, Cancer, Libra, or Capricorn) is action-oriented, and your daily lives will be busy and filled with energetic activities and people. Be sure to get enough rest and to occasionally look before you leap! What makes you feel grounded, nurtured, and comfortable: setting goals, being in motion, and starting new projects.

A fixed-sign Moon (Taurus, Leo, Scorpio, or Aquarius) is a bit like a pendulum: set it going and it will keep going exactly as it began. This steadiness is beneficial, as long as the relationship starts out in a positive way! What makes you feel grounded, nurtured, and comfortable: routines, stability, and predictability.

If you marry when the Moon is in a mutable sign (Gemini, Virgo, Sagittarius, or Pisces), there will be a light, changeable, and fluid quality to your daily lives together. Mutable signs also readily absorb the energies around them, so it's important to surround yourselves with positive people, in a calm and nourishing environment. What makes you feel grounded, nurtured, and comfortable: options, a flexible schedule, and the ability to retreat when you get overwhelmed.

The Moon's Element

The element of your marriage Moon sign describes the emotional food that keeps your daily lives nourished and thriving.

When you wed in a fire sign (Aries, Leo, or Sagittarius), you need a marriage rich in excitement, entertainment, challenges, and inspiration. Fire signs like to create, perform, and inspire others, so regular social engagements are in order—try hosting dinner parties, book clubs, and game nights for family and friends.

The earth marriage (Taurus, Virgo, or Capricorn) needs financial security, organization, and physical comfort in order to flourish. Making your home feel luxurious and orderly (without breaking the bank) and devising a winning system for handling your finances are imperative.

Communication, new ideas, and a network of interesting friends fuel the air-sign (Gemini, Libra, or Aquarius) marital engine. You won't be happy unless you have plenty to talk about with each other and abundant opportunities for social interaction with other people—whether in person, by telephone, or online.

A water marriage (Cancer, Scorpio, or Pisces) is nourished by empathy, emotional intensity, and spiritual rapport. Shared participation in religion or spiritual practice, regular heart-to-hearts, and small gestures that show your partner that you understand and are thinking of him or her will help your marriage flourish.

Marriage Moons by Sign

Moon in Aries (cardinal fire): The Pioneer Marriage

Aries is considered a challenging sign for the Moon in a wedding chart because the energy of Aries is about "me," while a congenial marriage tends to emphasize Libran pronouns like *we*. The Aries Moon has its strengths, however. As a couple, you will tend to move fast, make quick decisions, and be regarded by your family and friends as leaders and pioneers. You are unlikely to succumb to peer-pressure; you'll do things your own way.

Moon in Taurus (fixed earth): The Simple Marriage

Astrological tradition considers the Moon to be exceptionally strong in stable, contented Taurus. When you marry with the Moon in this sign, the natural rhythm of your day-to-day lives together will be peaceful and steady, and you will take enjoyment from life's simplest, most honest pleasures. Taurus enjoys the pleasures of the table, soothing music, and simple but beautiful surroundings. Your home will be comfortable and unpretentious, and you will likely cultivate a thriving garden together—or at least some window boxes.

Moon in Gemini (mutable air): The Convivial Marriage

The Gemini marriage needs conversation, variety, and movement in order for the two of you to feel centered and to recharge your emotional batteries. For you, variety truly is the spice of life; a stagnant routine will quickly derail your domestic happiness. You may be exceptionally sensitive to noise, so a peaceful household is essential. With your love of communication, a good high-speed Internet connection is a necessity, not a luxury, for your home!

Moon in Cancer (cardinal water): The Comforting Marriage

When you marry with the Moon in Cancer, you're not just taking on a spouse, you're creating a family. Your household is a revolving door of visiting relatives, friends who have fallen on hard times, and your children's latchkey friends. You will tend to flourish at home and may not travel much, although other factors in your marriage chart or your birth charts can make exploration much more likely. Cooking and caring for your home, children, and pets brings great contentment to your marriage.

Moon in Leo (fixed fire): The Fun Marriage

Leo emphasizes the importance of creativity, fun, loyalty, and inspiration in your union. You're a couple that, above all, offers warmth to your wide circle of friends and family. Children and young people will be especially drawn to your home because you make them feel important; they sense your sincere enjoyment of their company. People love to visit your home because they know they will laugh, eat, and drink well and meet other interesting people. If you are artistic or musical, your home will reflect these interests with an unusually colorful and creative décor and frequent meetings of like-minded friends.

Marriage by the Moon

Moon in Virgo (mutable earth): The Helpful Marriage

Virgo is among the sweetest and most giving signs, showing its affection with practical gestures and an honest desire to help. The Moon in Virgo excels at untangling emotional knots and bringing order to a chaotic world. But there is a caveat: if your relationship loses its balance, Virgo can manifest in an tendency toward destructive criticism. Focus on helping each other become your best selves, without feeling compelled to point out areas for improvement!

Moon in Libra (cardinal air): The Other-Oriented Marriage

Marry with the Moon in Libra, the sign of marriage and other important partnerships, and your instinctual approach to day-to-day life will be to figure out what your partner needs or wants and do everything you can to help achieve these goals. The natural rhythm of your day-to-day lives together will be busy but with a healthy work/life balance. Your gracious, welcoming home will be filled with artists, musicians, writers, and their creations. You may be much more inclined than other couples to spend nearly all your leisure time together; you thrive on togetherness.

Moon in Scorpio (fixed water): The Mysterious Marriage

Scorpio was traditionally considered a weak sign for the Moon. There is some logic to this, and it would be dishonest to say this placement describes an easygoing approach to life. Moon in Scorpio is not the most trusting placement, because Scorpio sees and understands so much of what other signs ignore; this can be a challenge in a relationship that requires total trust. So with a Moon in Scorpio marriage, your challenge is to remain absolutely, scrupulously honest and open with each other, and to patiently build the trust that Scorpio demands. Once that trust is in place, yours should be an unusually loyal and enduring union.

Moon in Sagittarius (mutable fire): The Globetrotting Marriage

Moon in Sagittarius emphasizes the themes of travel, academia, and religion. Your home will likely be filled with books and with cultural influences from many different lands and peoples. It will be chosen for its view, its square footage, and the size of the land on which it sits, which are generally more important to Sagittarius than the style of the structure. Sagittarius likes wide-open spaces—a limitless horizon for both the body and the mind! Even when you're unable to travel, new ideas and unfamiliar experiences can keep you both grounded and invigorated.

Moon in Capricorn (cardinal earth): The Administrative Marriage

This is not considered one of the Moon's stronger signs, because the pragmatic and worldly interests of Capricorn may conflict with the nurturing, emotional qualities of the Moon. Still, it can be an ideal lunar placement for a couple who are devoted to the notion of shared responsibility—to their families, their work, and society. You naturally assume caretaking roles with aging relatives and chronically ill friends. This is also an ideal lunar placement for a couple who work together, particularly in a home-based business.

Moon in Aquarius (fixed air): The Friendly Marriage

Moon in Aquarius needs a daily routine that emphasizes friendship, community, and societal progress. In fact, your friends will very likely serve as a kind of surrogate family for you, and your home is likely to be a popular place for friends to congregate. (Oddly, though, you may choose to maintain more of a distance from your actual families.) Though your fixed Moon sign is resistant to change, you may move from house to house relatively often, and you should always choose your home with an eye toward resale value!

Moon in Pisces (mutable water): The Spiritual Marriage

This is a particularly loving and happy placement for marriage. The Pisces Moon couple loves one another unconditionally, with compassion and an unshakable faith in one another's goodness. A long and intimate marriage will inevitably bring you to the moments when you must forgive one another for something, believe in one another when all evidence points to failure, or simply see things from one another's perspective. These are the moments when the Moon in Pisces comes through with flying colors.

The Care and Feeding of Your Marriage Moon

Just as your children's personalities may differ from yours, your marriage has needs of its own that require compromise and patience. But marriage, like having children, is also an incredible opportunity to see the world in a new way. Knowing your marriage Moon sign can help bring your daily lives into clearer focus and give your marriage the care it needs to endure and prosper.

About the Author

April Elliott Kent, a professional astrologer since 1990, graduated from San Diego State University with a degree in communications. Her book, Star Guide to Weddings, *was published by Llewellyn in 2008. April's astrological writing has also appeared in* The Mountain Astrologer (USA) *magazine, the online journals MoonCircles and Beliefnet, and Llewellyn's Moon Sign Book (2005–2010). April and her husband, who married with the Moon in Libra, live in San Diego with their two cats. Her website is: http://www.bigskyastrology.com.*

TELL US WHAT YOU WANT!

At Llewellyn our aim is to keep pace with your passion for lifelong learning and Earth-conscious living. Please help us to understand and serve you better by taking our short survey (approximately 5 minutes).

Please go to
http://www.llewellyn.com/surveys.php
to complete the online questionnaire and
let your voice be heard.

Thanks in advance for your feedback!